OLIVER CROMWELL AND THE RULE OF THE PURITANS IN ENGLAND

By *CHARLES FIRTH, M.A.*
(Originally published in 1900)

TABLE OF CONTENTS

CHAPTER I
EARLY LIFE, 1599–1629

CHAPTER II
THE PREPARATION FOR THE CIVIL WAR, 1629–1640

CHAPTER III
THE LONG PARLIAMENT, 1640–1642

CHAPTER IV
THE FIRST CAMPAIGN, 1642

CHAPTER V
CROMWELL IN THE EASTERN ASSOCIATION, 1643

CHAPTER VI
MARSTON MOOR, 1644

CHAPTER VII
NASEBY AND LANGPORT, 1645–1646

CHAPTER VIII
PRESBYTERIANS AND INDEPENDENTS, 1642–1647

CHAPTER IX
ARMY AND PARLIAMENT, 1647–1648

CHAPTER X
THE SECOND CIVIL WAR, 1648

CHAPTER XI
CROMWELL AND THE KING'S EXECUTION, 1648–1649

CHAPTER XII
THE REPUBLIC AND ITS ENEMIES, 1649

CHAPTER XIII
IRELAND, 1649–1650

CHAPTER XIV
CROMWELL AND SCOTLAND, 1650–1651

CHAPTER XV
THE END OF THE LONG PARLIAMENT, 1651–1653

CHAPTER XVI
THE FOUNDATION OF THE PROTECTORATE, 1653

CHAPTER XVII
CROMWELL'S DOMESTIC POLICY, 1654–1658

CHAPTER XVIII
CROMWELL'S FOREIGN POLICY, 1654–1658

CHAPTER XIX
CROMWELL'S COLONIAL POLICY

CHAPTER XX
CROMWELL AND HIS PARLIAMENTS

CHAPTER XXI
THE DEATH OF CROMWELL, 1658–1660

CHAPTER XXII
CROMWELL AND HIS FAMILY

CHAPTER XXIII
EPILOGUE

PREFACE

This *Life of Cromwell* is in part based on an article contributed by the author to the *Dictionary of National Biography* in 1888, but embodies the result of later researches, and of recently discovered documents such as the Clarke Papers. The battle plans have been specially drawn for this volume by Mr. B. V. Darbishire, and in two cases differ considerably from those generally accepted as correct. The scheme of this series does not permit a discussion of the reasons why these alterations have been made, but the evidence concerning the battles in question has been carefully examined, and any divergence from received accounts is intentional. The reader who wishes to see this subject discussed at length is referred to a study of the battle of Marston Moor printed in Volume XII. of the *Transactions of the Royal Historical Society* (new series), and to a similar paper on Dunbar which will appear in Volume XIV.

The quotations from Cromwell's letters or speeches are, where necessary, freely abridged.

C. H. F.

OXFORD, Feb. 6, 1900.

Charles Firth

INTRODUCTION

Oliver Cromwell was born in Huntingdon, England, 25th of April, 1599. He gained is education from a Puritan minister before attending Cambridge University.

Cromwell, as a young man, experienced a religious awakening and this motivated him to fight for Protestant rights in England. In 1628, Cromwell entered the House of Commons. In 1642, the English Civil War broke loss and Cromwell, several times, defeated the King's men. After which, he was promoted to Lieutenant-General.

The civil war saw the rise of the Parliament Army. This force defeated the King and his supporters, the Royalists. Cromwell consolidated this armed force and created the New Model Army. After the execution of Charles I and monarchical power, Cromwell was propelled to power and named the first chairman of the new Council of State. In 1653, Cromwell was named Lord Protector of the British Republic. This office gave him full power.

This manuscript explores in great detail the life of Oliver Cromwell, the fruits of his labour, and the impact he had on English affairs.

- Marshal Mason

Charles Firth

CHAPTER I
EARLY LIFE
1599–1629

"I was by birth a gentleman living neither in any considerable height nor yet in obscurity," said the Protector to one of his Parliaments. Cromwell's family was one of the many English families which rose to wealth and importance at the time of the Reformation. It owed its name and its fortune to Thomas Cromwell, Earl of Essex, the minister of Henry VIII., and the destroyer of the monasteries. In 1494, Thomas Cromwell's sister Katherine had married Morgan Williams, a wealthy brewer of Putney, whose family sprang from Glamorganshire. Her eldest son Richard took the surname of Cromwell, entered the service of Henry VIII., and assisted his uncle in his dealings with refractory Churchmen. Grants of land flowed in upon the lucky kinsman of the King's vicegerent. In 1538, he was given the Benedictine priory of Hinchinbrook near Huntingdon. In 1540, the site of the rich Benedictine abbey of Ramsey and some of its most valuable manors were added to his possessions. Honour as well as wealth fell to his lot. At the tournament held at Westminster on May Day, 1540, to celebrate the espousals of Henry VIII. and Anne of Cleves,—a marriage which was to unite English and German Protestantism,—Richard Cromwell was one of the six champions who maintained the honour of England against all comers. Pleased by his prowess with sword and lance, the King gave him a diamond ring and made him a knight.

Six weeks later fortune turned against the all-powerful Earl of Essex. He had pushed forward the Reformation faster than the King desired and bound the King to a woman he detested. "Say what they will, she is nothing fair," groaned Henry, and suddenly repudiated wife, policy, and minister. On June 10th, Thomas Cromwell was arrested in the Council Chamber itself and committed to the Tower on the charge of high treason. "He had left," it was said, "the mean, indifferent, virtuous, and true way" of reforming religion which his master trod. In his zeal to advance doctrinal changes, he had dared to say that if the King and all his realm would turn and vary from his opinions, he would fight in the field in his own person with his sword in his hand against the King and all others; adding that if he lived a year or two he trusted "to bring things to that frame that it should not lie in the King's power to resist or let it." On July 28th, Cromwell passed from the Tower to the scaffold.

Few pitied him and only one mourned him. Sir Richard Cromwell, said tradition, dared to appear at the Court in the mourning raiment which the King hated, and Henry, respecting his fidelity, pardoned his boldness. He retained the King's favour the rest of his life, was made a gentleman of the Privy Chamber and constable of Berkeley Castle, got more grants of lands, and died in 1546.

Sir Richard's son Henry built Hinchinbrook House, was knighted by Queen Elizabeth, whom he entertained during one of her progresses, and was four times sheriff of Huntingdonshire. As marshal of the county he organised its forces at the time of the Spanish Armada, raised, besides the four soldiers he was bound to furnish, twenty-six horsemen at his own cost, and called on the trained bands to practise "the right and perfect use of their weapons," and fight for "the sincere religion of Christ" against "the devilish superstition of the Pope." In their mixture of military and religious ardour his harangues recall the speeches of his grandson. People called him "the golden knight" because of his wealth and his liberality, and he matched his children with the best blood of the eastern counties. One daughter was the mother of Major-General Edward Whalley, one of the Regicides; another married William Hampden, and her son was John Hampden.

Of Sir Henry's sons, Oliver, his heir, was a man who from love of ostentation pushed his father's liberality to extravagance. When James I. came to England he was received at Hinchinbrook, "with such entertainment as had not been seen in any place before, since his first setting forward out of Scotland." James made him a Knight of the Bath at the coronation, and paid him three other visits during his reign.

Robert, Sir Henry's second son, inherited from his father an estate at Huntingdon, worth in those days about £300 a year, equal to three or four times as much now. He sat for Huntingdon in the Parliament of 1593, filled the office of bailiff for the borough, and was one of the justices of the peace for the county. Robert Cromwell married Elizabeth, widow of William Lynn, and daughter of William Steward of Ely. Her family were well off, and she brought with her a jointure of £60 a year. The Stewards were relatives of the last prior and first Protestant dean of Ely, who had obtained good leases of Church lands, and were farmers of the tithes of the see. Tradition, which loves curious coincidences, has connected them with the royal House of Stuart that their descendant overthrew, but history traces their origin to a Norfolk family originally named Styward. Oliver, the future Lord Protector, was the fifth child of Robert Cromwell, and the only one of his sons who survived infancy. He was born at Huntingdon, on April 25, 1599, baptised at St. John's Church in that town on April 29th, and christened Oliver after his uncle, the knight of Hinchinbrook. Little is known of his boyhood. A royalist biographer says that he was of "a cross and peevish disposition" from his infancy, while a contemporary panegyrist credits him even then with "a quick and lively apprehension, a piercing and sagacious wit, and a solid judgment."

Stories are told of his marvellous deliverances from danger, and of strange prognostications of his future greatness. It was revealed to him in a dream or by an apparition "that he should be the greatest man in England, and should be near the King." Another story was that he had acted the part of a king in a play in his school days, placing the crown himself upon his head, and adding "majestical mighty words" of his own to the poet's verses. These are the usual fictions which cluster round the early life of great men. All that is certain is that Cromwell was educated at the free school of Huntingdon under Dr. Thomas Beard—a Puritan schoolmaster who wrote pedantic Latin plays, proved that the Pope was Antichrist, and showed in his *Theatre of God's Judgments* that human crimes never go unpunished by God even in this world. Beard was an austere man who believed in the rod, and a biographer describes him as correcting the manners of young Oliver "with a diligent hand and careful eye," which may be accepted as truth. But these disciplinings did not prevent pupil and master from being friends in later life.

At the age of seventeen, Cromwell was sent to Cambridge, where on April 23, 1616, he was admitted a fellow commoner of Sidney Sussex College. The College, founded in 1598, was one of those two which Laud subsequently complained of as nurseries of Puritanism. Its master, Samuel Ward, was a learned and morbidly conscientious divine; a severe disciplinarian, who exacted from his scholars elaborate accounts of the sermons they heard, and had them whipped in hall when they offended. Cromwell did not distinguish himself, but he by no means wasted his time at Cambridge. He had no aptitude for languages. Burnet says he "had no foreign language but the little Latin that stuck to him from his education, which he spoke very viciously and scantily." When he was Protector he remembered enough Latin to carry on a conversation in that tongue with a Dutch ambassador.

Another biographer tells us that Cromwell "excelled chiefly in the mathematics," and his kinsman, the poet Waller, was wont to say that the Protector was "very well read in the Greek and Roman story." His advice to his son Richard bears out this account of his preferences. "Read a little history," he wrote to him; "study the Mathematics and cosmography. These are good with subordination to the things of God. These fit for public services for which a man is born." With Cromwell, as with Montrose, Sir Walter Raleigh's *History of the World* was a favourite book, and he urged his son to read it. "'Tis a body of history, and will add much more to your understanding than fragments of story."

Cromwell's tutor is said to have observed with great discrimination that his pupil was not so much addicted to speculation as to action, and royalist biographers make his early taste for athletics and sport a great reproach to him. One says: "He was easily satiated with study, taking more delight in horse and field exercise." Another describes him as "more famous for his exercises in the fields than in the schools, being one of the chief matchmakers and players of football, cudgels, or any other boisterous sport or game."

How long Cromwell remained at the university is not known, but it is certain that he left it without taking a degree. Probably he quitted Cambridge prematurely on account of the death of his father, who was buried at All Saints' Church, Huntingdon, on June 24, 1617. For a time Cromwell stayed at Huntingdon, no doubt helping his mother in the management of the estate and in the settlement of his father's affairs. Then he went to London to acquire the smattering of law which every country gentleman needed, and which one whose position marked him out as a future justice of the peace and member of parliament could not do without. "He betook himself," says a contemporary biographer, "to the study of law in Lincoln's Inn; that nothing might be wanting to make him a complete gentleman and a good commonwealthsman." Though his name does not appear in the books of that society, the fact is probable enough, and sufficiently well attested to be accepted.

Three years after his father's death, Cromwell married, on August 22, 1620, at St. Giles's Church, Cripplegate, Elizabeth Bourchier. She was the daughter of Sir James Bourchier, a city merchant living on Tower Hill and owning property at Felstead in Essex. It is probable that Cromwell's wife brought him a considerable dowry, for the day after marriage he contracted, under penalty of £4000, to settle upon her, as her jointure, the parsonage house of Hartford in Huntingdonshire with its glebe land and tithes. Elizabeth Cromwell was a year older than her husband, and is traditionally said to have been a notable housewife. In spite of royalist lampooners she was, if her portraits may be trusted, neither uncomely nor undignified in person. Her affection for her husband was sincere and lasting. "My life is but half a life in your absence," she writes to him in 1650. "I could chide thee," says Cromwell in answer to a complaint about not writing, "that in many of thy letters thou writest to me, that I should not be unmindful of thee and thy little ones. Truly, if I love you not too well, I think I err not on the other hand much. Thou art dearer to me than any creature; let that suffice."

After his marriage, Cromwell settled down at Huntingdon and occupied himself in farming the lands he had inherited from his father. Two-thirds of the income of the estate had been left by Robert Cromwell to his widow for the term of twenty-one years, in order to provide for the maintenance of the daughters, so that Oliver's means during the early years of his married life must have been rather narrow. It was understood, however, that he was destined to be the heir of his mother's brother, Sir Thomas Steward, and in 1628 another uncle, Richard Cromwell, left him a small property at Huntingdon. Ere long there was a proof that Cromwell had earned the good opinion of his neighbours, for, in February, 1628, he was elected to represent his native town in the third Parliament called by Charles I. The choice was partly due to the position of his family and its long connection with the borough, but more must have been due also to Cromwell's personal character and reputation, since the local influence of the Cromwell family, thanks to the reckless extravagance of its head, was already on the wane. In 1627, Sir Oliver to pay his debts had been obliged to sell Hinchinbrook to Sir Sidney Montague, and had retired to Ramsey. He had represented the county in eight Parliaments, but he sat for it no more, and the Montagues were henceforth the leading family in Huntingdonshire.

Cromwell's entry upon the stage of English politics took place at the moment when the quarrel between Charles I. and his Parliaments became a complete breach. To Henry VIII. Parliaments had been the servile tools with which he used to work his will in Church and State. To Elizabeth they had been faithful servants, obedient though sometimes venturing to grumble or criticise. During her reign, the House of Commons had grown strong and conscious of its strength. The spoils of the monasteries had enriched the country gentry, and the development of local government had given them political training, while the growth of commerce had brought wealth to merchants and manufacturers. Into upper and middle classes alike the Reformation had put a spirit which began by questioning authority in matters of religion, and went on to question authority in politics.

It was in religious matters, naturally, that this spirit of opposition first revealed itself. Henry VIII. had separated the English from the Catholic Church, not in order to alter its doctrine, but in order to make himself its master. The doctrinal change which Thomas Cromwell had prematurely attempted, Somerset and Northumberland carried out in the reign of Henry's son. The only result of the reaction under Mary was to inspire most Englishmen with a passionate hostility to the faith in whose name the Queen's bonfires had been kindled. Elizabeth restored Protestantism, and re-established the control of the State over the Church. She called herself "Supreme Governor" instead of "Head of the Church," but kept all the essentials of the supremacy which her father had established. To conciliate the English Catholics she made the doctrine and ritual of the National Church less offensively Protestant, but to impose her compromise she was obliged to use force. Year after year the penalties inflicted upon Catholics who refused to conform became heavier, and their lot was made harder, but thousands remained invincibly constant, and preferred to suffer rather than deny their faith.

Not only did the enforcement of the Elizabethan compromise fail to suppress Catholicism, but it created Puritanism and Protestant Nonconformity. Puritanism represented from the first "the Protestantism of the Protestant religion." The aim of those who called themselves Puritans was to restore the Church to what they thought its original purity in doctrine, worship, and government. Some remained within its pale, content to accept the rule of bishops and the supremacy of the Crown so long as doctrine and ritual were to their liking. Others, who desired a simpler ceremonial and a more democratic form of government, sought to transform the Anglican Church to the model of that of Scotland or Geneva, and were the predecessors of the Presbyterian party of Charles the First's time. A small band of extremists separated altogether from the National Church, and founded self-governing congregations, which defined their own creed and chose their own ministers. But though Independency sprang up first in England it made few converts, and never throve till it was transplanted to Holland or New England.

Elizabeth suppressed nascent Presbyterianism, and persecuted with equal vigour Catholic recusant and Protestant separatist. But within the National Church, in spite of repressive measures, the Puritan party grew continually stronger, while Parliament became more aggressively Protestant, and more eager for Church reform. While the Queen lived, no change in the ecclesiastical system was possible. When she died, wise men counselled her successor to adopt a different policy: to try comprehension instead of compulsion, and to make concessions to Puritanism. James refused. "I shall make them conform themselves," was his answer, "or I shall harry them out of the land." He began his reign by authorising new canons which enforced more rigid uniformity, and by driving three hundred ministers from their livings. The main cause of his breach with his first Parliament was his refusal to restrict the authority or to reform the abuses of the ecclesiastical courts.

The Church policy of James aggravated the divisions he should have tried to heal; his foreign policy ran counter to the national traditions of his subjects as well as their religious prejudices. It was an axiom with Englishmen that England's natural allies were the Protestant states of Europe, and that it was her duty when occasion demanded to come forward as the champion of Protestantism against the Catholic powers. But for more than ten years James made a close alliance with Spain his chief object in European politics, partly with the laudable aim of putting an end to religious wars, partly in the hope of paying his debts with the dowry of the Spanish Infanta. For the sake of this alliance he sent Raleigh to the block, declined to help the German Protestants, offered to suspend the penal laws against the Catholics, and forbade Parliament to discuss foreign affairs. The general joy which hailed the breaking off of the Spanish match revealed the depth of the hostility which the King's schemes had excited.

During the same years, the King's attitude towards English institutions called into life a constitutional opposition. His theory of monarchy found expression in persistent attempts to extend the power of the Crown and diminish the rights of Parliament. Backed by a judicial decision that the right to tax imports and exports was a part of the royal prerogative, James imposed new customs duties by his own authority, and dissolved his second Parliament when it voted them illegal. Members were imprisoned for their utterances in the House of Commons, and Parliament was forbidden to debate mysteries of State or matters touching the King's government. When the House asserted its right to freedom of speech James replied that its privileges were derived from the grace and favour of his ancestors, and erased the protest, which claimed that the liberties of Parliament were "the undoubted birthright and inheritance of the subjects of England."

Such a policy seemed to proceed from a formed design to destroy English freedom. Throughout Europe, absolute monarchies had risen on the ruins of national liberties, and now the same fate threatened England. When Charles

I. succeeded his father, he found the nation he had to govern not only discontented, but also full of suspicion. "We are the last monarchy in Christendom that maintains its rights," said a parliamentary orator in 1625, and the distrust and fear created by the pretensions of James flung their shadows across the path of his son.

Charles I., with his royal bearing and his kingly graces, seemed fitter to win back the hearts of his subjects than James, who lacked both majesty and manners. But he was as devoid of sympathy for the nation he governed as his father had been; as prone to cherish chimerical schemes, and as blind to facts. James had left him a courtier instead of a statesman to be his guide, and Charles gave Buckingham as complete trust as if he had possessed the experience of Burleigh or the wisdom of Bacon.

At the moment when the new reign opened, the rupture with Spain had given both Charles and his minister a factitious popularity. But on both foreign and domestic affairs King and Parliament speedily disagreed. Parliament was eager for war with Spain, but not ready either to furnish funds for a European coalition against the House of Hapsburg, or to buy the alliance of France by repealing the penal laws against English Catholics. It granted the King money to fit out a fleet, but its refusal of a more liberal supply, and its open declaration of want of confidence in the King's minister, brought the session to a sudden close.

Buckingham hoped to justify himself by success, and launched forth on the sea of European politics with all the boldness of an adventurer. He sent an expedition to sack Cadiz and to capture the Spanish plate-fleet. He promised subsidies to the King of Denmark for his campaigns in Germany. He courted popularity with the Puritans by repudiating the engagements made to France in the King's marriage treaty, and endeavouring to pose as the protector of the Huguenots. But when a second Parliament met there was nothing but a record of failure to lay before it. The expedition to Cadiz had ended in disaster and disgrace. "Our honour is ruined," cried Sir John Eliot to the Commons, "our ships are sunk, our men perished, not by the sword, not by the enemy, not by chance, but by those we trusted." All blame fell on the man who had monopolised power, but the King forbade

Parliament to call his servant to account, and put a stop to Buckingham's impeachment by a second dissolution.

During the next two years Charles tried the "new ways" he had threatened to adopt if Parliament declined to supply his necessities. A forced loan of £300,000 was levied, and those who refused payment were, if rich, imprisoned; if poor, impressed. There were schemes for raising an excise to support a standing army, and Ship-money to maintain a fleet. Judges were dismissed for denying the legality of the forced loan, and divines promoted for declaring it sinful to refuse payment. But abroad failure still dogged the King's foreign policy. In Germany the King of Denmark was crushed because Charles could not pay the promised subsidies. The French alliance ended in quarrels which grew into a war with France. Buckingham's expedition to the Isle of Rhé ended in a more ruinous failure than the expedition to Cadiz. "Since England was England," wrote Denzil Holles, "it received not so dishonourable a blow." Unable to continue the fight with France and Spain without money, Charles was forced once more to appeal to the nation.

Charles the First's third Parliament met on March 17, 1628. It opened its proceedings with a debate on the grievances of the nation, and almost the first speech Cromwell heard in the House must have been Eliot's appeal to his brother members to remember the greatness of the issue before them. "Upon this dispute," said the spokesman of the Commons, "not alone our goods and lands are engaged, but all that we call ours. Those rights, those privileges that made our fathers freemen are in question. If they be not now the more carefully preserved, they will render us to posterity less free, less worthy than our fathers." The House voted the King supplies, but made their grant dependent on the redress of grievances. Then followed the drawing up of the Petition of Right, declaring arbitrary imprisonment and taxation without the consent of Parliament henceforth illegal, and at last the Commons, by the threat of impeaching Buckingham again, wrung the acceptance of their petition from the reluctant King.

In the interval between the first and second session of the third Parliament, Buckingham died by Felton's hand, but his death did not put an end to the quarrel. Charles became his own prime minister, and made evident to all men that the King's will, not the favourite's influence, was the source of the policy against which the Commons protested. The beginning of the second session, in January, 1629, was marked by a new dispute about taxation. The Commons asserted that the levy of tonnage and poundage without its grant, and the continued collection of the new customs duties imposed by James I., were contrary to the Petition of Right. The King declared that these were rights he had never meant to part with, and persisted in exacting them despite the votes of the House. Louder still grew the cry against the High Church clergy and the ecclesiastical policy of the King. It was not only of sermons in favour of absolute monarchy or innovations in ritual that the Puritan leaders complained. The dispute about ceremonies had now developed into a dispute about doctrine too. The milder theories about justification and election—known as Arminianism and favoured by the High Church clergy—seemed to Puritans to be sapping the foundations of Protestantism and paving the way for Popery. The King endeavoured to put an end to doctrinal disputes by silencing controversial preaching; the Commons demanded the suppression of Arminianism, and the punishment of all who propagated views deviating from what they regarded as Protestant orthodoxy.

It was during these religious disputes that Cromwell first took part in the debates of the Commons. Inheriting the traditions of a family that owed everything to the Reformation, trained by a Puritan schoolmaster and at a Puritan college, he could take only one side, and he raised his voice to swell the attack upon the friends of Popery in the Church. The House was discussing some charges against Dr. Neile, the Bishop of Winchester, when Cromwell intervened with a story showing that prelate's leaning to popish tenets. A certain Dr. Alablaster, said Cromwell, had "preached flat Popery" in a sermon before the Lord Mayor, and when Dr. Beard, the next preacher there, came in turn to deliver his sermon, Neile sent for Beard, and "did charge him as his diocesan not to preach any doctrine contrary to that which Dr. Alablaster had delivered." Beard nevertheless persisted in refuting his predecessor, and was reprimanded by Neile for his disobedience.

Before the charges against Neile and other like-minded prelates were brought to a conclusion, and before the remonstrance of the Commons against the King's ecclesiastical policy was perfected, Charles put an end to the sitting of Parliament.

Ere it separated, the House of Commons, at Eliot's bidding, affirmed once more the principles for which it was fighting. Cromwell was one of the defiant crowd who refused to obey the King's orders for adjournment till they had passed by acclamation Eliot's three resolutions. Whoever, it was declared, should bring in innovations in religion, or seek to introduce Popery, Arminianism, or any opinion disagreeing from the true and orthodox Church, should be reported a capital enemy to this kingdom and commonwealth. Whoever counselled the levying of tonnage and poundage without a parliamentary grant should also be held an enemy to his country and an innovator in the government; and whoever willingly paid those taxes was proclaimed to be a betrayer of the liberties of England. The significance of the resolutions lay not merely in their challenge to the King, but in the union of political and religious discontents which they indicated. Elizabeth's policy had called into being a religious opposition. James had created a constitutional opposition. Under Charles the two had combined, and from their alliance sprang the Civil War.

To themselves the parliamentary leaders seemed defenders of the existing constitution in Church and State against the revolutionary changes of the King. In reality the greatest innovation of all lay in the claim of the Commons that Church and State should be controlled by the representatives of the people, not by the will of the King. When that claim was once made, the struggle for sovereignty was an inevitable and irrepressible conflict.

CHAPTER II
THE PREPARATION FOR THE CIVIL WAR
1629–1640

For the next eleven years Charles ruled without a Parliament. "Remember," he had warned the Commons in 1626, "that Parliaments are altogether in my power for their calling, sitting and dissolution; therefore as I find the fruits of them good or evil, they are to continue, or not to be." He now announced that their fruits were evil, and that henceforth it would be accounted presumption for anyone to prescribe to him a time for the calling of another. Henceforth he would govern by the authority which God had put into his hands, and so order the state that his people should confess that they lived more happily and freely than any subjects in the Christian world.

Taxation without parliamentary grant became thereafter the regular practice. Tonnage and poundage were levied from the merchants as if the right had never been disputed, and new impositions on trade were added to the old. Obsolete laws were revived and rigorously executed. In 1630, the law which required every person possessing an estate worth £40 a year to take up the honour of knighthood was put in force, and fines to the amount of £170,000 were levied on those who had omitted to comply with it. In 1634, the ancient forest laws were revived. Lands were now declared to be part of the royal forests which for three hundred years had been outside their boundaries, and landowners were heavily fined for encroachments.

The knighthood fines affected all the gentry and all men in easy circumstances; the extension of the forests threatened chiefly the nobility and persons of quality; the revival of the monopolies aggrieved all classes alike. The King, it was calculated, got £38,000 a year from the wine monopolists, the patentees received from the vintners £90,000, and the vintners raised the price of wine to the consumers so that the nation paid £360,000. And besides the wine monopoly there were monopolies of soap, of iron, of tobacco, of salt, of gunpowder, and of many other commodities.

On the one hand, the King's financial measures discontented the nation, and on the other they failed to meet the wants of the Government. In 1635, the ordinary revenue of the Crown was about £600,000, and the King's debts were about £1,200,000. When the safety of the seas and the exigencies of foreign policy required a fleet, it became necessary to resort to direct taxation, and Ship-money was invented. In 1634, it was levied on the maritime counties only, and brought in £100,000; in 1635, it was extended to the inland counties, and produced twice that amount.

It was useless to appeal to the law courts for protection or redress. The judges, removable at the King's pleasure, declined to arbitrate between King and people, and preferred to regard themselves as the servants of the Crown. When called upon to decide on the lawfulness of Ship-money, their decision was avowedly dictated by political rather than legal considerations. One judge declared that the law was the King's old and trusty servant, that it was not true that *lex* was *rex*, but common and most true that *rex* was *lex*. Another asserted that no acts of Parliament could take away the King's right to command the persons and the money of his subjects, if he thought a sufficient necessity existed. It was well said that the reasons alleged by the judges were such as every man could swear were not law, and that their logic left no man anything which he might call his own. To enforce his will, the King had at his disposal, besides the ordinary courts of law, the exceptional courts which the Tudors had created. Their jurisdiction was enlarged at the King's pleasure. In 1632, the powers of the Council of the North were increased. The Privy Council assumed legislative power by its proclamations, "enjoining this to the people that was not enjoined by law, and prohibiting that which was not prohibited by law." The Star Chamber enforced the proclamations by fine and imprisonment, and punished opponents or critics with inordinate severity.[1] The fate of Prynne, Burton, and Bastwick showed that no profession could exempt its members from barbarous and ignominious penalties.[2] The fate of Eliot and his friends proved that the privileges of Parliament were no protection against the King's vindictiveness.[3] There were Privy Councillors who "would ordinarily laugh when the word liberty of the subject was named," and to wise men it seemed that the very foundations of right were in danger of destruction.

If Englishmen wished to know what the aim of the King's ministers was they had only to look across St. George's Channel. "The King," wrote Wentworth from Ireland in 1638, "is as absolute here as any prince in the world can be."[1] Parliaments still existed, but the Lord Deputy managed them as he chose, and, as Pym said, Parliaments without parliamentary liberties were but plausible ways to servitude. Juries existed, but when they gave verdicts against the Crown they were fined for their contumacy. The highest officials and the richest noblemen felt the weight of Wentworth's hand, and submitted to do his bidding. Trade increased, order reigned where it had never reigned before, and the poor lived freer from the oppressions of the great than the poor in Ireland had ever dreamt of doing. But not a vestige of self-government remained save a few idle forms; the government was a machine in which all motion, all force, came from the royal authority. The people had nothing to do but to obey the King. "Let them," said Wentworth, "attend upon his will, with confidence in his justice, belief in his wisdom, and assurance in his parental affections," instead of feeding themselves "with the vain flatteries of imaginary liberty."

Amongst Englishmen the King's use of his absolute power did not foster this blind faith in his superior wisdom.

A vigorous foreign policy directed towards national ends might have reconciled some of his subjects to the substitution of personal rule for self-government. But Charles had no European policy. When he dissolved his third Parliament he was at war with France and Spain, and want of money obliged him to make peace as soon as possible. In European politics, his only object was to procure the restoration of the Palatinate to his sister and her children. For this he offered his alliance simultaneously to Gustavus Adolphus and to Ferdinand II. For this he negotiated with France and Spain as he negotiated a few years later with Presbyterians and Independents. His policy was a series of intrigues which failed, and a succession of bargains in which he asked much, offered little, and got nothing. As it was purely dynastic in its aim, and at once unprincipled and unsuccessful, it left him with no ally in Europe.

One result it had, attributed by panegyrists to his wisdom, and held by courtiers a compensation for the loss of freedom—England kept out of war. "It enjoyed," says Clarendon, "the greatest calm and the fullest measure of felicity that any people for so long a time together had been blessed with, to the wonder and envy of all the parts of Christendom." The Thirty Years' War was turning fruitful Germany into a wilderness, and its cities into heaps of ruins. All other countries were impoverished or devastated by war, but England was, as it were, "the garden of Christendom" and "the Exchange of Europe." "Here," sang a poet, "white peace, the beautifullest of things, had fixed her everlasting nest." Never had the English Court been gayer, more brilliant, more luxurious; never were masques and banquets more frequent than during the crisis of Protestantism in Germany.

"Let the German drum bellow for freedom," wrote the poet of the Court, "its noise disturbs not us, nor should divert our joys."

Puritans felt that these German drums were a call to England to be up and doing. With anxious or exultant eyes, they followed each turn of fate in the death-struggle of Catholicism and Protestantism. It cheered Eliot's prison in the Tower to think of the progress of "the work abroad." When Tilly fled before Gustavus at the Breitenfeld, Eliot cried that now "Fortune and Hope were met." When Gustavus fell at Lützen, every Puritan's heart sank within him. "Never," wrote D'Ewes, "did one person's death bring so much sorrow to all true Protestant hearts—not our godly Edward's, the Sixth of that name, nor our late and heroic Prince Henry's—as did the King of Sweden's at this present."

It seemed to Puritans as if the same struggle between Protestantism and Catholicism was beginning even now in England. While the foreign policy of Charles seemed to them a cowardly desertion of Protestantism, his ecclesiastical policy seemed an insidious attack upon it, and under Laud's influence the ecclesiastical policy of Charles was as uniform and consistent as his European policy was feeble and irresolute.[1] To himself, Laud appeared an eminently conservative reformer who sought to enforce only the discipline of the Church and the ecclesiastical laws of the State. His object was to bring the Church back to its true historical position as a branch of the great Catholic Church, and to purge it of the Calvinistic taint it had contracted since the Reformation. Not averse to a certain freedom of speculation amongst learned men, he sought to silence controversial preaching, and was intolerant of diversity in the forms of worship. Unity of belief was essential to the existence of a National Church, and the way to it lay through uniformity, "for unity cannot long continue in the Church when uniformity is shut out at the church door." "Decency and an orderly settlement of the external worship of God in the Church" was his own definition of the ends for which he laboured.

To the Puritans, Laud appeared an innovator and a revolutionary. Over half the country the observances he sought to enforce had fallen into disuse for years. Each restoration of an authorised form, every revival of ancient usage, brought the Church nearer to Roman practice, and in their opinion nearer to Roman doctrine. A bow was not an expression of reverence, but a confession of idolatry; a surplice, not a few yards of white linen, but a rag of Rome. Laud's attempts to silence their preachers aggravated their suspicion of his motives and confirmed them in the theory that he was a papist in disguise.

Much of the hostility which Laud brought upon himself was due to the means which he employed. The King's authority as supreme governor of the Church was the instrument by which the State could be used to carry out the views of a clerical reformer, and he had no scruples about using it. Laud's reliance on personal government in matters ecclesiastical allied him naturally with its supporters in things secular. Absolutism was with Strafford a political creed, with Laud an ecclesiastical necessity. Each needed the same tool: one to realise his dream of a well governed commonwealth, the other to shape a Church that had grown half Calvinistic into conformity with the Anglican ideal. Each had the same violent zeal. "Laud," says James I., "hath a restless spirit, and cannot see when things are well, but loves to bring matters to a pitch of reformation floating in his own brain." Strafford described himself as one "ever desiring the best things, never satisfied I had done enough, but did always desire to do better."

Laud and Strafford were alike in their impatience of opposition, whether it rose from indolence, corruption, or conscience; whether it pleaded legal technicalities or constitutional rights. Arbitrary though the government of Charles was, it was not vigorous enough to satisfy these two eager spirits. But Strafford's power to give his views effect was bounded by the Irish Sea, and outside the ecclesiastical sphere Laud's was hampered by conflicting influences. The correspondence of the Archbishop and the Lord Deputy is full of complaints of the remissness of the King's other ministers, and of sighs for the adoption of a system of "Thorough."

Opponents of Ship-money and Puritans in general must be put down with a strong hand. "The very genius of that people," wrote Strafford, "leads them always to oppose, as well civilly as ecclesiastically, all that ever authority ordains for them, but in good truth were they rightly served they should be whipped home into their right wits." "It might be done," answered Laud, "if the rod were rightly used, but as it is used it smarts not." Thus they took sweet counsel together, never dreaming of "that two-handed engine at the door" which waited to strike them both.

During these eleven years of arbitrary government, Cromwell's life was obscure, if not wholly uneventful. It was a period of unconscious preparation for his future action, a quiet seed-time which bore fruit hereafter. When the "great, warm, ruffling Parliament" of 1628 ended, Cromwell returned to his little estate at Huntingdon and busied himself with his farming. In May, 1631, he sold his property at Huntingdon for £1800, and rented some grazing lands at St. Ives, about five miles eastward, and farther down the Ouse. In 1636, Sir Thomas Steward of Ely, the brother of Cromwell's mother, died, and Oliver, whom his uncle had made his heir, succeeded Sir Thomas as farmer of the Cathedral tithes. He removed to Ely, where he lived in "the glebe house" near St. Mary's Church, which continued to be the residence of his wife and children till 1647. His family now numbered four sons, Robert, Oliver, Richard, and Henry; and two daughters, Bridget and Elizabeth, all born at Huntingdon. Two more daughters, Frances and Mary, were born in 1637 and 1638. The house he occupied is still standing; in 1845 it was an alehouse.

"By no means a sumptuous mansion," says Carlyle, "but may have conveniently held a man of three or four hundred a year, with his

family, in those simple times. Some quaint air of gentility still looks through its ragged dilapidations. It is of two stories, more properly of one and a half; has many windows, irregular chimneys, and gables."

Some writers, more especially poets, have spoken of these years of Cromwell's life as a time given up entirely to domesticity and agriculture. Marvell praises the Protector for an early abstention from public affairs which was by no means voluntary:

> "For neither didst thou from the first apply
>
> Thy sober spirit unto things too high;
>
> But in thine own fields exercisedst long
>
> A healthful mind within a body strong."

Elsewhere he pictures the ascent of the future general of the Republic:

> "From his private gardens, where
>
> He lived reservèd and austere,
>
> As if his highest plot
>
> To plant the bergamot."

Yet even to these private gardens and sequestered fields the echo of the German drums must have penetrated, and the Thirty Years' War must have stirred Cromwell as it stirred D'Ewes and Eliot. His later life suffices to prove it. In 1647, when the English Civil War seemed over, Cromwell thought of taking service in Germany himself. When he became Protector, his European policy was inspired by the passions of the Thirty Years' War. Its memories governed his attitude towards Austria and Sweden; he thought that Leopold I. would be a second Ferdinand II., and dreamt of finding a new Gustavus in Charles X. But to the Puritan farmer, prescient of a future struggle, the war was not merely a spectacle but a military education. Some of the best accounts of the battles and the mode of fighting of Gustavus were published in England, and between 1630 and 1640 few books were more popular than *The Swedish Intelligencer* and *The Swedish Soldier*. It cannot be doubted that Cromwell read these narratives, and absorbed from them that knowledge of military principles and military tactics which supplied for him the place of personal experience.

"I find him," says a modern military writer, "at the very first entrance into the war acting on principles which past experience had established, following closely upon just that stage which the art of war had reached under Gustavus, using the very same moral stimulus which Gustavus had made so effective, using the very words on one occasion which Gustavus used on another, and indicating in various ways that he had most carefully studied the past, though he had not had the opportunity of doing any peace parade work."

Cromwell watched the growth of arbitrary government in England with a still keener interest. In 1630, he was one of the many gentlemen prosecuted for omitting to go through the ceremony of knighthood, and finally had to pay ten pounds for his neglect. Presumably he also paid Ship-money, for there is no mention of his opposition to it amongst the State papers. If he refused to pay, the sheriff doubtless distrained upon his goods for the required amount, and there the matter ended. On another question Cromwell came into conflict with the local authorities, and was brought into collision with the King's Council. Up to 1630, Huntingdon had been an ancient prescriptive corporation, governed by two bailiffs and a common council of twenty-four inhabitants who were elected yearly. On July 15, 1630, the town obtained a new charter from Charles I. "To prevent popular tumult," the old common council was dissolved, and the government of the town vested in twelve aldermen elected for life, with a mayor, chosen annually out of the twelve, and a recorder. An oligarchy replaced a democracy. The chief agent of this change seems to have been Mr. Robert Barnard, a barrister who lived at Huntingdon, had lately bought an estate at Brampton hard by, and afterwards became Recorder of the town. The old common council had consented to the change in the government of Huntingdon, but when the terms of the new charter were examined a widespread discontent was aroused. Complaints were heard that it gave the mayor and aldermen power to deprive the burgesses of their rights in the common lands, and to levy exorbitant fines on burgesses who refused municipal office. Cromwell had assented to the change, and in the new charter he was appointed one of the three justices of the peace for the borough. But he thought these complaints well founded, and made himself the spokesman of the popular dissatisfaction. Perhaps Cromwell felt that he had been overreached by Barnard, whom in a later letter he significantly warns against too much subtlety. In his anger he made "disgraceful and unseemly speeches" to the new mayor and Barnard, and the corporation complained to the Privy Council. On November 2, 1630, the council committed Cromwell and one of his associates to custody. The case was heard on December 1st and referred to the arbitration of the Earl of Manchester, who, in his report, blamed Cromwell's conduct, but ordered the charter to be amended in three points to meet his objections. The rights of the poorer burgesses were secured by an order that "the number of men's cattle of all sorts which they now keep, according to order and usage, upon their commons, shall not be abridged or altered." As to the personal question Manchester's report was:

"For the words spoken of Mr. Mayor and Mr. Barnard by Mr. Cromwell, as they were ill, so they are acknowledged to be spoken in heat and passion and desired to be forgotten; and I found Mr. Cromwell very willing to hold friendship with Mr. Barnard, who with a good will remitting all the unkind passages past, entertained the same. So I left all parties reconciled."

This quarrel was doubtless one of the reasons why Cromwell left Huntingdon. At St. Ives and Ely, he showed the same zeal to defend the rights of his poorer neighbours. In 1634, a company was incorporated for the drainage of the fens round Ely, which were known as the Great Level. The "Adventurers," who were headed by the Earl of Bedford, were to be paid by a share of the lands they rescued from the water, and in 1637 the work was declared completed, and the reward claimed. By these drainage works the commoners lost the rights of pasturage and fishing they had previously enjoyed, and Cromwell made himself the champion of their interests against the "Adventurers."

"It was commonly reported," says a complaint, "by the commoners in Ely Fens and the Fens adjoining, that Mr. Cromwell of Ely had undertaken, they paying him a groat for every cow they had upon the commons, to hold the drainers in suit of law for five years, and that in the meantime they should enjoy every foot of their commons."

In 1638, the King intervened, declared the work of drainage incomplete, and undertook to complete it himself, announcing that the inhabitants of the district were to continue in possession of their lands and commons till the work was really finished. Nothing else is known of Cromwell's part in these disputes except a vague story told in the *Memoirs of Sir Philip Warwick*, that "the vulgar" grew clamorous against the scheme, and that Mr. Cromwell appeared as the head of their faction. Warwick, writing long after the events he referred to, assumed as a matter of course that Cromwell opposed the King, and the mistake found easy credence.

Some years later, Cromwell came forward in the same way to defend the rights of his old neighbours at St. Ives. The waste lands at Somersham near St. Ives had been enclosed without the consent of the commoners and sold to the Earl of Manchester. When the Long Parliament met, the aggrieved commoners petitioned the House of Commons for redress. The Lords intervened with an order in favour of Manchester. The commoners replied by proceeding "in a riotous and warlike manner" to break down the hedges and retake possession. Then the Lords sent the trained bands to reinstate Manchester, and Manchester issued sixty writs against the commoners. Without seeking to justify the violence of the commoners, Cromwell got the House of Commons to appoint a committee to consider the rights of the case. Hyde, its chairman, was greatly scandalised by the vehemence with which Cromwell advocated the rights of the commoners before it. Cromwell "ordered the witnesses and petitioners in the method of their proceeding, and enlarged upon what they said with great passion." He reproached the chairman for partiality, used offensive language to the son of the noble earl who claimed the land, and "his whole carriage was so tempestuous, and his behaviour so insolent," that the chairman threatened to report him to the House.

This persistent championship of the rights of peasants and small freeholders was the basis of Cromwell's influence in the eastern counties. Common rights were something concrete and tangible, which appealed to many who were not Puritans, and came home to men to whom parliamentary privileges were remote abstractions. Every village Hampden looked to Cromwell as a leader, and was ready to follow him. In 1643, a royalist newspaper nicknamed him "The Lord of the Fens," but his popularity with the fenmen began long before the military exploits which gained him the title.

In a more limited sphere Cromwell was well known as a zealous Puritan, but his opposition to Laud's ecclesiastical policy did not bring him into any general notoriety. Williams, Bishop of Lincoln, was Cromwell's kinsman, and lived during these years at Buckden near Huntingdon. He was wont to relate afterwards that his relative was in those days "a common spokesman for sectaries, and maintained their part with great stubbornness." A part of Laud's policy to which Cromwell was particularly hostile was the suppression of lectureships. The Puritans in the towns, discontented with the negligence of the established clergy in preaching, or with their doctrine, clubbed together to support lecturers, that is, clergymen whose sole business was preaching. Most corporations maintained a lecturer, and in 1625 a small society was formed for buying up impropriated tithes, and using the proceeds for the payment of lecturers. Laud sought to suppress these lectureships, and in 1633 the Star Chamber dissolved the Feoffees of Impropriations, and gave their patronage to the King.

At St. Ives or somewhere else in Huntingdonshire, there was a lectureship which Cromwell was anxious to keep up. It had been founded by some London citizens, and in 1636 was in danger of coming to an end through the stoppage of their subscriptions. Cromwell's first letter is an appeal to a forgetful subscriber, worded with singular care and tact. "Not the least of the good works of your fellow citizens," he begins,

"is that they have provided for the feeding of souls. Building of hospitals provides for men's bodies; to build material temples is judged a work of piety, but they that procure spiritual food, they that build up spiritual temples, they are the men truly charitable, truly pious. Such a work as this was your erecting the lecture."

He goes on to say that the lecturer is a good and able man, and has done good work; help him therefore to carry it on.

"Surely, it were a piteous thing to see a lecture fall in the hands of so many able and godly men, as I am persuaded the founders of this are; in these times, wherein we see they are suppressed, with too much haste and violence by the enemies of God his Truth.... To withdraw the pay is to let fall the lecture; for who goeth to warfare at his own cost. I beseech you therefore ... let the good man have his pay. The souls of God's children will bless you for it and so shall I."

The changes which Laud introduced in the externals of worship were as abhorrent to Cromwell as the suppression of Puritan preaching. "There were designs," said Cromwell, looking back on Laud's policy in 1658,

"to innovate upon us in matters of religion, and so to innovate as to eat out the core and power and heart and life of all religion, by bringing on us a company of poisonous popish ceremonies, and imposing them upon those that were accounted the Puritans of the nation and professors of religion among us, driving them to seek their bread in a howling wilderness. As was instanced to our friends who were forced to fly to Holland, New England, almost anywhither, to find liberty for their consciences."

A persistent tradition asserts that Cromwell himself thought of emigrating to New England, and there are many grounds for accepting it as true.

If he ever entertained such a design, it was probably between 1631 and 1636. When he left Huntingdon in May, 1631, he converted all his landed property into money, as a man intending to emigrate would naturally do. The cattle he bought and the lands he hired could be disposed of at short notice. The time at which this took place renders it more significant, for in

1630 and 1631 the Puritan exodus was at its height, and most of the New England colonists came from East Anglia. In March, 1632, the Earl of Warwick granted the old Connecticut patent to Lord Say and his associates, amongst whom was John Hampden. Nothing can be more probable than that Cromwell should have thought of settling in a colony of which his cousin was one of the patentees.

If Cromwell wished to emigrate, what was it that prevented him? The eighteenth century story that he was on board one of the ships stopped by order of council in May, 1638, is demonstrably false, for on the petition of the passengers they were allowed to continue their voyage. The contemporary story supplies a much more credible explanation. It is that a kinsman died leaving him a considerable fortune, and this kinsman is identified with Sir Thomas Steward, whose death took place in January, 1636. A story which fits in so well with ascertained facts, and is intrinsically so probable, should not be lightly put aside as a fiction.

There is another fact in Cromwell's history during this period of which one of his letters gives us evidence. If he had ever written an account of his own early life, little conflicts with local authorities or any alterations in his worldly fortunes would have seemed to us of less moment than the change which took place within him. Before 1628 he had become a professor of religion, and in all externals a Puritan, but by 1638 a formal acceptance of the Calvinistic creed had become the perfect faith which casts out all fears and doubts. His conversion had been followed by a time of depression and mental conflict which lasted for many years. Other Puritans passed through the same struggle. Bunyan relates how he "fell to some outward reformation in his life," and his neighbours thought him to be "a very godly man, a new religious man, and did marvel to see such a great and famous alteration." And yet for a long time afterwards he was "in a forlorn and sad condition," afflicted and disquieted by doubts. "How can you tell if you have faith?" said the inner voices. "How can you tell if you are elected? How if the day of grace be past and gone?" "My thoughts," he says, "were like masterless hell-hounds; my soul, like a broken vessel, driven as with the winds, and tossed sometimes headlong into despair."

By some such "obstinate questionings" Cromwell, too, was haunted and tormented. An unsympathetic physician who knew him at Huntingdon described him as splenetic and full of fancies; another whom he consulted at London wrote him down as "valde melancholicus." A mind diseased and a soul at war with itself were beyond their art. This internal conflict was at its height between 1628 and 1636. A friend who knew Cromwell then, wrote, many years afterwards, the following account of it:

"This great man is risen from a very low and afflicted condition; one that hath suffered very great troubles of soul, lying a long time under sore terrors and temptations, and at the same time in a very low condition for outward things: in this school of afflictions he was kept, till he had learned the lesson of the Cross, till his will was broken into submission to the will of God." Religion was thus "laid into his soul with the hammer and fire"; it did not "come in only by light into his understanding."

In 1638, at the request of his cousin, Mrs. St. John, Cromwell confided to her the story of this crisis in his life.

"You know," he said, "what my manner of life hath been. Oh, I lived in and loved darkness, and hated light; I was a chief, the chief of sinners. This is true, I hated godliness, yet God had mercy on me." Even now the struggle was not ended. "I live in Meshec, which they say signifies Prolonging; in Kedar, which signifies Blackness: yet the Lord forsaketh me not. Though He do prolong, yet He will I trust bring me to His tabernacle, to His resting-place. My soul is with the Congregation of the First-born, my body rests in hope.... He giveth me to see light in His light."

It would be wrong to take these self-accusings as a confirmation of the charges which royalist writers brought against Cromwell's early life. They refer to spiritual rather than moral failings, perhaps to the love of the world and its vanities against which he so often warns his children. They denote a change of feeling rather than a change of conduct, a rise from coldness to enthusiasm, from dejection to exaltation.

Full of thankfulness for this deliverance, Cromwell longed to testify to his faith. "If here I may honour my God, either by doing or suffering, I shall be most glad. Truly no poor creature hath more cause to put himself forth in the cause of his God than I have. I have had plentiful wages beforehand, and I am sure I shall never earn the least mite." The time for doing was near at hand, for when he wrote the resistance of the Scots had begun. The friend quoted before points out how strangely the turning-point in Cromwell's spiritual life coincided with the turning-point in the history of his cause. "The time of his extreme suffering was when this cause of religion in which we are now engaged was at its lowest ebb." When the cause began to prosper, "he came forth into comfort of spirit and enlargement of estate." And so "he suffered and rose with the cause, as if he had one life with it."

The year 1638 was the turning-point in the history of English Puritanism. When it began, the King's power seemed as firmly established as his heart could desire. The decision of the judges that Ship-money was lawful gave absolute monarchy a legal basis, and a vantage-ground for any future demands. The arguments which proved that the King had a right to levy taxes at will for the support of a navy, justified him, if he chose, in raising money for the maintenance of an army. Thus royalty, in Strafford's phrase, was "for ever vindicated from the conditions and restraints of subjects." "All our liberties," wrote a Puritan lawyer, "were now at one dash utterly ruined."

There had been rumours in 1637 of some tumults in Scotland. "Horrible ado against the bishops for seeking to bring in amongst them our service book," wrote Strafford's news-purveyor to the Lord Deputy, but neither thought it of much significance. At the end of March, 1638, the Scots took the Covenant, and the little cloud in the north became a threatening tempest. If Hampden and his friends could have read Laud's letters to Strafford, they would have laughed for joy. In May, the Archbishop was thoroughly uneasy about "the Scotch business." "If God bless it with a good end, it is more than I can hope for. The truth is that snowball hath been suffered to gather too long." Ten days after the decision against

Hampden, he was thoroughly alarmed. "It is not the Scottish business alone that I look upon, but the whole frame of things at home and abroad, with vast expenses out of little treasure, and my misgiving soul is deeply apprehensive of no small evils coming on.... I can see no cure without a miracle."

Charles was resolved to suppress the resistance of the Scots by arms. "So long as this Covenant is in force," he said, "I have no more power in Scotland than a Duke of Venice, which I will rather die than suffer." He sent the Marquis of Hamilton to negotiate with the Scots, "to win time that they may not commit public follies until I be ready to suppress them." But negotiations and intrigues failed to break their union, and in May, 1639, Charles gathered twenty thousand men and marched to the border to begin the work of suppression. Alexander Leslie, a soldier of Gustavus, with an equal force of Scots, barred his entrance to Scotland. Leslie's army was well disciplined, well paid, and well fed; his men "lusty and full of courage, great cheerfulness in the faces of all." The King's troops were ill-armed and ill-provided, and with no heart in their cause. The English nobility were as half-hearted as the troops, and the King had emptied his treasury to raise this army.

There was nothing left but to make peace, and on June 24, 1639, the Treaty of Berwick was signed. If the war had been a farce, the treaty was high comedy. Everything was forgiven, almost anything was promised. The King himself played the leading part in the negotiations with the Scots, who found him "one of the most just, reasonable, sweet persons they had ever seen." "His Majesty," wrote a Scot, "was ever the better loved of all that heard him, and he likewise was the more enamoured of us."

The Scots returned home full of loyalty, with permission to settle their ecclesiastical affairs in their own General Assembly, and their civil affairs in their own Parliament. Charles went back to London, and plotted to nullify his concessions. He refused either to rescind the acts establishing Episcopacy, or to confirm the acts of the Scottish Parliament, and summoned Strafford from Ireland to whip the Scots into their right minds. Strafford had ready both his plan of campaign and his policy. The English navy was to blockade the Scottish ports and destroy their trade. The Irish army was to threaten a landing in West Scotland, or to be transported to Cumberland. The English army was to invade Scotland and from a fortified camp at Leith keep Edinburgh and the Lowlands in awe, till the English Prayer-book was accepted and the bishops restored to their authority; "nay, perchance till I had conformed that kingdom in all, as well for the temporal as ecclesiastical affairs, wholly to the government and laws of England; and Scotland was governed by the King and council of England." Strafford's first step on reaching England was to procure the summoning of a Parliament. No Englishman, he thought, could refuse to give his money to the King in such an extremity, against so foul a rebellion. If any man resisted, he should be "laid by the heels," till he learnt to obey and not to dispute. But he repudiated the suggestion that the King had lost the affections of his people. In April, the Parliament met; its members were described as sober and dispassionate men of whom very few brought ill purposes with them. Amongst them was Cromwell, whose opposition to the "Adventurers" for the drainage of the fens had gained him a seat for the borough of Cambridge. All these sober and dispassionate men united in demanding the restoration of Parliament to its proper place in the constitution. Pym enumerated all the grievances in Church and State, and asserted that their source was the intermission of parliaments, for Parliament was the soul of the body politic. The Commons answered the King's demand for money by saying that "till the liberties of the House and the kingdom were cleared they knew not whether they had anything to give, or no." Charles tried to bargain with them, and offered to abolish Ship-money if they gave him £840,000 in return. They demanded not only the abolition of Ship-money but the abolition of the new military charges which the King had imposed on the counties for the support of their train-bands. Hearing that they meant to invite the Lords to make a joint protest against the intended war with the Scots, Charles cut short their project by a sudden dissolution (May 5, 1640). At this stroke moderate men were filled with melancholy, but the faces of the opposition leaders showed "a marvellous serenity." The cloudy countenance of Cromwell's cousin, St. John, was lit with an unusual light. "All was well," he said; "things must be worse before they could be better, and this Parliament would never have done what was necessary to be done."

With or without Parliament's aid, Charles was resolved to force the Scots to submission. Some of his council, knowing the emptiness of the exchequer, urged him to stand on the defensive.

"No defensive war," cried Strafford; "go on vigorously or let them alone. The King is loose and absolved from all rules of government. In an extreme necessity you may do all that your power admits. Parliament refusing, you are acquitted towards God and man. You have an army in Ireland you may employ here to reduce this kingdom. One summer well employed will do it."

At every step, however, the old difficulties gathered round the King's path. London refused a loan; France and Spain would lend nothing; even the Pope was applied to for men and money, but in vain. Not a tenth of the Ship-money imposed was paid, and Coat- and Conduct-money were universally refused. In his desperation, Charles thought of debasing the coinage and seizing the bullion which the Spanish Government had sent to England to be coined. The military outlook was equally depressing, for the army was smaller and worse than the army of 1639. The general of the cavalry at Newcastle described his task as teaching cart-horses military evolutions, and men fit for Bedlam and Bridewell to keep the ten commandments. The commander of the infantry in Yorkshire answered, that his mutinous train-bands were the arch-knaves of the country. Of this army, on August 18th, Strafford, half dead but indomitable, was appointed commander-in-chief.

Only a touch was needed to make the fabric of absolutism collapse. As the commander-in-chief was struggling towards his army in a litter, Leslie crossed the Tweed with twenty-five thousand Scots. On August 28th, he forced the passage of the Tyne at Newburn, driving before him the three thousand foot and fifteen hundred horse who strove to defend it. Newcastle was evacuated; Northumberland and Durham fell into Leslie's power; Strafford met his beaten troops streaming back into Yorkshire with the Scots close on their heels. "Never came any man to so lost a business," cried the unhappy statesman. It was not only that the army was untrained, necessitous, and cowardly, but the whole country was apathetic or hostile.

"An universal affright in all, a general disaffection to the King's service, none sensible of his dishonour." With desperate energy Strafford laboured to reorganise his shattered forces, and to keep the Scots out of Yorkshire. At his breath the dying loyalty of the country flashed up into a momentary blaze. It seemed as if the Scottish invasion might revive the forgotten hostility of the two nations.

Vain labours and vainer hopes. Twelve peers presented a petition demanding peace and a Parliament, and another to the same purpose came in from the City of London. Charles called a Council of Peers to patch up a truce with the Scots, and announced to them the summons of a Parliament for November 3rd. Absolutism had had its day.

CHAPTER III
THE LONG PARLIAMENT
1640–1642

The Long Parliament met at Westminster on November 3, 1640. Most of its members, even as Cromwell himself, had sat in the Parliament of the preceding May, but they came together now in a different temper, and with far greater power in their hands. Charles could not venture to dissolve them so long as the Scottish army was encamped on English soil. "No fear of raising the Parliament," wrote a Scot, "so long as the lads about Newcastle sit still."

There were three things which the Long Parliament was resolved to do. The first was to release the sufferers from arbitrary government; the second, to punish the men by whose hands the King had sought to establish his arbitrary power; the third, to amend the constitution so that arbitrary rule should be impossible hereafter. Pym's long experience in Parliaments made him the undisputed leader of the popular party, and his maxim was that it was not sufficient to remove grievances, but necessary to pull up the causes of them by the roots.

A master of parliamentary tactics in days when party discipline was unknown, Pym retained his ascendancy until the day of his death. But he remained to the end a great party leader rather than a great statesman. He was too much of a partisan to understand the feelings of his opponents, too closely attached to precedents and legal formulas to perceive the new issues which new times brought. When it was necessary to leave the beaten road, he was incapable of finding fresh paths. Pym was the chief orator of his party as well as its guiding spirit. In long, methodical expositions of the grievances of the nation, he pressed home the indictment against arbitrary government with convincing force. But sometimes he rose to a grave and lofty eloquence, or condensed the feeling of the hour in brief, incisive phrases that passed current like proverbs.

Hampden came next to Pym in authority with the House and had a far greater fame outside it. Ship-money had made him famous. "The eyes of all men were fixed on him as their *patriæ pater*, and the pilot that must steer their vessel through the tempests and rocks that threatened it." A poor speaker, but clear-sighted, energetic, and resolute, "a supreme governor over all his passions and affections," he was a man who swayed others in council, and whom they would follow when it came to action.

Next to these in importance came St. John—Hampden's counsel in the Ship-money case, and the ablest of the opposition lawyers,—Holles and Strode,—men who had suffered for their boldness in the Parliament of 1629,—and Rudyard, whose oratory had gained him renown in still earlier Parliaments. Of the younger men, the most prominent were Nathaniel Fiennes and Sir Henry Vane, notorious for their advanced religious views, and Sir Arthur Haslerig and Harry Marten, equally notorious for their democratic opinions. The headquarters of the popular party was Sir Richard Manly's house in a little court behind Westminster Hall, where Pym lodged. There, while Parliament was sitting, Pym, Hampden, and a few others kept a common table at their joint expense, and during their meetings much business was transacted. Cromwell, as the cousin of Hampden and St. John, was doubtless one of this group. Though he was known to the party in general only as a rather silent country squire who had been a member of the two last Parliaments, it is evident that he had some reputation for business capacity. During the first session of the Long Parliament, he was specially appointed to eighteen committees, not counting those particularly concerned with the affairs of the eastern counties, to which the member for Cambridge was naturally added. Cromwell's first intervention in the debates of the House was on November 9, 1640, when the grievances of the nation and the wrongs of those who had suffered under Star Chamber and High Commission were being set forth at large. He rose to deliver a petition from John Lilburn, a prisoner in the Fleet, and how he looked and spoke is recorded in Sir Philip Warwick's memoirs.

"The first time I ever took notice of him," says Warwick, "was in the beginning of the Parliament held in November, 1640, when I vainly thought myself a courtly young gentleman; for we courtiers valued ourselves much on our good clothes. I came into the House one morning, well clad, and perceived a gentleman speaking whom I knew not, very ordinarily apparelled; for it was a plain cloth suit which seemed to have been made by an ill country tailor; his linen was plain, and not very clean, and I remember a speck or two of blood upon his little band, which was not much larger than his collar; his hat was without a hatband; his stature was of a good size; his sword stuck close to his side; his countenance swollen and reddish; his voice sharp and untunable, and his eloquence full of fervour. For the subject matter would not bear much of reason, it being in behalf of a servant of Mr. Prynne's, who had dispersed libels against the Queen for her dancing, and such like innocent and courtly sports; and he aggravated the imprisonment of this man by the Council-table unto that height that one would have believed the very government itself had been in great danger by it. I sincerely profess it much lessened my reverence unto that great council, for he was very much hearkened unto."

When the grievances of the nation had been heard and the petitions of individual sufferers referred to committees, the Long Parliament turned to punish the King's ministers. Charles himself was never mentioned but with great honour, as a King misled by evil counsellors, who had prevented him from following the dictates of his native wisdom and goodness. In the interests of both King and subjects, argued Rudyard, these evil advisers must be removed and punished. As the Bible said: "Take away the wicked from the king and his throne shall be established."

Accordingly Strafford was arrested and impeached, just as he was himself about to accuse the parliamentary leaders of high treason for encouraging and aiding the invasion of the Scots (November 11th). A month later, Laud followed Strafford to the Tower. Windebank, the Secretary of State, and Lord Keeper Finch, likewise accused, fled beyond the seas. Two more bishops and six judges were impeached and imprisoned, while all monopolists were expelled from the House of Commons. It seemed "a general doomsday." Strafford was the first to suffer, and his trial in Westminster Hall riveted all eyes.

It was not only as "the great apostate to the commonwealth," the oppressor of the English colonists in Ireland, the moving spirit of the unjust war against the Scots, that Strafford was accused. The essence of the charge against him was that he had endeavoured by words, acts, and counsels to subvert the fundamental laws of England and Ireland, in order to introduce an arbitrary and tyrannical government. In him seemed incarnate the rule of arbitrary will as opposed to the reign of law which the Parliament strove to restore. Pym's speeches against Strafford are, throughout, a glorification of the reign of law. "Good laws," he said, "nay, the best laws, were no advantage when will was set above law." All evils hurtful to the State were comprehended in this one crime.

"The law is that which puts a difference betwixt good and evil, betwixt just and unjust. If you take away the law, all things will fall into a confusion. Every man will become a law to himself, which, in the depraved condition of human nature, must needs produce great enormities. Lust will become a law, envy will become a law, covetousness and ambition will become laws; and what dictates, what decisions such laws will produce, may easily be discerned in the government of Ireland."

Nor was the substitution of arbitrary power for law hurtful to subjects only.

"It is dangerous to the King's person, and dangerous to his Crown. If the histories of those Eastern countries be pursued, where princes order their affairs according to the mischievous principles of the Earl of Strafford, loose and absolved from all rules of government, they will be found to be frequent in combustions, full of massacres and of the tragical ends of princes."

Strafford struggled to show that the offences proved against him did not legally amount to high treason. Parliament through the Attainder Bill answered that it was necessary for the safety of the State to make them treasonable. "To alter the settled frame and constitution of government," said Pym, "is treason in any state. The laws whereby all other parts of a kingdom are preserved would be very vain and defective, if they had not a power to secure and preserve themselves."

Charles was anxious to save Strafford's life, but his blundering interventions during the course of the trial ended in failure. When it was discovered that the King's agents were plotting to get possession of the Tower and to bring the English army up from Yorkshire to overawe the Parliament, the Earl's fate was sealed. Pressed by both Houses to yield, and threatened by the London mob if he refused, Charles assented to the Bill of Attainder, and on May 12, 1641, Strafford was beheaded.

Side by side with the prosecution of the King's evil advisers went on the work of providing against arbitrary government in the future. The extraordinary courts which had been the instruments of oppression were swept away. Down went the Star Chamber and the High Commission Court, the Council of the North, and the Council of Wales and the Marches. The Tonnage and Poundage Act declared that henceforward it was illegal to levy customs duties without a parliamentary grant. The extension of the forests was prohibited, the exaction of knighthood fines forbidden, and Ship-money declared unlawful. Henceforward to govern without a Parliament was to be as impossible as to tax without a Parliament. On February 15, 1641, Charles assented to the Triennial Act, which bound him to call a Parliament every third year, and provided machinery for its convocation, if he neglected to summon it at the appointed time. On May 11th, he assented to a second act, which prohibited him from dissolving the present Parliament, or even proroguing it save by its own consent.

Cromwell had taken no part in the prosecution of Strafford, for he was neither an orator nor a lawyer, but his name is closely associated with one of these constitutional changes. The origin of the Triennial Act was a bill introduced by Strode for reviving the old law of Edward III. by which a Parliament must be summoned every year. On December 30th, Cromwell moved its second reading, and he was one of the committee from whose deliberations it finally issued as a bill for summoning a Parliament every three years. In ecclesiastical affairs, he was more prominent by far. On constitutional questions, the popular party had been almost unanimous, but on religious questions its unanimity ended. The general aim of its leaders was to subject the Church to the control of the State as represented by Parliament, instead of leaving it to the authority of the King as its "supreme governor." But while some desired to abolish the Prayer-book, and to make the doctrine of the Church more frankly Calvinistic, others wished merely the abolition of a few offensive formulas or ceremonies. On Church government there was the same diversity of opinion. A few wished to maintain bishops as they were, a few to abolish them altogether; the majority desired to retain Episcopacy, but to limit the power of the bishops. Hence the popularity of Ussher's plan for a limited Episcopacy, in which every bishop was to be assisted and controlled by a council of diocesan clergy. As yet there was no party in Parliament which proposed to introduce Presbyterianism or Independency, but those who wished for the complete extirpation of Episcopacy were very numerous. In the Commons, Fiennes and Sir Henry Vane were for its abolition, "root and branch," and Hampden afterwards joined them. Amongst these "root and branch" men was Cromwell, and he was more closely connected with the attack on the Church than with any other part of the proceedings of the Long Parliament. The only one of his letters which belongs to this period shows his interest in religious questions. It is addressed to a bookseller, and asks for a copy of the printed "reasons of the Scots to enforce their desire of uniformity in religion." "I would peruse it," he writes, "against we fall upon the debate, which will be speedily."

The only recorded speech of Cromwell in these ecclesiastical discussions was delivered on February 9, 1641, about the question whether a petition for the total abolition of Episcopacy, signed by fifteen thousand citizens of London, should be referred to a committee. A member urged its rejection, arguing that the bishops were one of the estates of the realm, and a part of the constitution. Equality (or, as he termed it, "parity") in the Church would lead to equality in the State. Cromwell stood up, and very bluntly denied his inferences and suppositions, on which "divers interrupted him and called him to the bar." Pym and Holles defended him, and he was allowed to continue.

"Mr. Cromwell went on and said: 'He did not understand why that gentleman that last spake should make an inference of parity from the

Church to the State, nor that there was any necessity of the great revenues of bishops. He was more convinced touching the irregularity of bishops than even before, because like the Roman hierarchy they would not endure to have their condition come to a trial.'"

In May, Cromwell took another opportunity of attacking the bishops. The Commons had passed a bill excluding clergymen in general from holding secular office either as judges, councillors, or members of the House of Lords, and the Upper House showed a resolution not to pass it. On this the "root and branch" men replied with a bill for the abolition of bishops altogether, which Sir Edward Dering, a noted speaker, was persuaded to introduce. Afterwards Dering repented and explained. "The Bill," he said, "was pressed into my hands by Sir Arthur Haslerig, being then brought to him by Sir Henry Vane and Mr. Oliver Cromwell."

The "root and branch" bill never got farther than committee, but its introduction further accentuated the division in the popular party. A section, headed by Hyde and Lord Falkland, severed themselves definitely from their former friends. Naturally conservative in temper, they were satisfied with the reforms already achieved, and were more willing to trust the King with the constitution than Parliament with the Church. Before the end of the session, Hyde was in communication with the King, and a party of constitutional Royalists based on the defence of the Church was in process of formation. Charles was equally determined to maintain the Church, and full of schemes for regaining his lost power. The prospect of obtaining support in the House of Commons itself increased his confidence of ultimate success, and in August he set out for Scotland, hoping to win the Scottish nobility to his side, and to use one kingdom against the other.

In October, 1641, when the second session of the Long Parliament began, the position of affairs was greatly altered. The popular party was weakened by its differences on the religious question, and the division was rapidly spreading to the nation. At the same time, the parliamentary leaders had lost, through the withdrawal of the Scottish army, the military force which had protected them from an attempted *coup d'état*. That the fear of such a stroke on the King's part was by no means groundless, the news from Scotland proved. It was rumoured that with the King's sanction a party of royalist soldiers had plotted to seize Hamilton and Argyle, whose hasty flight from Edinburgh had alone saved their lives. On the top of this came the news of a rebellion in Ireland, of an attempt to surprise Dublin Castle, and of a massacre of the English colonists in Ulster. The rebellion spread daily, and as tattered fugitives straggled into Dublin, each with his story of murder and pillage, the excitement in England rose to fever heat. It came to be an article of faith that fifty thousand Englishmen had been barbarously murdered, and some said 150,000.

To modern historians the Irish rebellion seems only the natural result of the English system of governing Ireland, but to contemporary Englishmen it came like a bolt from the blue. The native Irish were embittered and impoverished by the confiscations of the last sixty years, and filled with fury and fear by Strafford's intended plantation of Connaught. Now that the Puritans were in power, the complete suppression of the Catholic religion, only threatened before, seemed imminent and inevitable. The impeachment of Strafford and his most trusted counsellors had crippled the strong Government which Strafford had built up, and the disbanding of his army had filled the country with men trained to arms. The opportunity for a successful revolt had come at last, and it was no wonder that the Irish seized it. At its beginning, the rebellion of October, 1641, was a rising of the native Irish with the object of recovering the lands from which they had been expelled. It broke out first in the six counties of Ulster, planted in the reign of James I., and next in Wicklow, the most recent of the later plantations. But bloody and barbarous as the rebellion was, no general massacre was either planned or carried out. The first object of the rebels was simply to drive the colonists from their houses and lands, and in the process some were murdered, and all plundered. The number of persons killed in cold blood during the first month or two of the rebellion probably amounted to about four thousand, and perhaps twice as many perished from hardships and destitution.

To English Puritans, the only possible explanation of the rebellion was that it was the natural result of Popery. On December 4, 1641, the Long Parliament passed a resolution that they would never consent to any toleration of the Popish religion in Ireland, or in any other of his Majesty's dominions. Equally fatal was the resolve that the funds for the reconquest of Ireland should be raised by fresh confiscations of Irish land, and the assignment of two and a half million acres for the repayment of those who advanced the money. One vote turned a local insurrection into a general rebellion; the other made the rebellion an internecine war.

Both parties in Parliament approved of these votes. A public subscription was opened, to which members of Parliament and merchants of London contributed freely. "Master Oliver Cromwell," who knew nothing of Irish history, thought the plan wise and just, and put his name down for £500, which was about one year's income. He shared the general ignorance of his contemporaries about the causes of the rebellion, and believed the prevalent exaggerations about the massacre.

"Ireland," he told the Irish clergy eight years later, "was once united to England. Englishmen had good inheritances, which many of them had purchased with their money; they and their ancestors, from you and your ancestors. They had good leases from Irishmen, for long times to come; great stocks thereupon; houses and plantations erected at their own cost and charge. They lived peaceably and honestly among you. You had generally equal benefit of the protection of England with them; and equal justice from the laws, saving what was necessary for the State, out of reasons of State, to put upon some people apt to rebel upon the instigation of such as you. You broke this union. You unprovoked put the English to the most unheard-of and barbarous massacre (without respect to sex or age) that ever the sun beheld. And at a time when Ireland was in perfect peace."

To reconquer Ireland an army had to be raised at once, and it was impossible for the parliamentary leaders to trust the King with its control. Less than six months before, Charles had plotted to bring up an army to overawe their debates. In his recent journey to Scotland he had again been tampering with the officers of the same army, and its disbandment had only just been effected. If they gave him a new army, who could doubt that before six months were over he would be turning it against the Parliament? Pym had no doubts, and, on November 6th, he brought forward an address saying that unless the King would employ such ministers as Parliament approved "they would take such a course for the securing of Ireland as might likewise secure themselves." And while Pym proposed to seize upon the executive power as far as Ireland was concerned, Cromwell proposed to lay hands on it in England also. On November 6th he carried a motion that the two Houses should vote to the Earl of Essex power to command all the train-bands south of the Trent, and that those powers should continue till this Parliament should take further order. A month later, Haslerig brought in a militia bill, which gave a general appointed by the Parliament the supreme command of all the train-bands in England. The question whether the King or the Parliament should command the armed forces of the nation was thus definitely raised.

In the same November the Long Parliament appealed to the nation for support. The Grand Remonstrance set forth all the ills the nation had suffered in the fifteen years of the King's reign, and all the Parliament had done in the last twelve months to remove them. It pointed out the obstacles which hindered them in their task, and announced what they hoped to do in the future. The root of every evil was a malignant design to subvert the fundamental laws and principles upon which the religion and justice of the kingdom were based. Let "the malignant party be removed," and the reformation of Church and State could be completed. The Remonstrance bade the nation judge whether its representatives had been worthy of its confidence, and asked it to continue that confidence. It brought war nearer, not because it was an indirect indictment of the King, but because the ecclesiastical policy set forth in its last clauses divided the nation into two camps. In them the House declared its intention of taking in hand the work of church-reform, and demanded the calling of a general synod of divines to aid it in the task. Over these clauses of the Remonstrance the debate was long and bitter (November 22nd). When it passed by but eleven votes, and the majority proposed its printing, it seemed as if the Civil War would begin at once, and on the floor of the House. Members protested, and shouted, and waved their hats, and some took their sheathed swords in their hands as if they waited for the word to draw them. "I thought," said an eye-witness, "we had all sat in the valley of the shadow of death; for we, like

Joab's and Abner's young men, had catched at each other's locks, and sheathed our swords in each other's bowels."

When the tumult was allayed, and the members went home, Cromwell's whispered words to Falkland showed how much that night's decision meant. "If the Remonstrance had been rejected," he said, "I would have sold all I had the next morning, and never seen England more; and I know there are many other honest men of the same resolution."

Three days after the passing of the Remonstrance, Charles returned to Whitehall. He came back resolved to make no further concessions, and to rid himself of the parliamentary leaders under the form of law. Their relations with the Scots during the late war, their attacks on his royal power, and the changes they sought to make in the constitution were sufficient in his opinion to prove them guilty of high treason. His first step was to remove the guards round the House; his next, to ingratiate himself with the City; his third, to place a trusty ruffian in command of the Tower. When the Commons petitioned for the restoration of their guard, Charles told them that, on the word of a king, their security from violence should be as much his care as the preservation of his own children. On the day the House received this answer, Charles sent the attorney-general to impeach five members, and a sergeant-at-arms to arrest them.[8] The Commons refused to give them up. The next day he came to arrest them in person, with four hundred armed men at his back, but found the birds flown, and faith in the royal word fled too (January 4, 1642). The House of Commons adjourned to the City, which refused, as the House itself had done, to surrender the accused members. Petitioners poured in from the country in thousands to support their representatives, and it was evident that the feeling of the nation was overwhelmingly on the side of the Parliament. The King's *coup d'état* had completely failed. On the 11th of January, the House of Commons returned to Westminster, while the King left London to avoid witnessing their triumph.

Charles had not intended to act treacherously, and believed that his actions were perfectly legal, but it was natural that the parliamentary leaders, refusing to trust him, should press with renewed vigour for the control of the armed force. Cromwell felt this as strongly as his leaders, and three days after the return to Westminster he moved for a committee to put the kingdom in a posture of defence (January 14th). The motion was a little premature. It was necessary, Pym felt, that the two Houses should act together, and the Lords were slow to move. It was not till Pym told them that unless they would join the Commons in saving the kingdom the Commons would save the kingdom without them, that the Upper House gave way. In February, they passed the bill for the exclusion of the bishops, and joined in the demand for the control of the militia. In March, they united with the Commons in a vote to put the kingdom in a posture of defence by authority of both Houses.

For the present, however, both King and Parliament were unwilling to appeal to arms: the King strove to gain time in order to gain strength; the Parliament still hoped that the King would grant the securities they sought. So for six months they argued and negotiated, each appealing to the nation by declarations and counter-declarations, and preluding by these paper skirmishes the opening of real hostilities. Charles had two policies which he followed alternately, each of which demanded time for its success. The one was the policy of the Queen and the courtiers; the other was the policy of Hyde and the constitutional Royalists. The Queen's policy was active preparation for the inevitable war, regardless of any constitutional doctrines that stood in the way. Help was to be sought from France, or Denmark, or the Prince of Orange, and a port was to be secured, in which foreign troops could be landed. Hyde's policy was that the King should remain passive, that he should "shelter himself wholly under the law," granting anything which the law obliged him to grant, and denying anything which the law enabled him to deny and his position made it inexpedient to concede. "In the end," said Hyde, "the King and the Law together would be strong enough for any encounter that might happen."

Neither the King's character nor his position made it possible for him to adopt an entirely consistent policy. Some concessions he was obliged to make, either to conciliate public opinion by a show of yielding, or to gain time for his preparations for war. He withdrew the impeachment of the Five Members; he removed the governor of the Tower; he temporised about the Militia Bill; he even consented to the exclusion of the bishops from the House of Lords. Sorely against his own conscience was the latter concession granted, but the Queen insisted upon it, and to secure her safe passage to the continent Charles yielded. She bore with her to Holland the crown jewels to be pawned to provide arms and ammunition, and when she had sailed Charles took his way to Yorkshire to gather his friends around him and to secure the indispensable seaport. As he journeyed north, a deputation met him at Newmarket, and renewed the petition for the militia. But the necessity for concessions was past, and he refused even a temporary grant. "By God," he cried, "not for an hour! You have asked that of me in this, was never asked of a king, and with which I will not trust my wife and children."

When the King reached York, he set in operation an attempt to get possession of Hull. It was not only the most convenient port for the landing of succours from Holland and Denmark; it was also the great arsenal where the arms and munitions collected for the Scottish war had been stored. On April 23rd, Charles appeared before Hull with three hundred horsemen and demanded admission. But Sir John Hotham, the Governor, drew up the drawbridge, and taking his stand on the wall refused to admit the King. After proclaiming him a traitor, Charles rode away.

While the policy which the Queen had urged met with failure, the policy of which Hyde was the advocate gained for Charles adherents every day. Opinion veered to the King's side. The change was mainly due to the ecclesiastical policy of the Parliament, for those who loved the Church feared to see its liturgy and its government delivered up to the rough hands of a Puritan Parliament and a synod of Puritan divines. But Hyde's skilful advocacy did much to further the reaction. The declarations he wrote for the King, with their fluent, florid rhetoric, and their touches of humour and sarcasm, were far more effective than the ponderous legal arguments published by the Parliament. More was due to the art with which he represented the King as the guardian of the constitution, and the Parliament as its assailant. Pym's panegyric of the law was turned against Pym himself. The King was made the champion of "the known laws of the land," against revolutionists who wished to make the long-established rights of king and subject dependent on a vote of the House of Commons. He was made the defender of the "ancient, equal, happy, well poised, and never-enough-commended constitution," against those who sought to introduce "a new Utopia of religion and government."

That the Parliament was claiming new powers and the King standing on old rights it was impossible to deny, and it was difficult for the Parliament to prove the necessity which justified its demands. They could intimate the "fears and jealousies" which made them distrust the King, but the reality of their grounds for distrusting him is proved by evidence which they could only conjecture, and which later historians were to bring to light.

A mere argumentative victory could do nothing to solve the question the English nation had to decide. It was no longer a dispute whether the law gave certain powers to King or Parliament, but whether King or Parliament was to be sovereign. In the Nineteen Propositions which formed the Parliament's ultimatum, they demanded all the branches of sovereignty for themselves. The control of foreign policy, of ecclesiastical policy, of the army and the navy, the appointment of ministers, councillors, and judges, the right to punish and the right to pardon, were all included. Government, in short, was to be carried on by persons chosen by the Parliament, instead of persons chosen by the King. The King might reign, but henceforth he should not govern.

In that sense Charles understood the Nineteen Propositions.

"These being passed" he answered, "we may be waited upon bareheaded, we may have our hand kissed, the style of majesty continued to us, and the King's authority declared by both Houses of Parliament may still be the style of your commands, we may have swords and maces carried before us, and please ourselves with the sight of a crown and sceptre, but as to true and real power we should remain but the outside, but the picture, but the sign of a king."

On the other side, their demand, as it presented itself to the minds of the Parliamentarians, was rather defensive than aggressive in its intention. Without this transference of sovereignty, they held it impossible to transmit to their descendants the self-government they had received from their ancestors.

"The question in dispute between us and the King's party," says Ludlow, "was, as I apprehended, whether the King should govern as a god by his will and the nation be governed by force like beasts; or whether the people should be governed by laws made by themselves, and live under a government derived from their own consent."

Only the sword could decide. On July 4th, Parliament appointed a Committee of Safety; on July 6th, they resolved to raise ten thousand men; on July 9th, they appointed the Earl of Essex their general. The King set up his standard at Nottingham on August 22nd.

CHAPTER IV
THE FIRST CAMPAIGN
1642

From the day when King Charles raised his standard at Nottingham, and even before that date, England was divided into two camps, according as men elected to obey the King or the Parliament. The country was about to learn by experience what civil war meant, and to suffer as it had not suffered since the fifteenth century. In the Wars of the Roses, two rival houses had laid claim to the allegiance of the people; now its obedience was demanded by two rival authorities.

Moreover, apart from the question which authority ought to be obeyed, the fact that the Parliament itself was divided made a choice difficult and obscured the main issue. The House of Commons was no longer the almost unanimous body which it had been in November, 1640. About 175 members followed the King's flag, while nearly three hundred remained at Westminster. In the Upper House the preponderance was overwhelmingly on the King's side. Rather more than thirty peers threw in their lot with the popular party, while about eighty supported the King, and about twenty took no part in the struggle.

Very various, therefore, were the motives which led men to choose one side or the other. To many peers, the fate of the King and the nobility seemed inseparably linked together, and like Newcastle they loved monarchy as the foundation and support of their own greatness. Some, lately ennobled by Charles and his father, had personal obligations to the House of Stuart, which they were ready to repay by any sacrifice. "Had I millions of crowns or scores of sons," wrote Lord Goring to his wife, "the King and his cause should have them all with better will than to eat if I were starving.... I had all from the King, and he hath all again." Of the parliamentary peers, a few like Brooke, Saye, and Warwick were ardent Puritans and were moved by religious zeal quite as much as by political motives. In Northumberland, "the proudest man alive," the independent spirit of the feudal baron seemed to live again. Holland was ambitious and in disfavour at Court; he hoped to be one of the Parliament's generals. Others thought the Parliament stronger than the King, and were resolved to be on the winning side. "Pembroke and Salisbury," says Clarendon, "had rather the King and his posterity should be destroyed than that Wilton should be taken from the one and Hatfield from the other."

Amongst the gentry, there was the same mixture of motives. The bulk of them indeed adhered to the King, but great numbers supported the Parliament, especially in districts where Puritanism was prevalent.

Of the towns, cathedral cities such as York and Chester were usually royalist in feeling. The universities of Oxford and Cambridge were for the King, but the representatives of the towns were in each case Parliamentarians. "London," which Milton calls "the mansion house of liberty," and Clarendon, "the sink of the ill-humours of the kingdom," was the headquarters of Puritanism, and most manufacturing or trading towns were anti-royalist. "Manchester," says Clarendon, "from the beginning, out of that factious humour which possessed most corporations and the pride of their wealth, opposed the King and declared magisterially for the Parliament." Birmingham, though little more than a village, "was of as great fame for hearty, wilful, affected disloyalty to the King as any place in England." The clothing towns of the West Riding of Yorkshire and the manufacturing districts of Somersetshire and Gloucestershire were also hostile to Charles. In the latter counties, according to Clarendon,

"the gentlemen of ancient families were for the most part well affected to the King, yet there were a people of inferior degree, who by good husbandry, clothing, and other thriving arts, had gotten very great fortunes, and by degrees getting themselves into the gentlemen's estates were angry that they found not themselves in the same esteem and reputation with those whose estates they had; and therefore studied all ways to make themselves considerable. These from the beginning were fast friends to the Parliament."

In purely agricultural districts, the influence of the great landowners was generally decisive, but there were many notable exceptions. In the eastern counties, many of the chief gentry were disposed to take up arms for the King, but "the freeholders and yeomen in general adhered to the Parliament."

Yet, though the bulk of the upper classes was on one side, the war never became a social war, but remained a struggle of opinions and ideas. From the very beginning, men who were determined to maintain the Church intact adopted the King's cause, and those who desired to change the government of the Church, or sought freedom of worship outside of it, supported the Parliament. At first, even to Puritans, the political question seemed more important than the religious. Colonel Hutchinson read the manifestos of both parties till "he became abundantly informed in his understanding and convinced in his conscience of the righteousness of the Parliament's cause in point of civil right." But "though he was satisfied of the endeavours to bring back Popery and subvert the true Protestant religion, he did not think that so clear a ground for the war as the defence of English liberties."

No contemporary record reveals the precise motives which led Cromwell to take up arms: we are left to infer them from his earlier acts and his later utterances. "I profess," he wrote in 1644, "I could never satisfy myself of the justness of this war, but from the authority of the Parliament to maintain itself in its rights." Like Hutchinson, he regarded the King's Church policy as subversive of Protestantism, and defined the war as undertaken for "the maintenance of our civil liberties as men, and our religious liberties as Christians." As the war progressed, religious liberties grew more and more important in his eyes, and what had been originally a struggle against innovations became an attempt to establish freedom of conscience.

"Religion," said Cromwell in 1654, "was not the thing at first contested for, but God brought it to that issue at last, and gave it unto us by way of redundancy, and at last it proved to be that which was most dear to us. And wherein consisted this more than in obtaining that liberty from the tyranny of the bishops to all species of Protestants to worship God according to their own light and conscience?"

In every civil war, political and religious convictions must often conflict with family ties. Few families were like the Fairfaxes and Sheffields, of whom it was said that there was not one of those names but was on the side of the Parliament. Royalists might have made a like boast of the Byrons, the Comptons, and many less distinguished houses, but in very many cases the nearest relations took opposite sides. At Edgehill, the Earl of Denbigh and the Earl of Dover charged in the King's guard, while their sons, Lord Feilding and Lord Rochford, fought under Essex. In Cromwell's own family, his uncle, Sir Oliver, and his cousin, Henry Cromwell, were both ardent Royalists, and owed the preservation of their estates, after the defeat of their party, to the intercession of their kinsman.

While this division of families and friends made the war more painful, it tended to humanise the manner in which it was conducted. The men who found themselves reluctantly arrayed in arms against each other could not forget old friendship and old kinship.

"My affections to you," wrote Sir William Waller to his old comrade, Sir Ralph Hopton, when their two armies were about to meet in battle, "are so unchangeable that hostility itself cannot violate my friendship to your person, but I must be true to the cause wherein I serve. The great God, who is the searcher of my heart, knows with what reluctance I go upon this service, and with what perfect hatred I look upon a war without an enemy. The God of peace in His good time send us peace, and in the meantime fit us to receive it. We are both upon the stage, and we must act the parts that are assigned us in this tragedy. Let us do it in a way of honour, and without personal animosities."

On the whole, the war was honourably and humanely carried on. The savage cruelty which marked the Thirty Years' War in Germany is absent in the contemporaneous war in England. Little blood was shed except in the heat of battle; quarter was liberally granted, and the lives of non-combatants were respected. But inevitably the prolongation of the war embittered the temper of both parties, and when, as in Scotland and Ireland, their hostility was inflamed by national animosity a fiercer spirit showed itself.

War broke out in England in the summer of 1642, and there were many local struggles between the partisans of King and Parliament before the royal standard was set up at Nottingham (August 22, 1642). In many counties a royalist lord-lieutenant endeavoured to put in force the King's commission of array, while a parliamentary lord-lieutenant tried to carry into effect the Parliament's militia ordinance. Each called on the local train-bands to gather round him, and sought to obtain possession of the magazine in which the arms and munitions of the county were stored. The first of these collisions—a bloodless one—took place at Leicester in June; blood was shed in an affray at Manchester on July 15th. In July, the King attempted to besiege Hull, and some lives were lost in a sally. In August, the Marquis of Hertford proclaimed the commission of array in Somersetshire, the Governor of Portsmouth declared for the King, and the flame spread from the north and the midlands to the western counties. As yet there was no serious fighting, but everywhere men gathered in arms, and preparations for the campaign began.

In this preliminary trial of strength, no man was more active for the Parliament than Cromwell. On June 5th, he subscribed five hundred pounds to the fund for raising an army. Next month, after sending to his constituents at Cambridge a hundred pounds' worth of arms at his own expense, he obtained a vote empowering them to train and exercise volunteer companies. The King sent to the university for its money and its plate, but Cromwell, aided by his brothers-in-law, Valentine Walton and John Desborough, raised men and beset the north road to intercept them. Early in August, he marched to Cambridge, seized the county magazine, and secured most of the plate, worth, it is said, twenty thousand pounds, for the Parliament's service. At the same time he prevented the attempt to execute the commission of array in the county, and sent the heads of three of the colleges, Jesus, Queen's, and St. John's, prisoners to London. The House of Commons passed a vote for his indemnity, but the promptitude with which he assumed responsibility and anticipated their orders by his acts was extremely characteristic. There were many gentlemen of greater rank in Cambridge and Huntingdonshire willing to fight for the Parliament, but from the very first Cromwell's energy and readiness to act made him a leader. At the end of August, Cromwell returned to London, and shortly afterwards joined with a troop of sixty horse the army which Parliament was gathering under the Earl of Essex.

From the moment that preparations for war began, the Parliament had two great advantages over the King, which it retained as long as the war lasted. In July, the fleet in the Downs accepted the Earl of Warwick as its admiral and declared for the Parliament. The possession of the navy meant the command of the sea and the interception of the King's communications with the continent. He looked to Holland and France for arms and ammunition, but the parliamentary cruisers constantly captured his ships and stopped his supplies. All the chief ports were in the power of the Parliament; Charles held Newcastle and Chester, but the recapture of Portsmouth was one of the first results of the defection of the navy. Thanks to its ships, in 1643 and 1644 the Parliament was able to preserve Hull when the rest of Yorkshire was subdued, and to keep Lyme and Plymouth when the King's forces were triumphant in the west. Thanks to its ships, the King's plans for procuring French or Danish or Walloon mercenaries to restore his falling cause were made impossible to carry out, even if he could raise money to hire them.

The second advantage of the Parliament was that it had far more money at its disposal than the King. It was strongest in the richest parts of the country. With London and the trading classes in general devoted to it, it had no difficulty in raising loans. The possession of London and most of the seaports secured it the customs, which formed the largest and the most expansive part of the revenue of the State. As the war continued, voluntary loans developed into forced loans, customs were supplemented by the imposition of an excise, monthly assessments were levied on all counties under the Parliament's rule, and the sequestration of the lands of Royalists provided a new source of income. Yet, great though the resources of the Parliament were, its financial system was so imperfect that after the first few months the pay of the soldiers was constantly in arrears.

On the other hand, Charles had scarcely any regular sources of income, and very little money to equip or support an army. To provide arms and ammunition for his men he was driven to pawn the Crown jewels and to mortgage the Crown lands. Loans from corporations or men of means, the sales of peerages or other titular dignities, customs duties in the few ports under his control, and contributions levied in the districts within range of his garrisons made up his scanty budget. Throughout, the King's chief resource was the devotion of his followers. Loyal merchants in London secretly forwarded him their offerings. The University of Oxford sent him ten thousand pounds, and its colleges gave up their plate to be coined for his cause. Rich noblemen contributed regiments or troops, and poor gentlemen served at their own expense. The Marquis of Newcastle raised some thousands of men on his own estates; the Earl of Worcester and his son, Lord Herbert, furnished the King with £120,000 between March and July, 1642. Thanks to the zeal of his followers, and above all to the territorial influence of the great landowners, Charles was able ere long to oppose Parliament with forces equal to its own. At the end of August the King had with him at Nottingham only a few hundred half-armed foot. His artillery and several regiments of infantry were left behind at York, and his cavalry under Prince Rupert in the Midlands. The general of his little army told the King that he could not secure him against being taken in his bed, if the enemy made a brisk attack. The parliamentary forces assembling at Northampton amounted early in September to fourteen thousand men, and Essex had in all about twenty thousand men under his command. This was "an army which," as the historian of the Long Parliament said, "was too great to find resistance at that time from any forces afoot in England."

But instead of hastening to crush the King while he was weak, Essex gave him time to grow strong. From Nottingham, Charles moved to Shrewsbury, increasing his forces as he went, and equipping them with weapons taken from the train-bands, or from the armouries of loyal noblemen. Essex moved to Worcester and established himself there, making no effort to find the King and fight him, and reducing his forces by leaving garrisons in different towns. Now that he had an army, Charles boldly took the offensive and marched to London, hoping to end the war at a blow. Essex hurried eastwards to defend the capital, and at Edgehill, on October 23rd, Charles was obliged to turn and give battle to his pursuer.

The two armies were now not unequally matched. Each numbered about fourteen thousand men, but the Parliamentarians were far better armed than the Royalists. Clarendon thus describes the equipment of the King's army:

"The foot, all but 300 or 400 who marched without any weapons but cudgels, were armed with muskets, and bags for their powder, and pikes, but in the whole body there was not one pikeman who had a corselet and very few musketeers who had swords. Amongst the horse, the officers had their full desire if they were able to procure old backs and breasts and pots (*i. e.*, helmets), with pistols or carbines for their two or three front ranks and swords for the rest; themselves and some soldiers by their example having gotten besides their pistols and swords a short poleaxe."

The regiments who followed Essex, thanks to the Parliament's control of money and its possession of the magazines of Hull and the Tower, were armed with more uniformity and more completeness. His musketeers had their swords, his pikemen, who constituted a third of each foot regiment, had their corselets, and his horsemen pistols and defensive armour. In both armies, the officers consisted mostly of gentlemen who had neither military training nor experience of war, mixed with a certain number of soldiers of fortune who had served in the armies of France, or Holland, or Sweden. In foot regiments, the major or lieutenant-colonel was usually an old soldier; in troops of horse, the lieutenant. "The most part of our horse were raised thus," says a royalist playwright: "The honest country gentleman raises the troop at his own charge, then he gets a low-country lieutenant to fight his troop for him, then sends for his son from school to be cornet."

On both sides, the generals possessed the training which their soldiers lacked. Essex had fought with honour in the Palatinate and Holland; Balfour, who led his cavalry, had served many years in the Dutch army. The King's commander-in-chief, the Earl of Lindsey, was another Dutch officer, and Prince Rupert had seen some fighting under the Prince of

Orange, and one disastrous campaign in Germany. Yet despite Rupert's lack of experience the King gave him charge of all his horse as an independent command, and followed his advice rather than Lindsey's in the ordering of the battle. One great advantage Charles had which counterbalanced the superior armament of the parliamentary forces. His cavalry was superior to theirs both in quantity and quality. He had four thousand horse to Essex's three thousand, and his troopers were flushed with confidence by their easy victory in a skirmish near Worcester. Rupert resolved to utilise this advantage to the full. Massing the bulk of the cavalry on the right wing under his own command, he swept the horse opposed to him from the field, routed four regiments of Essex's foot, plundered Essex's camp at Kineton, and followed the fugitives for some miles. Wilmot, with the cavalry of the left, charged with like success, and even the reserves joined in the chase. Meanwhile, Essex and those of his foot regiments who stood firm attacked the royalist infantry front to front, while Balfour, with two regiments of cavalry forming the parliamentary reserve, fell upon their exposed flanks. The Earl of Lindsey was mortally wounded and made prisoner, the King's standard taken and regained, several regiments were cut to pieces, and two only held their ground. When Rupert returned from the chase, his cavalry were too disordered to be brought to attack, but their arrival saved the King's infantry from further attack, and night brought the dubious battle to a close. Before day broke, Hampden, with two fresh regiments of foot and ten troops of horse, joined Essex, and urged him to advance and drive the King from his position. Essex, discouraged by the misbehaviour of his cavalry, and by his heavy losses, was disinclined to risk anything, and retreated to Warwick. All the fruits of victory fell to the King, and, capturing Banbury Castle without a blow, he pursued his march to Oxford and made that city his headquarters for the remainder of the war (October 29th).

Early in November, Charles resumed his advance upon London. Reading was abandoned as he drew near, but by this time Essex had placed his army between the King and the capital, and there was no ground for the panic which filled the citizens. In the Parliament, the peace party for a moment gained the upper hand and sent commissioners to open negotiations. Charles expressed his willingness to treat, but said nothing about a suspension of hostilities, and still continued to advance. By his orders, on November 12th, Rupert, taking advantage of a mist which concealed his movements, fell upon Essex's outposts at Brentford, and cut to pieces the two regiments of Holles and Brooke. Hampden came to their rescue and covered the retreat of the survivors, but Brentford was thoroughly sacked by the Royalists. The City expected to share the same fate, and, says Clarendon, "the alarum came to London with the same dire yell as if the army were entered their gates." Negotiations were broken off, with loud accusations of treachery against the King. The train-bands rushed to arms, and, all night, regiments streamed forth from the City to reinforce Essex. Next day, Charles found twenty thousand men blocking his way at Turnham Green, while three thousand more occupied Kingston and threatened his line of retreat. Some cannon shots were exchanged, but the King was too weak to attack, and Essex too cautious. Once more Hampden urged him to action, and for a moment he seemed inclined to take the offensive. He had two men to the King's one, and his citizen soldiers were eager to fight, and cheered "Old Robin" whenever he appeared amongst them. But, as after Edgehill, "the old soldiers of fortune, on whose judgment the general most relied," were against fighting, and he called back Hampden, evacuated Kingston, and suffered Charles to draw off his troops undisturbed. The march on London was stopped, at least for this year; the shops of its citizens were safe, and neither "captain or colonel or knight-at-arms" threatened the "defenceless doors" of Puritan poets. Charles retired to Oxford; the parliamentary army went into winter quarters, and the campaign ended as indecisively as Edgehill had ended. With a larger and better equipped army, and with greater pecuniary resources at his disposal, Essex had throughout allowed the King to take the initiative, and neglected every opportunity offered him by fortune. Charles, on the other hand, as soon as he got together an army, adopted a consistent strategic plan, and pursued it with energy and even audacity. His outposts were now within thirty miles of London, and all over England his followers were gaining ground and gaining heart.

Ever since September, Cromwell had been serving under Essex, and this unsuccessful campaign was his sole training in the art of war. At Edgehill, his troops formed part of the regiment commanded by Sir Philip Stapleton, one of the two regiments which did such splendid service on that day. In later years, it pleased party pamphleteers to assert that he was not even present in the battle, but a contemporary account specially mentions Captain Cromwell in a list of officers who "never stirred from their troops, but fought till the last minute." One lesson at least he learned at Edgehill: that was the necessity of keeping a reserve in hand, and the importance of energetically using it. Another thing which the battle taught him was that the Parliament's arms would never be victorious till its cavalry was equal in quality to the King's. Some of Essex's foot regiments were excellent, but the ranks of his cavalry were filled with men attracted solely by high pay and opportunities of plunder-men who were neither soldiers nor good material for making soldiers. The consequences were what might have been expected. "At my first going out into this engagement," said Cromwell, "I saw our men beaten at every hand." Accordingly he spoke to his cousin, Hampden, and urged him to procure the raising of some new regiments to be added to Essex's army.

"I told him I would be serviceable to him in bringing such men in as I thought had a spirit that would do something in the work. 'Your troops,' said I, 'are most of them old decayed serving-men, tapsters, and such kind of fellows; do you think that the spirits of such base, mean fellows will ever be able to encounter gentlemen that have honour, and courage, and resolution in them? You must get men of a spirit that is likely to go as far as gentlemen will go, or you will be beaten still.'"

Hampden answered that the notion was a good notion, but impracticable. Impracticable was not a word which Cromwell understood. He obtained leave of absence for himself and his troop and went down into the eastern counties in January, 1643, "to raise such men as had the fear of God before them, and made some conscience of what they did."

CHAPTER V
CROMWELL IN THE EASTERN ASSOCIATION
1643

At the opening of the campaign of 1643, the strength of the Royalists had greatly increased, and before its close the advantage had passed to the King. In almost every county, towns and castles were garrisoned, and rival leaders, raising troops for King or Parliament, waged war against each other with varying fortunes. In the north and in the west of England, the Royalists rapidly gained the upper hand, and these local successes exercised a decisive influence on the course of the general war.

In April, 1643, Essex with sixteen thousand foot to three thousand horse advanced towards Oxford and captured Reading (April 27th). Hampden urged him to follow up this advantage by besieging Oxford, which was weakly fortified and ill provisioned. But Essex's army was mutinous for want of pay, and decimated by a great sickness which broke out in his camp after the fall of Reading. He did not resume the movement on Oxford till June, and in the meantime the King had been strongly reinforced. With his diminished numbers, Essex was unable to invest Oxford, and in the small encounters which took place round it his troops were generally worsted. At Chalgrove Field, on June 18th, Hampden was mortally wounded, and his death a week later was as great a blow to his party as the loss of a battle. "Every honest man," wrote a fellow officer, "hath a share in the loss, and will likewise in the sorrow. He was a gallant man, an honest man, an able man, and, take all, I know not to any living man second." In his short military career, he had shown an energy, a decision, and a strategic instinct which seemed to mark him out as a future general.

After Hampden's death, Essex fell back from Oxford and remained inactive, permitting the King to effect a junction with the Royalists of the north and the west. In the north, the Marquis of Newcastle had overrun the greater part of Yorkshire and cooped up Lord Fairfax and his son Sir Thomas in the West Riding. On June 30th, he routed the two Fairfaxes at

Adwalton Moor, near Bradford, and forced them to take refuge in Hull—the only fortress which the Parliament now held in Yorkshire. The Queen had landed at Bridlington in February, and these successes enabled her to march south and join Charles at Oxford with arms, ammunition, and reinforcements.

In the west, during the same period, a little army of Cornishmen under Sir Ralph Hopton won victory after victory over the Parliamentarians. At Bradock Down, on January 19, 1643, Hopton defeated General Ruthven; at Stratton, on May 16th, he beat Lord Stamford. Then, joined by Prince Maurice and the Marquis of Hertford, he advanced into Somersetshire and fought a drawn battle with Sir William Waller at Lansdown, near Bath, on July 5th. Followed by Waller, Hopton continued his march towards Oxford, and was blocked up in Devizes with his infantry by his pursuer. But the retreat of Essex had enabled the King to move freely, and had left Waller unsupported. On July 13th, the very day when the Queen reached Oxford, Wilmot and a body of horse sent from Oxford routed Waller's army at Roundway Down, and rescued Hopton's hard-pressed army.

Thus by the end of July the Royalists were masters in the field, and Charles could take the offensive. The King's original plan had been that he should hold Essex in check, whilst Newcastle advanced from the north into Essex, and Hopton made his way through the southern counties toward Kent. All three were then to close in upon London, and strike down rebellion in its headquarters. But now Newcastle's army refused to march southwards whilst Hull was uncaptured, and the western army hesitated to advance farther whilst Plymouth was not taken. Local feeling was too powerful to be neglected, and Charles was forced to complete the subjugation of the west instead of advancing upon London.

On July 26th, Bristol, the second port in the kingdom, surrendered to Prince Rupert. Gloucester was besieged on August 10th, and though vigorously defended by Colonel Massey it seemed certain to fall, for the Parliament had no army available to relieve it. "Waller," exulted the Royalists, "is extinct, and Essex cannot come." Once more Pym and the Parliament appealed to the City, and London responded with a zeal which no disasters could chill. The citizens closed their shops, six regiments of

London train-bands joined the shattered army of Essex, and with fifteen thousand men at his back the Earl marched for Gloucester. Vainly Rupert and the King's horse strove to delay his progress; at his approach, the besiegers drew off their forces without fighting, and Gloucester was saved.

As the Parliamentarians returned to London, the King barred their way at Newbury, and forced them to cut their way through or perish (September 20th). This time the parliamentary horse fought well, but it was the firmness and courage of Essex's infantry which preserved the army. The London train-bands, whom the Cavaliers had derided, "stood as a bulwark and rampire to defend the rest," and received charge after charge of Rupert's horse with their pikes as steadily as if they had been drilling on their parade ground. Long training in military exercises had given them a "readiness, order, and dexterity in the use of their arms," which compensated for their inexperience of actual war. Step by step the parliamentary army gained ground, till the failure of the King's ammunition obliged him to retreat and leave the passage free. Essex re-entered London in triumph. Gloucester was safe, and his army was safe, but Reading, the one trophy of his year's fighting, was abandoned again to the Royalists.

The year 1643 closed gloomily for the Parliament. Except Gloucester, Plymouth, and a few ports in Dorsetshire, all the west was the King's; the north was his except Hull and Lancashire, and in the midlands the Parliamentarians held their own with difficulty. Only in the eastern counties had the Parliament gained strength and territory, and it was to Cromwell more than any other man that this isolated success was due. At the close of 1642, Parliament had passed an ordinance associating the five counties of Norfolk, Suffolk, Essex, Cambridge, and Hertfordshire for the purpose of common defence (December 10, 1642). The Eastern Association, as it was termed, was completed by the accession of Huntingdonshire (May 26, 1643) and finally of Lincolnshire (September 20, 1643). Cambridge was its headquarters and Cromwell was from the first its guiding spirit. On his march from London in January, 1643, Cromwell seized the royalist high sheriff of Hertfordshire as he was proclaiming the King's commission of array in the market-place of St. Albans, and sent him up to London (January 14th). In February, he was at Cambridge busily fortifying the town and collecting men to resist a threatened attack from Lord Capel. In March, he suppressed a royalist rising at Lowestoft, taking prisoners many gentlemen and "good store of pistols and other arms." A few days later, he disarmed the Royalists of Lynn; in April, those of Huntingdonshire shared the same fate, and on April 28th he recaptured Crowland where the King's party had established a garrison. Whenever royalist raiders made a dash into the Association, or disaffected gentry attempted a rising, Colonel Cromwell and his men were swift to suppress them. "It's happy," he wrote, "to resist such beginnings betimes," and he never failed to do so.

Meanwhile the notion which Hampden had thought impracticable was rapidly becoming a fact. Cromwell's one troop of eighty horse had become the nucleus of a regiment. By March, 1643, he had five troops, and by September, ten. When the New Model army was constituted, his regiment had become a double regiment of fourteen full troops, numbering about eleven hundred troopers. Above all they were men of the same spirit as their colonel. His original troop had been carefully chosen. "He had a special care," writes Baxter, "to get religious men into his troop; these men were of greater understanding than common soldiers ... and making not money but that which they took for public felicity to be their end, they were the more engaged to be valiant." The new additions were of the same quality. "Pray raise honest, godly men and I will have them of my regiment," Cromwell promised the town of Norwich. "My troops increase," he told a friend a few weeks later; "I have a lovely company; you would respect them did you know them; they are no Anabaptists, they are honest, sober Christians."

The officers were selected on the same principle. "If you choose godly, honest men to be captains of horse, honest men will follow them; and they will be careful to mount such," wrote Cromwell to the Committee of Suffolk. When he could get gentlemen he preferred them, but godliness and zeal for the cause were the essentials.

"I had rather have," said he, "a plain russet-coated captain that knows what he fights for and loves what he knows, than that which you call 'a gentleman,' and is nothing else. I honour a gentleman that is so indeed.... It may be it provokes some spirits to see such plain men made captains of horse. It had been well that men of honour and birth had entered into these employments—but why do they not appear? But seeing it was necessary the work must go on, better plain men than none."

What struck observers first was the rigid discipline which Cromwell enforced not only in his own regiment but in all men under his command. No plundering was permitted, reported a newspaper; "no man swears but he pays his twelvepence; if he be drunk he is set in the stocks or worse. How happy were it if all the forces were thus disciplined!" The next notable fact was that they were better armed than other regiments, as well as better disciplined. Besides the sword, each trooper had a pair of pistols, but not carbines or other firearms. For defensive arms, they had simply a light helmet or "pot," and a "back and breast" of iron. Thus while adequately protected they were lighter and more active than fully equipped cuirassiers, and while adequately armed they had no temptation to adopt the tactics of mounted infantry or dragoons. Moreover, from the beginning, Cromwell's men were taught to charge home, and to rely on the impact of their charge and the sharpness of their swords. They were well mounted and many of them owned the horses they rode, being, as Whitelocke says, "freeholders or freeholders' sons, who upon matter of conscience engaged in this quarrel." Others were provided from the stables of Royalists, and one of Cromwell's letters is a defence of an officer who had seized the horses of "Malignants" to mount his troop. A great lover of horses and arms himself, Colonel Cromwell made his men keep both in good condition. "Cromwell," says a royalist writer, "used them daily to look after, feed, and dress their horses, and, when it was needful, to lie together on the ground; and besides taught them to clean and keep their arms bright and to have them ready for service." Men of such a spirit, armed, mounted, drilled, and disciplined with care, soon proved their superiority both to the King's troops and to those of Essex and Waller.

"That difference," says Clarendon, "was observed shortly from the beginning of the war: that though the King's troops prevailed in the charge, and routed those they charged, they never rallied themselves again in order, nor could be brought to make a second charge again the same day, whereas Cromwell's troops if they prevailed, or though they were beaten and routed, presently rallied again, and stood in good order till they received new orders."

In May, 1643, Essex ordered the forces of the eastern counties and the east midlands to unite in order to relieve Lincolnshire, and if possible to penetrate to Yorkshire and assist the Fairfaxes. Cromwell was eager to carry out his orders, but first one then another local commander declined to leave his particular locality unprotected. "Better it were that Leicester were not," said Cromwell, "than that there should not be found an immediate taking of the field by our forces to accomplish the common ends." He himself set out for Lincolnshire, and at Grantham on May 13th defeated a royalist force twice the size of his own. The Royalists were beaten mainly through their inferior tactics. Their commander had twenty-one troops and some dragoons to Cromwell's twelve, but he never attempted to charge. The two bodies of horse stood about musket-shot from each other, and their dragoons exchanged shots for about half an hour.

"Then," says Cromwell's despatch, "they not advancing toward us we agreed to charge them ... we came on with our troops at a pretty round trot, they standing firm to receive us: and our men charging fiercely upon them, by God's providence they were immediately routed and ran all away, and we had the execution of them two or three miles."

Ten days later, Cromwell reached Nottingham and joined the forces of Lincolnshire and Derbyshire, but with all his eagerness he could get no farther. The three commanders quarrelled, and one of them, Captain John Hotham, was secretly in correspondence with the Royalists. To add to Cromwell's difficulties, some of his soldiers were unpaid and mutinous, though he wrote urgently for money. It was a trouble continually recurring in his letters throughout this campaign, because parts of the Association were always behindhand in paying the men they raised.

"Lay not too much," he appealed to one defaulter, "upon the back of a poor gentleman, who desires, without much noise, to lay down his life and bleed the last drop to serve the cause and you. I ask not your money for myself; if that were my end and hope—viz: the pay of my place—I would not open my mouth at this time. I desire to deny myself, but others will not be satisfied."

Till the end of June, Cromwell stayed at Nottingham, defeating the Newark garrison in skirmishes, and hoping at least to bar the Queen's march south, but his fellow commanders left him, and so he was obliged to fall back into the Association, and leave the Fairfaxes to be crushed at Adwalton Moor.

Now came the hour of danger for the Association. Backed by Newcastle's army, the Royalists of the neighbouring counties began to press over its borders. One party threatened Peterborough, and garrisoned Burleigh House near Stamford. Another body besieged Lord Willoughby, the commander of the Lincolnshire Parliamentarians, in Gainsborough. Cromwell came to the rescue with his usual speed, captured Burleigh House and its garrison on July 24th, and, gathering what force he could get from Nottinghamshire and Lincolnshire, hurried to the relief of Gainsborough. Colonel Cavendish faced him with a body of royalist horse posted on the edge of a sandy plateau outside the town, and Cromwell's men had to mount it before they could attack. Before they were completely formed, the royalist horse advanced, but Cromwell would not wait to receive their charge.

"In such order as we were," says he, "we charged their great body. We came up horse to horse, where we disputed it with our swords and pistols a pretty time, all keeping close order, so that one could not break the other. At last they a little shrinking, our men, perceiving it, pressed in upon them, and immediately routed the whole body."

Part of the Parliamentarians followed the chase five or six miles, but Cromwell halted three troops of his regiment as soon as he could, and it was well he did so; for in the meantime Cavendish and his reserve beat the Lincoln troops forming the parliamentary second line, and were hotly pursuing them when Cromwell with his three troops fell on their rear, and drove them down the hill and into a bog. Cavendish was killed by

Cromwell's lieutenant, and his regiment scattered to the winds. Powder and provisions were thrown into the besieged town, and the van of the Parliamentarians were actively engaged in attacking a body of Royalists discovered on the other side of Gainsborough, when Newcastle's army arrived, fifty companies of foot, "and a great body of horse." To fight was hopeless. There was nothing left for the Parliamentarians but to retreat if they could. The foot drew off with some confusion and took refuge in the town; the horse, under Cromwell's command, were withdrawn in good order from position to position. Four troops of his regiment under Major Whalley, and four Lincoln troops under Captain Ayscough, alternately retiring and facing the enemy, covered the withdrawal.

"They with this handful faced the enemy, and dared them to the teeth in, at the least, eight or nine several removes, the enemy following at their heels; and they, though their horses were exceedingly tired, retreating in order near carbine shot of the enemy, who thus followed them, firing upon them; Colonel Cromwell gathering up the main body and facing them behind those two lesser bodies."

In this order he effected his retreat to Lincoln without loss.

Without a greater force it was impossible to drive Newcastle back, and in announcing his victory Cromwell appealed for reinforcements.

"God follows us with encouragements.... They come in season; as if God should say, 'Up and be doing, and I will stand by you and help you.' There is nothing to be feared but our own sin and sloth.... If I could speak words to pierce your hearts with the sense of our and your condition I would."

Two thousand foot must be raised at once if they meant to save Gainsborough. "If somewhat be not done in this you will see Newcastle's army march up into your bowels, being now, as it is, on this side Trent. I know it will be difficult to raise thus many in so short a time: but let me assure you, it's necessary and therefore to be done."

Parliament realised the imminence of the danger. On the day of Cromwell's victory at Gainsborough, it had appointed him Governor of the Isle of Ely. A week later, he received the special thanks of the House for his "faithful endeavours to God and the kingdom," and was voted three thousand pounds for his troops. On August 10th, an ordinance passed authorising the Associated Counties to raise ten thousand foot and five thousand horse to be commanded by the Earl of Manchester. It seemed, however, as if the eastern counties would be overrun before the new army could be raised. Gainsborough was taken, Lincoln was abandoned, all Lincolnshire except Boston fell into the power of the Royalists. In Norfolk, Lynn raised the King's standard. However, Newcastle turned back with the bulk of his forces to besiege Hull, and while Manchester with all the foot he could get together besieged Lynn, Cromwell with his cavalry made a bold march into Lincolnshire. Sir Thomas Fairfax, who was shut up in Hull with his father, had with him twenty-one troops of horse, useless for the defence of the town, but capable of changing the fortune of the campaign if added to Cromwell's force. Fairfax shipped them down the Humber in boats to Saltfleet in Lincolnshire, thus evading the attempts of Newcastle's cavalry to intercept him, and effected his junction with Cromwell. Both then joined Manchester, who had by this time captured Lynn, and in October the joint army set about the reconquest of Lincolnshire.

The Cavaliers of Lincolnshire and part of Newcastle's cavalry, headed by Lord Widdrington and Sir John Henderson, fought them at Winceby on October 11th. Cromwell led the van, seconded by Sir Thomas Fairfax.

"Immediately after their dragooners had given the first volley," says a parliamentary narrative, "Colonel Cromwell fell with a brave resolution upon the enemy; yet they were so nimble, as that within half pistol shot, they gave him another; his horse was killed under him at the first charge, and fell down upon him; and as he rose up he was knocked down again by the gentleman who charged him; but afterwards he recovered a poor horse in a soldier's hands, and bravely mounted himself again. Truly this first charge was so home given, and performed with so much admirable courage and resolution by our troops, that the enemy stood not another;

but were driven back upon their own body which was to have seconded them; and at last put them into a plain disorder; and thus in less than half an hour's fight they were all quite routed."

Thirty-five colours, and nearly a thousand prisoners were the trophies of the victors; Lincoln and Gainsborough fell into their hands a few weeks later. Moreover, on the very day of the victory of Winceby, Lord Fairfax sallied forth from Hull, beat Newcastle from his trenches, and forced him to raise the siege in disorder. Thus the Association was secured from invasion, Lincolnshire conquered, and the Parliament's hold on Yorkshire maintained.

So closed Cromwell's second campaign. He had shown a skill in handling cavalry very rare amongst the courageous knights and squires who "rode forth a-colonelling." He kept his promise to Hampden,—raised men of such a spirit that they never turned their backs to the enemy, and disciplined them so that they were an example to all the troops of the Parliament in camp or in battle. The general recognition of his great services was shown by two facts. On February 16, 1644, Parliament appointed a new committee for the management of the war, called, because it included representatives of Scotland, the Committee of Both Kingdoms. Cromwell had not been a member of the Committee of Safety appointed when the war began, but he was from the first a member of this new one. The second fact was Cromwell's appointment as Lieutenant-General of the army of the Eastern Association. He had been practically Manchester's second in command since the army was formed, and on January 22, 1644, he received his commission. The appointment had important results, political as well as military. Manchester himself, "a sweet, meek man," says the Presbyterian Baillie, "permitted his Lieutenant-General to guide all the army at his pleasure." Of Cromwell he adds: "the man is a very wise and active head, universally well-beloved as religious and stout; being a known Independent most of the soldiers who loved new ways put themselves under his command." Thus Cromwell's influence spread to the whole army of the Eastern Association, and officers and men became permeated by the spirit of his regiment. By March, 1644, Manchester's army was reported to be fifteen thousand strong.

"Neither," said a newspaper, "is his army so formidable in number as exact in discipline; and that they might be all of one mind in religion, as of resolution in the field, with a severe eye he hath looked into the manners of those all who are his officers, and cashiered those whom he found to be in any way irregular in their lives or disaffected to the cause."

CHAPTER VI
MARSTON MOOR
1644

As yet neither party had decidedly gained the upper hand, though the tide seemed setting against the Parliament. Both parties, therefore, looked outside England for allies, one to make its success complete, the other to regain what it had lost. The King turned to Ireland, and to the army there, which with little support from the Parliament was striving to put down the rebellion. On September 15, 1643, Ormond, the Lord-Lieutenant, concluded a cessation of arms with the rebels, and was able to send several regiments of experienced soldiers to the King's assistance during the following months. The English Puritans turned to their brethren in Scotland; in September, the Solemn League and Covenant pledged the two nations to unite for the reformation of religion according to the word of God and the example of the best reformed churches; in November, the Scottish Parliament agreed to send twenty-one thousand men to the assistance of the English Parliamentarians. In January, 1644, Alexander Leslie, now Earl of Leven, crossed the Tweed with the promised army.

The campaign of 1644 opened badly for the King. In January, Sir Thomas Fairfax defeated Lord Byron and the King's Irish forces at Nantwich. In March, Waller defeated Hopton at Cheriton in Hampshire, and frustrated his intended advance into Sussex. In April, Newcastle, after striving in vain to bar Leslie's progress in Durham, was forced to throw himself into York, where Leslie and the Fairfaxes besieged his army. In May, the forces of Waller and Essex advanced upon Oxford. The Royalists evacuated Reading and Abingdon, and Charles, fearing to be blockaded in Oxford, left the city to be defended by its garrison, and with about six thousand men made his escape to Worcester. But Essex, instead of pursuing and crushing the King's weak army as he ought to have done, delegated the task to Waller, and set out himself to recover the south-western counties and relieve Lyme.

In April, while Waller and Essex were preparing for their movement on Oxford, the army of the Eastern Association under Manchester took the field. Its first business was to reconquer Lincolnshire,—the debatable land between the north and east,—for Rupert's defeat of the besiegers of Newark in March, 1644, had thrown Lincolnshire once more into the hands of the Royalists. On May 6th, Manchester's army recaptured Lincoln, and at the beginning of June he joined the two armies which beleaguered York with about nine thousand men. Of these nine thousand, three thousand were cavalry under the command of Cromwell. York held out stubbornly; some detached forts were taken and the suburbs burnt, but an attempted assault was bloodily repulsed. At the end of June, news came that Prince Rupert with fifteen thousand men had crossed the hills from Lancashire, and was marching to the relief of the city. The three generals, Leven, Fairfax, and Manchester, raised the siege in order to give battle to Rupert's army, but when they assembled their forces on the south bank of the Ouse, Rupert crossed to the northern bank, and reached York without striking a blow. On the morning of July 2nd, the parliamentary generals, finding themselves outmanœuvred, and the resumption of the siege rendered impossible, were in full retreat to the south, when Rupert's attacks on their rearguard forced them to halt and offer battle. They drew up their army on some rising ground between Tockwith and Marston, overlooking the open moor on which the Royalists had taken their post. Between the armies, and marking the southern boundary of the moor, ran a hedge, and ditch, which Rupert had lined with musketeers, and some similar obstacles strengthened the royalist left flank. Rupert's army, reinforced by Newcastle's forces from York, numbered about eighteen thousand men, while the Parliamentarians amounted to about twenty-seven thousand, but the Royalists had the advantage of a strong defensive position, and of open ground on which their cavalry could manœuvre freely.

For three hours the two armies faced each other in battle array; a few cannon-shots were exchanged, but neither army advanced. The Roundheads fell to singing psalms, and the royalist generals came to the belief that there would be no fighting that day. About five, the whole parliamentary line began to move forward, and Cromwell, with the cavalry forming its left wing, attacked Lord Byron and the royalist right. Cromwell had under his command all the horse and dragoons of the Eastern Association, half a regiment of Scottish dragoons, and three weak regiments of Scottish cavalry who formed his reserve,—in all not less than four thousand men, of whom one thousand were dragoons. The dragoons rapidly drove the royalist musketeers from the ditch, and enabled the cavalry to pass it. Cromwell led the way, and with the first troops who crossed charged the nearest regiment of Royalists. His own division, says a contemporary narrative, "had a hard pull of it; for they were charged by Rupert's bravest men both in front and flank." But as fast as they could form, the other troops of Cromwell's first line charged in support of their leader, erelong the foremost regiments of the Royalists were broken, and, pursuing their victory, Cromwell's men engaged the second line.

In this hand-to-hand combat Cromwell was wounded in the neck by a pistol-shot fired so near his eyes that it half blinded him, but, though for a short time disabled, he did not leave the field. Meanwhile Rupert himself, who had been at supper in the rear when the attack began, galloped up with fresh regiments and, rallying his men, drove back Cromwell's troopers. It was but a temporary check, for David Leslie with Cromwell's second line fell on Rupert's flank, and the royalist cavalry was irretrievably routed. Sending the light Scottish regiments of the reserve in pursuit of the flying Cavaliers, Cromwell and Leslie reformed their tired squadrons, and halted to find out how the battle had gone in other quarters of the field. Tidings of disaster soon reached them, and it became plain that the battle was more than half lost for the Parliament. Sir Thomas Fairfax, wounded and almost alone, came with the news that the horse of the right wing under his command were defeated and flying. His own regiment had charged with success, and broken through the enemy; those who should have supported him, disordered by the furze and the rough ground they had to pass through to debouch upon the moor, had been charged by the Royalists, and completely scattered. The infantry of the parliamentary centre had fared little better. The advance had been at first successful all along the line, some guns had been taken, and the ditch passed. On the left, Manchester's foot, led by Major-General Crawford, had outflanked the infantry opposed to them, and were still gaining ground. In the centre, Lord Fairfax's foot and the Scottish regiments supporting them, repulsed by Newcastle's white-coated north-countrymen, and trampled down by their own flying horse, were in full flight. On the right, the main body of the Scottish infantry was hard pressed; some regiments gave way as their brethren in the centre had done; others maintained their ground manfully. Yet with the centre of the parliamentary line pierced, and the cavalry of the right wing driven from the field, the position of these isolated regiments, exposed to attack in front and flank both, seemed hopeless. So thought old Leven, who, after striving in vain to rally the runaways, gave up the day for lost, and galloped for Leeds. Lord Fairfax, too, was carried off the field in the rout of his infantry, though he returned later.

While Goring's victorious horse pursued the fugitives, or stopped to plunder the baggage, Sir Charles Lucas, with another division of Goring's command, employed himself in attacking the Scottish infantry. Maitland's and Lindsey's regiments on the extreme right of the line stood like rocks, and beat off three charges with their pikes. Like their ancestors at Flodden, and with better fortune,

> *"The stubborn spearmen still made good*
>
> *Their dark, impenetrable wood,*
>
> *Each stepping where his comrade stood*
>
> *The instant that he fell."*

Help was now at hand. Sweeping across the moor behind the royalist centre, Cromwell and Leslie came with their whole force to the relief of the Scots. With them too marched Crawford and the three brigades of Manchester's foot. As they advanced, Lucas's horse suspended their attack, and Goring's men streamed back from pursuit and pillage to meet this new antagonist.

Cromwell's cavalry now occupied the very ground where Goring's men had been posted when the battle began, and met them at "the same place of disadvantage" where Sir Thomas Fairfax had been routed. The struggle was short but decisive, and when the last squadrons of the royalist horse were broken, Cromwell turned to co-operate with Crawford and the Scots in attacking the royalist infantry. Some of Rupert's veteran regiments made good their retreat to York; Newcastle's white-coats got into a piece of enclosed ground, and sold their lives dearly; the rest scattered and fled under cover of the protecting darkness. About three thousand Royalists fell in the battle, while sixteen guns, one hundred colours, six thousand muskets, and sixteen hundred prisoners were the trophies of the victors. Rupert left York to its fate, and made his way back to Lancashire with some six thousand men, and the city itself surrendered a fortnight later.

In the despatch which the three Generals addressed to the Committee of Both Kingdoms, they gave no account of the details of the battle, and made no mention of Cromwell's services. Private letters were more outspoken. One described him as "the chief agent in obtaining the victory." Some people spoke of him as "the saviour of the three kingdoms," though Cromwell repudiated the title with some anger. The friends of the Scottish army depreciated his services, attributed what his cavalry achieved to David Leslie, and circulated reports that Cromwell had taken no part in the battle after his first charge.

The utterances of the royalist leader both before and after the battle showed that he appreciated Cromwell's importance more justly. "Is Cromwell there?" asked Rupert of a prisoner taken just before the battle, and it was Rupert too who, after the battle, gave Cromwell the nickname of "Ironside" or "Ironsides." The title was derived, according to a contemporary biographer, "from the impenetrable strength of his troops, which could by no means be broken or divided," and it was extended later from the leader to the soldiers themselves.

Cromwell's only account of the battle is contained in a few lines written to his brother-in-law, Colonel Valentine Walton.

"England," he said, "and the Church of God hath had a great favour from the Lord in this great victory given unto us, such as the like never was since this war began. It had all the evidences of an absolute victory, obtained by the Lord's blessing upon the godly party principally. We never charged but we routed the enemy. The left wing, which I commanded, being our own horse, saving a few Scots in our rear, beat all the Prince's horse. God made them as stubble to our swords. We charged their regiments of foot with our horse, and routed all we charged. The particulars I cannot relate now; but I believe of 20,000 the Prince hath not 4000 left. Give glory, all the glory, to God."

Cromwell's letter has been charged with concealing the services of David Leslie and the Scots. But every word of his brief account was true. He did not give the particulars of the fight, because he was writing a letter of condolence, not a despatch. Walton's son, a captain in Cromwell's own regiment, had fallen in the battle, and Cromwell wrote to tell the father details of his son's death. He began with the news of the great victory in order that Walton might feel that his son's life had not been idly thrown away. Then he turned suddenly to the real subject of the letter. "Sir, God hath taken your eldest son away by a cannon shot. It brake his leg. We were necessitated to have it cut off, whereof he died." Next he praised the dead—the "gallant young man," "exceeding gracious," "exceedingly beloved in the army of all that knew him," who had died "full of comfort," lamenting nothing save that he could no longer serve God against his enemies, and rejoicing in his last moments to "see the rogues run." In the spring, Cromwell had lost his own son, Captain Oliver, who died not in battle, but of smallpox in his quarters at Newport. "A civil young gentleman, and the joy of his father," said a newspaper recording it. He referred to this now while seeking to comfort Walton. "You know my own trials this way; but the Lord supported me with this, that the Lord took him into the happiness we all pant after and live for." Let the same faith support Walton, and let "this public mercy to the Church of God" help him to forget his "private sorrow." So closed the letter, revealing in its tenderness and sympathy, its enthusiasm and its devotion to the cause, the depths of Cromwell's nature, and the secret of his power over his comrades in arms.

After the fall of York, the three parliamentary armies separated. Leven and the Scots turned northwards again to besiege Newcastle, the Fairfaxes remained to capture the royalist strongholds in Yorkshire, and Manchester, taking on his way Sheffield Castle and a few smaller garrisons, returned to Lincoln. All August he remained there idle, declining even to besiege Newark. He was weary of the war, anxious for an accommodation with the King, and shocked at the spread of sectarian and democratic opinions in his army and in the kingdom. Cromwell, as the protector of the sectaries, was at daggers-drawn with Major-General Crawford, who attempted to suppress them; Crawford cashiered an officer on the ground that he was an Anabaptist, and Cromwell and some of his colonels threatened to lay down their commissions unless Crawford was removed. A compromise of some kind was patched up, but Cromwell's influence over Manchester was at an end.

Meanwhile, in the south of England the campaign so prosperously begun was ending in disaster. Charles had turned on his pursuer, and defeated Waller at Cropredy Bridge, in Oxfordshire, on June 29th. Leaving Waller's disorganised and mutinous army too weak to do any harm, he followed Essex into the west, and, joined by the forces of the western Royalists, threatened to overpower him. At the end of August, the Committee of Both Kingdoms ordered the army of the Eastern Association to go to the succour of Essex. Cromwell was eager to do so. "The business," he wrote to his friend Walton, "has our hearts with it, and truly, had we wings we would fly thither." Manchester's army, though ill provided with necessaries, and slandered by evil tongues as factious, was ready to serve anywhere. "We do never find our men so cheerful as when there is work to do." But he went on to hint that there were obstructives in high places, who were less willing to fight than their soldiers. "We have some amongst us much slow in action; if we could all intend our own ends less, and our own ease too, our business would go on wheels for expedition."

Before Manchester stirred from Lincoln the anticipated disaster came. At Lostwithiel on September 2nd, Skippon and the infantry of Essex's army were forced to capitulate and to lay down their arms. The horse escaped by a night march through a gap in the royalist lines, while Essex himself and a few officers fled by sea. After his victory the King returned slowly to Oxford, and Manchester with the greatest reluctance moved south-west to meet him. "My army," he said openly, "was raised by the Association and for the guard of the Association. It cannot be commanded by Parliament without their consent." It was imperative that Charles should be fought before he could get to his old headquarters at Oxford, while his army was weakened by the forces left behind in the west, but Manchester's refusal to advance allowed the Royalists to reach Newbury before the King was obliged to fight. At Newbury, on October 27th, Manchester's army, strengthened by Waller's forces and by what remained of Essex's troops, made a joint attack on the King. Charles had only ten thousand men to oppose to the nineteen thousand brought against him, but he had chosen a strong position between two rivers, protected on one side by Donnington Castle, and covered, where it was most assailable, by intrenchments. Above all, his army was under a single commander, while the Parliament's was directed by a committee. Essex was absent from illness, and the Committee of Both Kingdoms hoped to avoid disputes by putting the command in commission.

The parliamentary scheme was that Skippon's foot, with the horse of Cromwell and Waller, should attack the King's position on the west, while Manchester assaulted it on the north-east. It failed through lack of combination. Skippon's infantry carried the royalist intrenchments, and recaptured several guns they had lost in Cornwall, but the cavalry, impeded by the nature of the ground, could effect little. Manchester delayed his attack till it was too late to assist them, and was repulsed with heavy loss. Nevertheless the result of the day's fighting was that the King's position was so seriously compromised that only a retreat could save his army. In the night, the royalist army silently marched past Manchester's outposts, and by morning it was half way to Wallingford. Waller and Cromwell set out in pursuit with the bulk of the cavalry, but as Manchester and the majority of the committee refused to support them with infantry Charles made good his retreat to Oxford. A fortnight later, the King, reinforced by Rupert with five thousand men, returned to relieve Donnington Castle and carry off the artillery he had left there (October 9, 1644). He offered battle, and Cromwell was eager to fight, but Manchester and a majority of the committee declared against it. Foot and horse alike were greatly reduced in numbers, and the latter "tired out with hard duty in such extremity of weather as hath been seldom seen." Manchester, in addition to military reasons, urged political arguments against risking a battle.

"If we beat the King ninety-nine times, yet he is King still, and so will his posterity be after him; but if the King beat us once we shall all be hanged, and our posterity made slaves." "My Lord," retorted Cromwell, "if this be so, why did we take up arms at first? This is against fighting ever hereafter. If so, let us make peace, be it ever so base."

But much as he might despise Manchester's logic, he had to bow to the logic of facts, and to accept the view of the committee in general.

So ended the campaign of 1644. The north of England had been definitely won, and with capable leadership the defeat of Essex in Cornwall might have been compensated by the defeat of the King in Berkshire. When Cromwell came to reflect on the incidents of the last few months, he attributed the failure to obtain this victory entirely to Manchester. He had failed, apparently, not through accident or want of foresight, but through backwardness to all action. And this backwardness, concluded Cromwell, came "from some principle of unwillingness to have the war prosecuted to a full victory; and a desire to have it ended by an accommodation on some such terms to which it might be disadvantageous to bring the King too low." On November 25th, Cromwell rose in the House of Commons, told the story of the Newbury campaign, and made this charge against Manchester. Manchester vindicated his generalship in the House of Lords, alleging that he had always acted by the advice of the council of war, and that Cromwell was a factious and obstructive subordinate. Then, leaving military questions alone, he made a bitter attack on Cromwell as a politician. He had once given great confidence to the Lieutenant-General, but latterly he had become suspicious of his designs, and had been obliged to withdraw it. For Cromwell had spoken against the nobility, and had said that he hoped to live to see never a nobleman in England. He had expressed himself with contempt against the Assembly of Divines, and with animosity against the Scots for attempting to establish Presbyterianism in England. Finally, he had avowed that he desired to have none but Independents in the army of the Eastern Association, "so that in case there should be propositions for peace, or any conclusion of a peace, such as might not stand with those ends that honest men should aim at, this army might prevent such a mischief."

Cromwell did not deny these utterances, and their revelation produced the effect which Manchester had anticipated. An enquiry into errors in the conduct of the war developed into a political quarrel. The Lords took up the cause of Manchester as the cause of their order. The Scots intrigued against Cromwell as the enemy of their creed. "For the interest of our nation," wrote Baillie, "we must crave reason of that darling of the sectaries," and talked of breaking the power of that potent faction "in obtaining his removal from the army, which himself by his over-rashness has procured." Some of the Scottish leaders consulted together on the feasibility of accusing Cromwell as an "incendiary" who had sought to cause strife between the two nations, but the English lawyers consulted advised against it.

"Lieutenant-General Cromwell," said Mr. Maynard, "is a person of great favour and interest with the House of Commons, and with some of the peers likewise, and therefore there must be proofs, and the most clear and evident proofs against him, to prevail with the Parliament to judge him an incendiary."

As the controversy proceeded, the Lower House declared on Cromwell's side, and the conviction of Manchester's incapacity spread amongst its members. But, instead of pressing the charge home, Cromwell drew back. A personal triumph, to be gained at the cost of a rupture between the two Houses, and perhaps a rupture between England and Scotland, was not worth gaining. What he wanted was military efficiency and the vigorous conduct of the war, and he resolved to use the dissatisfaction which Manchester's slackness had roused in order to obtain these ends, and to abandon the personal charges to secure them. The moment was propitious, for on November 23rd the Commons had ordered the Committee of Both Kingdoms to consider the reorganisation of the whole army. On December 9th, when the report on the charges against Manchester was brought in to the House of Commons, Cromwell turned the debate to the larger issue. The important thing now, he said, was to save the nation out of the bleeding, almost dying condition, which the long continuance of the war had brought it into.

"Without a more speedy, vigorous, and effectual prosecution of the war, we shall make the kingdom weary of us, and make it hate the name of a Parliament."

"For what do the enemy say? Nay what do many say that were friends at the beginning of the Parliament? Even this: That the members of both Houses have got great places and commands, and the sword into their hands; and what by interest in Parliament, what by power in the army, will perpetually continue themselves in grandeur, and not permit the war speedily to end, lest their own power should determine with it.... If the army be not put into another method and the war more vigorously prosecuted, the people can bear the war no longer, and will enforce you to a dishonourable peace."

He went on to abandon his attack upon Manchester, by recommending the House not to insist upon any complaint against any commander. Oversights could rarely be avoided in military affairs, and he acknowledged that he had been guilty of them himself. The essential was not to enquire into the causes of these failures, but to apply a remedy to them. That remedy, as he had already suggested, was the reorganisation of the army, and a change in its commanders. "And I hope," he concluded, "we have such true English hearts and zealous affections towards the general weal of our mother country, as no members of either House will scruple to deny themselves, and their own private interests for the public good."

Cromwell's suggestion was at once adopted, and, before the debate ended, a resolution was passed that no member of either House of Parliament should during the war hold any office or command either military or civil. Ten days later, on December 19th, the Self-Denying Ordinance passed the House of Commons and was sent up to the Lords. The Lords demurred, and delayed, and at last rejected it, on the ground that they did not know what shape the new army would take. The Commons immediately formulated their scheme, nominated Sir Thomas Fairfax as the future General, and fixed the new army at twenty-two thousand men. On the 15th of February, 1645, the Lords accepted it, much against their will;

and on April 3rd, with still greater reluctance, they accepted a second Self-Denying Ordinance. But the new ordinance was much less stringent than the old. It simply ordained that all members of the two Houses holding office should lay down their commissions within forty days of its passing, and said nothing to prevent their reappointment in the future if the two Houses thought fit. So much at least the Peers had gained by their resistance.

Cromwell had been a leader in the earlier portion of this struggle. He had been one of the tellers for the majority which voted Fairfax General in place of Essex, and had urged that Fairfax should have full liberty in the choice of his officers. His own military career seemed over, for he could scarcely expect to retain his command when all other members lost theirs. If he had sought to keep it, he would have continued the prosecution of Manchester rather than striven to erect a legal barrier against his own employment. But before the struggle ended, and before the second Self-Denying Ordinance was passed or even introduced, he was once more in the field. In the west of England, Weymouth and Taunton were hard pressed by a royalist army under Goring. Waller was ordered to advance and relieve them, but without reinforcements he was too weak to do so. Parliament ordered Cromwell's regiment to join Waller; it murmured, grew mutinous, and seemed about to refuse obedience. On March 3rd, the House ordered Cromwell to go with it, its murmurs ceased, and obedience was immediately restored. Cromwell made no objection to putting himself under Waller's command, and Waller found him an admirable subordinate. There was nothing in his bearing, wrote Waller, to show that he was conscious of having extraordinary abilities; "for although he was blunt, he did not bear himself with pride or disdain. As an officer he was obedient, and did never dispute my orders, or argue upon them." What struck Waller most was that, whilst a man of few words himself, Cromwell had a way of making others talk, and a singular sagacity in judging their characters, and discovering their secrets.

Waller's expedition accomplished its object: a royalist regiment of horse was captured, an imperilled body of parliamentary foot successfully brought off, and at the end of April Cromwell returned to headquarters to lay down his commission. It remained to be seen whether Parliament could dispense with his services, and above all whether the army would be content to lose a general who had gained the confidence of the soldiers more than any leader whom the war had produced.

CHAPTER VII
NASEBY AND LANGPORT
1645–1646

The "New Model" army which Fairfax commanded had a better chance of success than that of Essex. Essex had failed partly through incapacity, but partly because his forces were never properly maintained or recruited. His regiments melted away without much fighting, because their pay was always in arrears and their supplies irregular and insufficient. But now Parliament had rectified the worst defects of its financial system, and provided for the regular payment of the soldiers during the campaign by a monthly assessment levied on all the counties under its power. The new army consisted of eleven regiments of horse, each numbering six hundred men, twelve regiments of foot, each of twelve hundred, with a thousand dragoons, and a small train of artillery. About half the infantry was composed of men who had served under Essex, Manchester, and Waller; the rest were pressed-men raised by the county authorities. Of the cavalry, more than half was drawn from the former army of the Eastern Association. Cromwell's old regiment was made into two, one commanded by his cousin, Edward Whalley, the other by Sir Thomas Fairfax himself.

Fairfax owed his appointment partly to his military reputation, partly to his freedom from political objections. He was religious, but the question whether he was a Presbyterian or an Independent was a riddle none had solved. Though he had served a campaign in Holland, his real training-school had been the long struggle with Newcastle and the northern Royalists. Swift marches and dashing attacks, resourcefulness in difficulties and persistency in defeats had made him famous. "Black Tom" was the idol of his troopers, and whilst friends complained that he exposed himself too recklessly, enemies spoke of his "irrational and brutish valour," and denied him all higher qualities. He was looked upon as essentially a leader of cavalry, and his selection as General instead of Lieutenant-General surprised even his friends. To most of the officers of his army, Fairfax was unknown, except by reputation. When he took up his command, they saw a man of about thirty-three, tall in stature and very dark, with the scars of old wounds upon his face. His bearing was quiet and reserved, but it was soon observed that though he said little in council he was very tenacious of his opinions, and very prompt in acting upon them. In battle he seemed transformed, threw off his reserve, lost his stammer, and was all fire, energy, and decision.

Skippon had been made Major-General of the army to supply the scientific knowledge and the long experience which the commander-in-chief lacked, but the second place in the army was still unfilled, for no lieutenant-general had been appointed to command the horse. There can be little doubt that it was designedly left open in order that Cromwell might fill it.

Ever since March, Cromwell had been employed in his expedition to the west. On the 19th of April, he returned to the headquarters at Windsor in order to take leave of Fairfax, and to lay down his commission as the Self-Denying Ordinance required. Next morning, a letter came from the Committee of Both Kingdoms giving him fresh duty to do. The King was about to take the field and the "New Model" was not ready to fight him. Ever since the beginning of April, Fairfax had been labouring hard at the reorganisation of the army, but recruits were slow in coming in, and the obstructiveness of the Lords had thrown all preparations back. The most efficient part of the army and the readiest for immediate action was the brigade of cavalry Cromwell had brought back from the west, and with it he was now despatched to Oxfordshire to prevent the King from joining Prince Rupert. Charles lay at Oxford with part of the royal army, including the artillery train; Rupert with the rest, and with the bulk of the cavalry, was quartered about Hereford and Worcester. Cromwell set out at once, and at daybreak on April 24th he routed three regiments of the King's horse at Islip, killing two hundred and taking two hundred prisoners. Part of the fugitives took refuge in Blechington House, which Cromwell at once attacked and forced, under threat of an assault, to surrender. By the terms granted, the garrison were allowed to retire to Oxford, but had to give up their horses and arms. "I did much doubt the storming of the house," wrote Cromwell in explanation, "it being strong and well manned, and I having few dragoons, and this not being my business." Two days later, at Bampton in the Bush, he intercepted a regiment of foot marching from Faringdon to Oxford, took a couple of hundred, and killed or scattered the rest. On the 29th, he appeared before Faringdon House, and made an attempt to storm it, but was repulsed with loss. In spite of this check, Cromwell had effected the work he was sent to do. The King's march was stopped. His cavalry was shattered by defeats, and his artillery could not be moved because Cromwell had swept up all the draught-horses in the country round. Charles was obliged to summon Goring's cavalry from the west to cover his junction with Rupert, and could not start till the 7th of May.

Meanwhile Fairfax had got his army into marching order, and on May 1st, leaving Cromwell to observe the King, he set out to relieve Taunton. His operations were determined not by his own judgment, but by the orders of the Committee of Both Kingdoms. Half-way to Taunton he got fresh orders instructing him to send a brigade to relieve it, and to turn back with the rest of his troops to besiege Oxford. For a fortnight therefore he invested Oxford, limiting himself to a blockade because his siege train had not come up, and without heavy guns and intrenching tools he could do nothing more. During these weeks Rupert and the King with nine thousand or ten thousand men were marching unopposed about the midlands. On May 15th, Charles took Hawkesley House in Worcestershire, and then turned north to relieve Chester, but heard on his way that the siege was raised. Some of his advisers urged him to march north still in order to relieve Pontefract and beat Leven and the Scots; others proposed a raid into the Eastern Association. But reports of the danger of Oxford kept him in the south, and as a diversion it was resolved to attack Leicester. On May 31st, that city was stormed and sacked by the King's army.

The King's movements had completely upset the plans of the Committee of Both Kingdoms. As soon as the news of the capture of Leicester came, Fairfax was ordered to leave Oxford, and to march against the King. Taught by experience, the amateur strategists of the Committee left him free to order his movements as he thought fit, and removed all limitations they had before imposed. In the alarm caused by the King's successes, public opinion imperatively called for Cromwell's employment. All felt he was too necessary to be spared. On May 10th, Parliament had prolonged his command for another forty days. On the 28th, when the King threatened the eastern counties, Cromwell was sent in hot haste to Ely to see to their defence. A week later London petitioned that he might have power to raise and command all the forces of the Association. Finally, on June 10th, Fairfax and his council of war petitioned Parliament to appoint Cromwell Lieutenant-General. For they were now advanced within a few miles of the King's position, and Fairfax had a great body of horse, but no general officer to command it in the coming battle. No one but Cromwell would do, urged Fairfax.

"The general esteem and affection which he hath both with the officers and soldiers of this whole army, his own personal worth and ability for the employment, his great care, diligence, courage, and faithfulness in the services you have already employed him in, with the constant presence and blessing of God that have accompanied him, make us look upon it as the duty we owe to you and the public, to make it our suit."

The Lords made no answer to this unwelcome petition, but the Commons agreed to the appointment for so long a time as Cromwell was needed in the army. So, on June 13th, Cromwell rode into Fairfax's camp with six hundred horse from the Association, and was welcomed by the soldiers "with a mighty shout." "Ironsides," they cried, "is come to head us," calling him by the name which Rupert had given him after the battle of Marston Moor.

In the King's camp there were great divisions of opinion. Rupert, the commander-in-chief, advocated one course, and the King's civilian advisers another. Charles hesitated and delayed till he found Fairfax at his heels, and then he was forced to fight. On June 14th, the two armies met. Rupert's original intention had been to deliver a defensive battle in a chosen position at Harborough, but his scouts deluded him into the belief that Fairfax's troops were retiring, and he advanced to find them drawing up in battle order on a high plateau in front of the little village of Naseby. The King's army amounted at most to about five thousand horse and four thousand or five thousand foot. Fairfax had thirteen thousand men, of whom six thousand were horse. In spite of these odds, the Royalists expected an easy victory. Many of the parliamentary foot were raw conscripts, whilst the King's were old soldiers. Charles himself spoke confidently of beating "the rebels' new brutish general" as he had beaten the experienced Essex, and even supporters of the Parliament had little faith in their untried army. "Never," wrote one, "did any army go forth to war who had less of the confidence of their own friends, or were more the objects of the contempt of their enemies." But Cromwell, for his part, had no doubts of the issue of the battle.

"I can say this of Naseby," he wrote a month later. "When I saw the enemy draw up and march in gallant order towards us, and we a company of poor, ignorant men, to seek how to order our battle—the General having commanded me to order all the horse—I could not, riding alone about my business, but smile out to God in praises, in assurance of victory, because God would, by things that are not, bring to naught things that are. Of which I had great assurance, and God did it."

As the royalist line advanced, Fairfax's artillery fired a few shots, which went high and did no execution. The King's guns were too far behind to do any service. The foot on each side fired one volley, and then charged each other with levelled pikes and clubbed muskets. So fierce was the onset of the royalist infantry that four out of the five regiments in Fairfax's front line gave way before it. Skippon's regiment was broken, its lieutenant-colonel killed, and Skippon himself severely wounded. But Fairfax's own regiment stood its ground, and the second line, coming up, drove the Royalists back and gave the broken regiments time to rally.

Still worse fared Colonel Ireton and the left wing of the parliamentary horse. Ireton's five regiments advanced to meet Rupert, but their charge was badly delivered and badly supported. At the outset, Ireton himself gained a temporary success, but, turning prematurely to attack a regiment of foot, he was unhorsed, wounded, and for a short time a prisoner. Rupert pushed his advantage with his usual vigour, and, not content with driving Ireton's horse from the field, attacked the train and the baggage guard of the Parliamentarians behind Naseby. As they stood firm he abandoned the attempt, and returned to see how the battle went on the plateau.

During this time, the horse of the parliamentary right wing under Cromwell decided the fate of the day. Cromwell did not wait to be charged by Sir Marmaduke Langdale, but met his horsemen as they advanced, and after a stiff struggle swept them back in disorder, and forced them to take shelter behind their reserve. Cromwell's troopers, said an eye-witness, were like a torrent, driving all before them. Charles put himself at the head of his guards and the rest of the reserve, and prepared to lead a desperate charge against the advancing Roundheads. "Will you go upon your death?" said a nobleman, seizing his bridle rein; so the guards halted, and wheeled about, and drew back for a quarter of a mile from the field. Leaving four regiments to keep them in check, Cromwell with the rest of his horse, and with what he could collect of Ireton's, turned to fall upon the royalist centre. The royalist infantry fought with great tenacity, but, attacked simultaneously by horse and foot, they were soon broken, and regiment after regiment laid down its arms. A brigade of bluecoats stood "with incredible courage and resolution" beating back charge after charge with their pikes. At last Cromwell charged one face of the square with Fairfax's regiment of foot, while Fairfax, bareheaded, led his life-guard against another. It too was broken, and Fairfax took the colours with his own hand. Of the King's infantry, scarcely a man escaped capture.

Fairfax halted the victorious cavalry till the main body of his foot came up, and then, forming a fresh line of battle, ordered a general advance. The King's guards and Langdale's routed horse had now been joined by Rupert's victorious troopers, and were drawn up to make a second charge. But discouraged as they were, and without artillery or foot to support them, their position was hopeless. In a few moments they wavered and broke, and every man, turning his horse's head towards Leicester, rode as hard as he could.

The pursuit lasted some thirteen miles. Nearly five thousand prisoners, more than one hundred colours, all of the King's baggage and artillery, and his private papers fell into the hands of the victors. Leicester surrendered four days later, and Fairfax, leaving the King to take refuge in Wales, set forth in haste to engage General Goring and the western army. At the news of his approach, Goring raised the blockade of Taunton, and took up his position about ten miles from Bridgwater, with his front covered by the rivers Yeo and Parret. The two armies came into collision near Langport on July 10th. Goring had posted his men on the brow of a hill, with enclosures and a marshy valley in their front. There was a ford across the little stream at the bottom of the valley, and a lane led up the hill to the open ground at the top where Goring's cavalry stood, while the hedges and enclosures on each side of the lane were filled with his musketeers. Intending to retreat to Bridgwater, Goring had sent thither his baggage, and all his guns but two.

Langport was one of the few battles of the Civil War in which field artillery played an important part. Fairfax began by overwhelming Goring's two guns with the fire of his own, and forcing the cavalry to move farther back and leave their musketeers unsupported. Then he ordered forward fifteen hundred musketeers, who, advancing down one hillside and up the other, drove Goring's skirmishers from hedge to hedge, and cleared the enclosures. Finally, under Cromwell's direction, six troops of horse (all drawn from Cromwell's own old regiment) dashed through the ford, and up the lane at Goring's cavalry. Major Bethell headed the charge, which he performed, writes Cromwell, "with the greatest gallantry imaginable," and Major Desborough seconded him with equal courage. Bethell beat back two bodies of Goring's horse and "brake them at sword point"; but, oppressed with numbers, his three troops were being driven back when Desborough and the other three came up to relieve them. Then they charged again, and both together routed another body of Goring's horse. At the same time, Fairfax's musketeers, coming close up to the cavalry, poured in their shot, and Goring's men began to run. Cromwell halted Desborough and Bethell on the ground they had won, allowing no pursuit till the rest of the horse joined them. Two miles farther back, the royalist cavalry made another stand, but one charge proved sufficient, and they were sent flying towards Bridgwater. Through the burning streets of Langport Cromwell dashed after them, capturing during the chase both their two guns and fourteen hundred prisoners.

Immediately after his victory, Fairfax laid siege to Bridgwater. Like Gustavus Adolphus, his method was to risk an assault wherever success seemed possible, rather than to spend time on elaborate siege works. The part of the town on the east bank of the Parret was taken by escalade on July 21st, and the other half surrendered after a short bombardment. The possession of Bridgwater, added to that of Taunton, Langport, and Lyme, gave Fairfax a line of garrisons which cut off Cornwall and Devon from the rest of England, and confined what remained of Goring's army to those two counties. He turned back, therefore, to complete the conquest of the west by taking the strongholds he had left in his rear. Bath was captured on July 29th, the strong castle of Sherborne stormed after a fortnight's siege on August 15th, and a week later Bristol was invested. Rupert with thirty-five hundred men held the city, but its fortifications were very extensive, and in many places weak. On September 10th, about one o'clock in the morning, Fairfax made a general assault on the whole circuit of the works, and by daybreak the most important fort and a mile of the line were in his possession. Rupert had no choice but to capitulate at once.

Cromwell was now put in command of four regiments of foot and three of horse, and sent to clear Wiltshire and Hampshire of hostile garrisons. Devizes and Laycock House surrendered to him on September 23rd; Winchester cost a week's siege, but gave in as soon as a breach was made. "You see," wrote Cromwell to the Speaker, "God is not weary in doing you good. His favour to you is as visible, when He comes by His power upon the hearts of your enemies, making them quit places of strength to you, as when He gives courage to your soldiers to attempt hard things." Basing House, the next place attacked, was very strong, had stood many sieges, and was garrisoned by determined men. Its owner, the Marquis of Winchester, was a Catholic, and many of its defenders were of the same creed. Cromwell breached its walls with his cannon and ordered a storm. The night before it, he spent much time in prayer. "He seldom fights," said his chaplain, "without some text of Scripture to support him." This time his eye fell upon a text in the Psalms foretelling the doom of idols and idolaters—"They that make them are like unto them; so is every one that putteth his trust in them." To a Puritan it seemed a promise of certain victory, and Cromwell gave the word to assault in complete assurance of success. His soldiers "fell on with great resolution and cheerfulness," clapped their scaling ladders to the walls, beat the enemy from their works, and made the house their own. Some three hundred of the garrison were killed, and about as many taken prisoners, while the house itself was thoroughly sacked by the soldiers, and then burnt. "I thank God," wrote Cromwell to the Speaker, "I can give you a good account of Basing."

At the end of October, Cromwell, having completed his task, joined Fairfax before Exeter. Except Devon and Cornwall, all the west had now been cleared of the Royalists. On the Welsh border, the King had Worcester and Hereford and a number of smaller places, but Chester was besieged, and in the north Newark was the only important fortress in his possession. Between these different places and his headquarters at Oxford, Charles, attended by two or three thousand horse, had aimlessly wandered, since his defeat at Naseby. At first, he thought of joining Goring and Prince Charles in the west, but Langport put an end to that plan. In August, he tried a raid into the Eastern Association, and took and plundered Huntingdon. In September, the rumour of his approach led Leven and the Scots to raise the siege of Hereford. More than once the King thought of joining Montrose in Scotland. In September, 1644, Montrose had begun the marvellous series of victories which threatened to oblige the Covenanters to withdraw their army from England. He beat them at Tippermuir, Aberdeen, Inverlochy, Auldearne, and Alford, and dreamt of subduing all Scotland and coming to the assistance of the King. At Kilsyth, on August 15, 1645, he won a still greater and more decisive victory than all the rest. Glasgow was occupied; Edinburgh and the south of Scotland submitted; the Covenanting leaders took refuge at Berwick. Montrose sent a triumphant message to the King saying that he would soon cross the border with twenty thousand men. But his Highlanders went home with their plunder, the Lowland Scots declined to enlist under his banner, and he had less than two thousand men with him when David Leslie, with four thousand horse from the Scottish army in England, surprised his little force at Philiphaugh, and cut it in pieces (September 13th). Ignorant of this disaster, Charles set out from Raglan Castle with three thousand horse to join Montrose. At Rowton Heath, on September 24th, he was defeated by Major-General Poyntz in an attempt to relieve Chester, and lost nine hundred men. Forced to abandon the plan of marching north through Lancashire, the King made his way to Newark, and thence, in November, back to Oxford. From Newark, Lord Digby made a desperate attempt to get to Scotland, but the sole result was the loss of the fifteen hundred horse he took with him.

From a military point of view, the King's position was now utterly hopeless. If after Naseby he had collected the men wasted in petty garrisons he could have got together a force sufficient to meet the "New Model" in the field. But he neglected the moment, one after another his garrisons were taken, and his new levies were scattered before they could combine. His generals lost hope, and while the quarrels of Goring and Grenville paralysed the King's western army, Rupert urged his uncle to make peace. Charles obstinately refused to listen either to him or to the rest of the peace party.

"If I had any other quarrel but the defence of my religion, crown, and friends," wrote Charles, "you had full reason for your advice; for I must confess that speaking as a mere soldier or statesman, there is no probability but of my ruin. Yet as a Christian I must tell you that God will not suffer rebels to prosper, nor His cause to be overthrown, and whatever personal punishment it shall please Him to inflict upon me must not make me repine, much less give over this quarrel."

The nation in general was weary of the war and impatient for peace. In the west and the south of England the country people began to form associations in order to keep all armed men of either party out of their districts, and to put an end to free quarter and the plunder of their cattle. In the south-west, these "Clubmen," as they were called, fell under the influence of royalist agents, but generally they remained neutral. When Fairfax marched into Dorsetshire, he employed Cromwell to disperse gathering after gathering of rustics armed with clubs and muskets.

"I assured them," wrote Cromwell to Fairfax, "that it was your great care, not to suffer them in the least to be plundered, and that they should defend themselves from violence, and bring to your army such as did them any wrong, where they should be punished with all severity; upon this very quietly and peaceably they marched away to their houses, being very well satisfied and contented."

Another body fired on Cromwell's men, and had to be dispersed by a cavalry charge. Some dozen were killed, and about three hundred made prisoners—"poor silly creatures" whom he released with an admonition. The moderation and just dealing of Cromwell and Fairfax, and the excellent discipline of their soldiers, speedily restored confidence. The countrymen came to perceive that the best hope of peace lay in the triumph of the Parliament. At the siege of Bristol, the Clubmen of the neighbourhood helped in the investment of the city, and at its surrender Rupert had to be guarded to prevent their taking vengeance for the plunderings he had sanctioned.

The feeling in favour of the parliamentary cause was still further strengthened by the discovery of the King's negotiations for the introduction of foreign forces into England. The letters taken at Naseby in June showed that the King was negotiating with the Duke of Lorraine to send an army of ten thousand men into England. Those captured when Digby was defeated in his attempt to reach Scotland proved that Charles was trying to get troops from Denmark. In October, some more captured correspondence revealed a treaty made with the Irish rebels in the previous August, by which they were to furnish Charles with ten thousand men in return for the legal establishment of Catholicism in Ireland. Finally, in January, 1646, Fairfax intercepted letters from royalist agents in France concerning five thousand Frenchmen who were to be landed in the west. These successive discoveries alienated men who had fought for the King, and turned neutrals into supporters of the Parliament.

It was to anticipate any such landing of foreign forces in England that Fairfax took the field so early in 1646. During the last two months of 1645 he had been blockading Exeter, but at the beginning of January, though the snow was on the ground and there was a hard frost, a general advance was ordered. The royalist forces in Cornwall and Devon numbered not less than twelve thousand men, besides the garrisons, but, as Clarendon confesses, they were a "dissolute, undisciplined, wicked, beaten army," more formidable to their friends than to their foes. Goring, to whose misconduct this disorganisation was due, had resigned his command at the end of 1645, and the brave and blameless Hopton, who succeeded him, could effect nothing with such troops. In two months, the resistance of the west collapsed. Cromwell opened the campaign by surprising Lord Wentworth's brigade at Bovey Tracy on January 9th; Wentworth and most of his men escaped in the darkness, but four hundred horses were taken, and the whole brigade scattered. Ten days later, Fairfax took the strong fortress of Dartmouth by storm, capturing one hundred guns and over one thousand prisoners. On February 16th, a chance collision between outposts at Torrington in North Devon developed into a general engagement in which Hopton was driven from the town with the loss of six hundred men, and his infantry were completely dispersed. Hopton had still about five thousand horse left, so, in spite of the sufferings of his soldiers from hard marches and winter weather, Fairfax resolved to follow him into Cornwall, "the breaking of that body of horse there being the likeliest means to prevent or discourage the landing of any foreign forces in those parts." When he entered the county, the Cornishmen, won by his good treatment of his prisoners and by the good behaviour of his soldiers, offered no opposition. Hopton's troopers deserted daily, and those who stayed by their colours had no fight left in them. The Prince of Wales and his councillors fled to the Channel Islands, and on the 14th of March Hopton's army capitulated. Fairfax wisely granted liberal terms, and every common soldier, on giving up horse and weapons, and promising not to bear arms any more against the Parliament, was given twenty shillings to carry him to his home.

From Cornwall, Fairfax now marched back to Exeter, which surrendered to him on April 9th, and thence to besiege Oxford, which he invested at the beginning of May. Cromwell stayed with Fairfax until Exeter fell, and then went to London at the General's desire, to give Parliament an account of the state of the west. On April 23rd, he was thanked by the House of Commons for his "great and faithful services." Rewards of another nature they had already conferred upon him. On December 1, 1645, the Commons, in drawing up the peace propositions to be offered to the King, had resolved that an estate of twenty-five hundred pounds a year should be settled on Lieutenant-General Cromwell, and that the King should be asked to make him a baron. The negotiations fell through, but on January 23rd the House ordered that the lands in Hampshire belonging to the Marquis of Worcester and his sons should be settled on Cromwell, and an ordinance for that purpose finally passed both Houses. As the rents of these lands fell short of the income promised, other estates of the same nobleman in Glamorganshire, Gloucestershire, and Monmouthshire were subsequently added to make up the sum.

Cromwell rejoined Fairfax at Oxford in time to take part in the negotiations for its surrender. Contemporary rumour attributed the leniency of the terms granted to the garrisons of Exeter and Oxford largely to his influence with Fairfax and the council of war. Oxford was strongly fortified, and it would have cost many men to take it, but, apart from this, there were political reasons of great weight which must have appealed to Cromwell. Just before Fairfax invested Oxford, King Charles escaped in disguise from the city, and took refuge in the camp of the Scottish army at Newark. For some months he had been negotiating with the Scots through the French Ambassador, and he hoped to be able to persuade them to adopt his cause against the English Parliament. There were rumours that the Scots meant to employ their army on his behalf, their complicity in his flight seemed proved, and an open breach between the two nations seemed more than possible. "The scurvy, base propositions which Cromwell has given to the Malignants of Oxford," writes Baillie, "have offended many more than his former capitulation at Exeter; all seeing the evident design of these conscientious men to grant the greatest conditions to the worst men, that they may be expedited for their northern warfare."

Even if the political situation had been otherwise, the necessity of healing the wounds of the war by liberal treatment of the conquered was an axiom with the army and its leaders. Politicians were as usual less generous than soldiers. The articles were reluctantly ratified by Parliament, and there were repeated complaints of their infringement. Cromwell and the officers of the army never ceased to represent that honour and policy alike demanded their exact observance. "There hath been of late a dispute about the Oxford articles," said a royalist news-letter in February, 1648. "One gentleman being discontented at the largeness of them told the Lieutenant-General they should lose two hundred thousand pounds by keeping them; he replied they had better lose double as much than break one article."

With the capitulation of Oxford on June 24, 1646, the war was over. Worcester, it is true, held out till July, and isolated castles in Wales, such as

Raglan, Denbigh, and Harlech, for some months longer, but their reduction was only a question of a short time.

Cromwell left these little sieges to be conducted by others, and returned to his duties in Parliament. He removed his family from Ely to London, and took a house in Drury Lane, moving thence about a year later to King Street, Westminster. His household was diminished by the marriage of his two elder daughters. Bridget, the eldest, had married, on June 15, 1646, Commissary-General Henry Ireton, her father's most trusted subordinate, and Elizabeth, Cromwell's favourite daughter, became, on January 13, 1646, the wife of John Claypole, a Northamptonshire squire. Only the two youngest daughters, Mary and Frances, were still at home. Of his four sons, two were already dead: Robert died in May, 1639, before the war began, and Captain Oliver five years later, while serving in his father's regiment. Richard, the elder of the two who survived, was now in Fairfax's life-guard, and Henry, who was about nineteen, was a cornet or lieutenant in some cavalry regiment. Cromwell had offered his sons to the cause as freely as he gave himself to it.

CHAPTER VIII
PRESBYTERIANS AND INDEPENDENTS
1642-1647

The settlement of the kingdom after the war ended was a task of far greater difficulty than the defeat of the King's armies. It could not be solved by putting Charles upon his throne again as if nothing had happened. Measures had to be devised for securing permanent guarantees against misgovernment in the future, and for rendering a new war impossible. Moreover, these ends must be attained by means of an agreement between the King and the Parliament, because the working of the constitution depended on the co-operation of the two powers, and on the reconciliation of the two parties which had followed their flags. Nor was it possible to effect a lasting settlement without taking into account the new ideas and the new forces which had come into existence during the four years' struggle.

Since the beginning of the Civil War an ecclesiastical revolution had taken place in England. As soon as hostilities commenced the Root and Branch party gained the ascendancy in Parliament, and in the first negotiations with the King, the total abolition of Episcopacy was one of the demands made. In July, 1643, Parliament summoned an assembly of divines to meet at Westminster, and undertake the reformation of the Church. Then followed the acceptance by Parliament of the Solemn League and Covenant, the implied promise to model the Church of England upon that of Scotland, and the inclusion of representatives of the Scottish clergy in the Assembly of Divines.

Step by step the English Church was transformed. In January, 1645, the two Houses passed a series of resolutions for the reorganisation of the Church upon a Presbyterian basis, followed by ordinances which established one after another the component parts of the system. By the close of 1646, the use of the Prayer-book had been prohibited, and a "Directory," drawn up by the Assembly, had been enjoined in its stead, while new Articles of Belief, a new Confession of Faith, and a new Catechism were in preparation. Bishops and all the ecclesiastical hierarchy dependent on them had been abolished, and their lands vested in trustees for the payment of the debts of the State (October, 1646). The work was still incomplete, but under all outward conformity there would be an essential difference between the Presbyterian Churches of England and Scotland. In Scotland the Church was dependent upon no one; in England it would be dependent upon Parliament. Whatever the Westminster Assembly might decide was established only by the authority of Parliament, which revised its conclusions, criticised its formularies, and limited its functions as it thought fit. Compared to an ideal Presbyterian Church ruling by its inherent right as the one divinely ordained form of Church government, the English Church would be, as a Scottish divine complained, "only a lame Erastian presbytery." Such as it was, however, its clergy were as high in their claim to authority as English bishops, and as intolerant as Scottish ministers. They proved in a hundred different ways the truth of Milton's maxim that "new presbyter is but old priest writ large."

During the years which saw the growth of English Presbyterianism, a rival system of ecclesiastical organisation had also taken root in England. The Independents drew their inspiration not from Scotland, but from the Puritan exiles in Holland and the Puritan colonists in New England. To the idea of a national Church with its local basis and its hierarchy of authorities, they opposed the idea that a true Church was a voluntary association of believers, and that each congregation was of right complete, autonomous, and sovereign. Most of them accepted the theology of Calvin even when they rejected his ecclesiastical organisation; all claimed the right to interpret the Bible for themselves without regard to tradition or authority. Their principle was that set forth in the advice which John Robinson gave to the Pilgrim Fathers—to be ready to receive whatever truth should be made known to them from the written word of God. Hence came their ardent faith in new revelations, with the diversity of doctrines and the multiplicity of sects which were its natural consequence. Hence the horror with which Presbyterians and Episcopalians alike regarded a system which began by a denial of their theory of Church and State, and ended by an attack upon the fundamentals of their creed.

Just as the two divisions of the parliamentary party differed as to the constitution of the Church, so they differed as to the constitution of the State. Each was a political as well as a religious party. The aim of the Presbyterians was to make King and Church responsible to Parliament, and so far the Independents went with them. But while one party proclaimed the sovereignty of Parliament, and justified its claim by historical precedent, the other proclaimed the sovereignty of the people, and based its claim on an appeal to natural rights. Church democracy, as Baxter called Independency, brought in its train State democracy. Applied to politics, the ecclesiastical theories of the Independents developed into the fundamental principles of democratic government. Those who held that a Church was a voluntary association of believers bound together by a mutual covenant, naturally adopted the corollary that a State was an association of freemen based on a mutual contract. If it was the right of the members of a religious body to elect their own ministers, it was evidently equally just that the members of a civil society should elect their own magistrates. More than once in its paper wars with the King, Parliament had put forward the view that Kings were but officers, whose power was a trust from the people, but it shrank from the distinct enunciation or the practical application of the principle its declarations contained. It was therefore in opposition to the Long Parliament that the sovereignty of the people was first asserted in English political life. In 1646, when John Lilburn was imprisoned by the Lords for libelling Manchester he appealed to the House of Commons as "the supreme authority of the nation," and denied the authority of the Peers because they were not elected by the people. When the House of Commons refused to hear him he appealed "to the universality of the people," as "the sovereign lord" from whom they derived their power, and by whom they were to be called to account for its use.

As yet, however, Lilburn's principles found little acceptance in Parliament, and the Lower House had no intention of quarrelling with the Upper on a question of abstract rights. In the Commons, even after the new elections of 1645 and 1646 had recruited the numbers of the House, the Independents were a minority both on political and ecclesiastical questions. On a purely religious issue they could muster fifty or sixty votes, of whom probably less than half were convinced democrats. But the ties of party allegiance were weak, and the ability of the Independent leaders gave them an influence beyond the circle of their followers. On questions such as the conduct of the war, the control of the pretensions of the Westminster Assembly, and the claim of the Scots to dispose of the King, a majority of the House adopted the policy of the Independents. But when the war was over, and the dispute with the Scots settled, the ascendancy passed to the Presbyterian leaders, and remained with them.

On the other hand, the army had been from the beginning a stronghold of Independency, and there its adherents grew more numerous every day. In the summer of 1645, when Richard Baxter became chaplain to a regiment of cavalry, he found it full of hotheaded sectaries. Every sect and every heresy was represented in its ranks. "Independency and Anabaptism were most prevalent; Antinomianism and Arminianism equally distributed." One day he had to confute the opponents of Infant Baptism, and another to vindicate Church order and Church government. But the most universal belief amongst officers and soldiers, and the error he most often had to controvert, was that the civil magistrate had no authority in matters of religion either to restrain or to compel, and that every man had a right to believe and to preach whatever he pleased.

In the army, too, the political principles of Independency had reached their fullest and freest development. Baxter found officers and soldiers "vehement against the King and against all government but popular."

"I perceived" he writes, "that they took the King for a tyrant and an enemy, and really intended absolutely to master him or to ruin him, and that they thought, that if they might fight against him they might kill or conquer him; and if they might conquer they were never more to trust him further than he was in their power; and they thought it folly to irritate him by wars or contradictions in Parliament, if so be they needs must take him for their King, and trust him with their lives when they had thus displeased him."

These were the principles upon which they thought any settlement should be based, and they meant to make their views heard. "They plainly showed me," continues Baxter, "that they thought God's providence would cast the trust of religion and the kingdom upon them as conquerors."

In peace, even more than in war, the army looked to Cromwell to lead it. Apart from his splendid military gifts, he had all the qualities required to win popularity with soldiers. Cromwell had none of the reserve or reticence of Fairfax. A large-hearted, expansive, vigorous nature found expression in his acts and utterances. "He was of a sanguine complexion," says Baxter, "naturally of such a vivacity, hilarity, and alacrity, as another man is when he hath drunken a cup of wine too much." Elsewhere he speaks of Cromwell's "familiar rustic carriage with his soldiers in sporting," and one of Cromwell's officers tells us that "Oliver loved an innocent jest." Nor did it make him less popular that underneath this geniality lay a fiery temper, which sometimes flamed up into vehement utterances or sudden bursts of passion. Partly for this very reason he was generally credited with much more democratic opinions than he really had. People remembered his hard sayings about the Lords during his quarrel with Manchester, and took a practical man's irritation against half-hearted and incapable leaders for rooted hostility to an institution. His patronage of Lilburn seemed another proof of his extreme views. Cromwell had procured Lilburn's release from imprisonment in 1640, obtained him a commission in Manchester's army in 1643, and intervened on his behalf with the House of Commons in 1645. People attributed to sympathy with advanced democracy what was really due to hatred of oppression and injustice. Lilburn's praises fostered the illusion. Great as Cromwell was in the field, argued Lilburn, he was still more useful in Parliament.

"O for self-denying Cromwell home again ... for he is sound at the heart and not rotten-cored, hates particular and self-interests, and dares freely to speak his mind." "Myself and all others of my creed," wrote Lilburn to Cromwell in 1647, "have looked upon you as the most absolute single-hearted great man in England, untainted or unbiassed with ends of your own."

In religion, however, Cromwell represented the army more completely than in politics. Cromwell was, as Baillie truly termed him, "the great

Independent"—a type of Independency itself, representing not any particular species of Independent, but the whole genus which the term included. He called himself by the name of no sect, "joined himself to no party," and "did not profess of what opinion he was." "In good discourse" he would sometimes "very fluently pour himself out in the extolling of Free Grace," but he refused to dispute about doctrinal questions. There are indications in some of Cromwell's utterances that he was attracted to those who called themselves "Seekers," because they found satisfaction not in any visible form or definite creed, but in the perpetual quest for truth and perfection. "To be a Seeker," says Cromwell in a letter written about this time, "is to be of the best sect next after a Finder, and such an one shall every faithful humble Seeker be in the end." But while standing a little apart from every sect, Cromwell seemed to share the aspirations and enthusiasms of each. "Anabaptists, Antinomians, Seekers, Separatists," he sympathised with all, welcomed all to the ranks of the army, and "tied all together by the point of liberty of conscience, which was the common interest in which they all did unite."

Of this demand for freedom of conscience, Cromwell had ever made himself the spokesman. At the outset of the war, he and his officers had proposed to make their regiment "a gathered Church." While he was governor of Ely, he and his deputy-governor, Ireton, had filled the island with Independents until people complained that for variety of religions the place was "a mere Amsterdam." When he became Lieutenant-General of Manchester's army, Independency had spread from his regiment to the rest of the troopers he commanded.

"If you look on his regiment of horse," said an opponent, "what a swarm there is of those that call themselves godly men; some profess to have seen visions and had revelations. Look on Colonel Fleetwood's regiment with his Major Harrison, what a cluster of preaching officers and troopers there is. To say the truth almost our horse be made of that faction."

Cromwell protected them against Manchester's Presbyterian chaplains and against the hostility of Presbyterian officers. In March, 1644, when

Major-General Crawford cashiered the lieutenant-colonel of his regiment on the ground that he was an Anabaptist, Cromwell at once remonstrated. If any military offence were chargeable upon the lieutenant-colonel, he must be tried by court-martial; if none, Crawford must restore him to his command. "Admit he be an Anabaptist, shall that render him incapable to serve the public? Sir, the State in choosing men to serve it, takes no notice of their opinions; if they be willing to serve it faithfully, that suffices." Six months later, after a second quarrel with Crawford on the same subject, Cromwell procured from Parliament what was known as "the Accommodation Order." A committee was to be appointed

"to take into consideration the differences in opinion of the members of the Assembly of Divines in point of Church government, and to endeavour a union if it be possible; and in case that cannot be done, to endeavour the finding out some way, how far tender consciences, who cannot in all things submit to the common rule which shall be established, may be borne with according to the Word, and as may stand with the public peace" (September 13, 1644).

After every victory of the "New Model," Cromwell reminded Parliament of the necessity of legally establishing the toleration which this vote promised. "Honest men served you faithfully in this action," he wrote from the field of Naseby; "they are trusty; I beseech you in the name of God not to discourage them. He that ventures his life for the liberty of his country, I wish he trust God for the liberty of his conscience, and you for the liberty he fights for." So little did the Commons share his feeling, that they mutilated his letter by omitting in the published copies his plea for toleration, but he repeated it in still plainer language after the storming of Bristol.

"Presbyterians and Independents, all here have the same spirit of faith and prayer ... they agree here, have no names of difference; pity it should be otherwise anywhere. All that believe have the real unity which is most glorious because inward and spiritual.... For being united in forms, commonly called Uniformity, every Christian will for peace sake study and do as far as conscience will permit. And from brethren in things of the mind we look for no compulsion, but that of light and reason."

Parliament had answered by mutilating this letter as it had mutilated the other. What prospect was there, now that the swords of the Independents were no longer needed, that their political and religious demands would be listened to, or that no compulsion save that of light and reason would be exercised against their consciences? As to religion, if Parliament allowed the Presbyterian clergy to work their will, Independents could expect nothing but persecution. "To let men serve God according to the persuasion of their own consciences," wrote one Presbyterian divine, "was to cast out one devil that seven worse might enter." Toleration, wrote another, was "the Devil's Masterpiece." "If the devil had his choice whether the hierarchy, ceremonies, and liturgy should be established in the kingdom, or a toleration granted, he would choose a toleration." "We detest and abhor the much endeavoured toleration," declared a meeting of the London ministers. The corporation of London backed their declaration by a petition for the suppression of all heresies. In Parliament itself it was evident that the anti-tolerationists had gained the upper hand. As late as April, 1646, the Commons had promised a due regard for tender consciences, providing only that they differed not in any fundamentals of religion. In September, however, the House passed the second reading of a bill which punished with death those who denied doctrines relating to the Trinity and the Incarnation, and with imprisonment for life those who opposed Infant Baptism and other less important doctrines. In December, when a bill was introduced prohibiting laymen from preaching in churches or elsewhere, Cromwell could only muster fifty-seven members in favour of allowing them at least to expound the Scriptures. Nor was there in the proposals of Parliament for the settlement of the kingdom any sign that the constitutional settlement would include in it toleration for Independency.

As little hope was there from the King. Ever since May, 1646, Charles had been a prisoner in the camp of the Scots, first at Newark, and then at Newcastle. The chief demands contained in the propositions sent to him at Newcastle were, that the King should enforce the taking of the Covenant through all the three kingdoms, and accept the Presbyterian Church which Parliament had set up. At the same time he was to give Parliament the control of the naval and military forces of the nation for the next twenty years, and when that period ended the two Houses were to decide as to their future disposal. Backed by the Church, and with the sword as well as the purse in their hands, the power of Parliament would be securely established.

As long as he could, Charles evaded a direct answer. He believed that bishops and apostolical succession were necessary to a true Church. If he gave way to the abolition of Episcopacy "there would be no Church," and to yield against the dictates of his conscience would be "a sin of the highest nature." Political motives reinforced conscientious objections. To accept or impose the Covenant would be a "perpetual authorising rebellion." As to establishing Presbyterianism by law,

"under pretence of a thorough reformation in England they intend to take away all the ecclesiastical power of government from the Crown, and place it in the two Houses of Parliament. Moreover they will introduce the doctrine which teaches rebellion to be lawful and that the supreme power is in the people, to whom kings, as they say, ought to give account, and to be corrected when they do amiss.... There was not a wiser man since Solomon than he who said 'no bishop, no king.'"

The utmost that Charles, after months of negotiation, would concede was to grant the establishment of Presbyterianism for three years, and the control of the army and navy for ten. At the end of the ten years he stipulated that the control of army and navy should return to the Crown, and at the end of the three he was firmly resolved to re-establish Episcopacy.

After eight months of futile negotiating, the Scots, disgusted by the King's obstinate refusal to accept Presbyterianism, resolved to abandon the King's cause and hand him over to his English subjects. They settled their own differences with the English Parliament about their arrears of pay, received two hundred thousand pounds on account, and evacuated Newcastle on January 30, 1647, leaving Charles in charge of the parliamentary commissioners. In February he was brought to Holmby

House in Northamptonshire in custody of the commissioners and of a guard of cavalry.

But the moment when the King seemed to have fallen lowest marked the success of his policy. His refusal to accept the terms offered him at Newcastle rested mainly on the conviction that he was indispensable. "Men," he said in one of his letters, "will begin to perceive that without my establishing there can be no peace." Even his adversaries must see it: "without pretending to prophesy I will foretell their ruin unless they agree with me." Sooner or later, he felt certain some party amongst his opponents must, for their own sake, accept his terms and come to an understanding with him. What he had anticipated was now coming to pass. Before he arrived at Holmby, a number of the Presbyterian Peers had agreed to accept the King's concessions as the basis of an agreement, upon the completion of which Charles was to be restored to the exercise of his power. It was the beginning of that alliance between the Royalists and the Presbyterians which produced the Second Civil War, and finally the restoration of Charles II. On May 12th, a new message from the King embodying these concessions reached Westminster, and it was not doubtful that a majority in the two Houses would accept them as satisfactory.

An agreement on such a basis was a truce, not a peace. It left unsettled the questions which had caused the war, and threw away all the fruits of the victory. Parliament and the King had fought for sovereignty, but now, at the price of temporary concessions, sovereignty would be left in the King's hands. As long as the King's right to veto bills was left intact he could prevent any of his temporary concessions from becoming permanent, and he meant to do so. The Independents felt all the danger of such a one-sided compromise, but they were now in a hopeless minority in both Houses. When the army was disbanded, they would be entirely without influence. Its disbandment would have taken place in October, 1646, but for the strained relations of Parliament with the Scots, and a scheme for disbandment was voted on, February, 1647. Out of the forty thousand men in arms in England, Parliament proposed to form a new army consisting of six thousand four hundred horse, and about ten thousand foot for garrison service. It seized the opportunity to get rid of all the Independent officers of the "New Model." Fairfax was to be retained as General, but all the other general officers were to be dismissed. No member of Parliament was to hold a commission in the new army, and no officer was to be employed who did not conform to the Presbyterian Church. Of the soldiers of the "New Model," four thousand horse were to be retained in service in England; the rest of the horse and the infantry were to be employed for the reconquest of Ireland.

In Ireland, ever since the cessation of 1643, Ormond, the King's Lord-Lieutenant, had maintained himself in Dublin, struggling ever to turn the cessation into a peace, and to send help to the King in England. But the refusal of the Catholic clergy to accept less than the establishment of Catholicism in Ireland frustrated his negotiations, and, in 1646, Dublin was again besieged. With few troops and with no money to pay them, Ormond found himself obliged to submit to either Irish or English rebels. He chose the latter as the only way to preserve Ireland to the English nation, and in February, 1647, offered to deliver up his charge to the Parliament. Nothing could have fallen in more opportunely for the plans of the Presbyterians, and on March 6, 1647, Parliament voted that 12,600 men, drawn from the ranks of the "New Model," should be promptly despatched to Ireland, and sent commissioners to the headquarters of the army to persuade the soldiers to enlist for Irish service.

If the soldiers had been justly treated there would have been no difficulty in persuading them either to volunteer for Ireland or to disband quietly. But the folly of the Presbyterian leaders created a military revolt which changed the face of English politics. As was natural, the soldiers wanted to be paid for their past service before disbanding or re-enlisting. The pay of the foot was eighteen weeks in arrears; that of the horse, forty-three weeks. They petitioned Fairfax to represent their desires to Parliament, asking particularly to be indemnified against legal proceedings for acts done in the late war, and to be guaranteed their back pay. The House of Commons ordered the petition to be suppressed, and declared those who persisted in petitioning to be enemies of the State and disturbers of the public peace. As to their arrears, it offered only six weeks' pay, and even that offer was delayed till the end of April. The result was that out of the whole twenty-two thousand men of the "New Model," only twenty-three hundred volunteered for Ireland, and the discontent of the army swelled to a formidable agitation. In April, the horse regiments elected representatives, called Agitators or Agents, to concert united action, and in May the foot followed their example. At the end of April, the Agitators of eight regiments sent a joint letter to Skippon and Cromwell, urging them to represent the wrongs of the army to Parliament, and to procure redress. Cromwell and Skippon laid the letter before the House, and the House ordered the two, accompanied by Ireton and Fleetwood, to go down to the army, and endeavour to quiet the distempers of the soldiers. It promised the soldiers a considerable part of their arrears on disbanding, and good security for the payment of the remainder. The six weeks' pay offered was increased to eight.

Up to this point Cromwell had taken no part in the negotiations with the soldiers, much less in the movement amongst them against disbanding. In February, 1647, when the first votes for disbanding were passed, he was dangerously ill, and for some time absented himself both from the House and from the Committee of Both Kingdoms. All men knew his dissatisfaction with the policy which the Presbyterian leaders were following, and some attributed his abstention to that cause. "We are full of faction and worse," was Cromwell's comment on the state of affairs in Parliament, in August, 1646. He marked with anxiety the growth of royalist feeling in London and the increasing hostility of the citizens to the army and the Independents.

"We have had a very long petition from the City," he wrote to Fairfax on December 21, 1646; "how it strikes at the army and what other aims it has you will see by the contents of it; as also what is the prevailing temper at this present, and what is to be expected from men. But this is our comfort, God is in heaven, and He doth what pleaseth Him; His and only His counsel shall stand, whatsoever the designs of men and the fury of the people be."

In March, 1647, the feeling in the city was still worse.

"There want not in all places," he told Fairfax, "men who have so much malice against the army as besots them.... Never were the spirits of men more embittered than now.... Upon the Fast-day divers soldiers were raised, both horse and foot, near two hundred in Covent Garden, to prevent us soldiers from cutting the Presbyterians' throats! These are fine tricks to mock God with."

He was irritated also by the suspicions with which he himself was regarded and the reception they met with from people who ought to have known better.

"It is a miserable thing," he told Ludlow, "to serve a Parliament, to which, let a man be never so faithful, if one pragmatical fellow amongst them rise and asperse him, he shall never wipe it off; whereas when one serves a general he may do as much service, and yet be free from all blame and envy."

Cromwell even thought of leaving England, with as many of his fellow soldiers as he could take with him, to fight for the cause of the German Calvinists under the flag of the Elector Palatine. He had long conferences with the Elector on the subject in March or April, 1647.

But, in spite of Cromwell's dissatisfaction, there is no sign either in his words or action that he contemplated resisting the policy of Parliament or thought of stirring up a military revolution. There were bitter complaints from some of his greatest admirers that he persistently discouraged the petitions of the soldiers.

"I am informed this day," wrote Lilburn to Cromwell on March 25th, "by an officer out of the army, that you and your agents are like to dash in pieces the hopes of our outward preservation, their petition to the House, and will not suffer them to petition till they have laid down their arms; because forsooth you have engaged to the House they shall lay down their arms whenever it shall command them."

Cromwell's action during the last few months, continued Lilburn, had filled him with grief and amazement. Could it be that he was held back by temporising politicians, "covetous earthworms," such as Vane and St. John, or bribed into inaction by the estate Parliament had given him? Let him pluck up resolution "like a man that will persevere to be a man for God," and risk his life to deliver his fellow soldiers from ruin, and his country from vassalage and slavery.

Cromwell turned a deaf ear to these appeals. He feared to encourage the intervention of soldiers in politics, and dreaded still more the anarchy which might follow a breach between Parliament and the army. In May, he went to the headquarters of the army at Saffron Walden with his three colleagues, examined carefully the grievances of the petitioners, communicated the votes of Parliament, and did his best to persuade officers and soldiers to submission.

"Truly, gentlemen," he said to the officers, "it will be very fit for you to have a very great care in making the best use you can both of the votes, and of the interest that any of you have in your regiments, to work in them a good opinion of that authority that is over both us and them. If that authority falls to nothing, nothing can follow but confusion."

The commissioners reported that they found the whole army "under a deep sense of some sufferings" and the common soldiers "much unsettled." On May 21st, Cromwell received the thanks of the Commons, and told them that the soldiers would certainly not go to Ireland, but that he thought they would disband quietly. Under his influence, the House for a moment seemed disposed to adopt a conciliatory policy, and passed ordinances redressing some of the minor grievances of the soldiers. But no steps were taken to give them the promised security for the payment of their arrears, and on May 27th a scheme for the immediate disbandment was voted. It was to begin on June 1st, with Fairfax's own regiment, and to prevent any concerted action the regiments were to be separately disbanded at widely distant places.

The Presbyterian leaders had made up their minds to resort to force to carry their policy through. In secret they were discussing with the French Ambassador and the commissioners of the Scottish Parliament a plan for bringing the Scottish army into England. The Prince of Wales was to be sent to Scotland to head the projected invasion. As soon as possible, the

King was to be brought from Holmby to London, where the City militia was entirely under the control of the Presbyterians. At the same time, in order to cripple the resistance of the army, the train of artillery was to be removed from Oxford to the Tower. Then, backed by the Scots and the City, they would force the soldiers to submit to their terms, and punish the officers who had taken their part. It meant a new civil war.

Simultaneously a general mutiny began. The votes for disbanding the soldiers before redressing their grievances robbed the tardy and trifling concessions of Parliament of all their value. The ulterior schemes of the Presbyterian leaders were known in the army almost as soon as they were formed. At the bidding of the Agitators the army refused to disband. "Be active," wrote one, "for all lies at stake." It was no longer simply a question of arrears of pay. "The good of all the kingdom and its preservation is in your hands." So thought most of the officers, and pledged themselves to stand by their men. So thought Fairfax's council of war, and at the petition of the soldiers ordered a general rendezvous of the whole army on June 3rd. "I am forced," apologised Fairfax, "to yield something out of order to keep the army from disorder or worse inconveniences." Without his orders, a party of horse secured the artillery train at Oxford, and seized the King at Holmby on June 3rd. The same day Cromwell left London, resolved to throw in his lot with the army.

CHAPTER IX
ARMY AND PARLIAMENT
1647–1648

Cromwell joined the army because he wished to prevent the outbreak of anarchy or civil war. War was inevitable, if the Presbyterian leaders were allowed to bring Scottish forces into England to suppress the Independent army. Anarchy was inevitable, unless the Independent army was held in by a strong hand. If Cromwell remained passive, the mutiny would become a military revolution, and a bloody collision would take place between Independents and Presbyterians. He could prevent these things only by immediate action. It was too late now to attempt mediation, for with or without his aid the Agitators had determined to act. "If he would not forthwith come and head them," they told Cromwell, "they would go their own way without him."

As soon as Cromwell's mind was made up, he struck with swiftness and decision. The King was the key of the situation, and the possession of his person was to either party nine points of the law. His co-operation was indispensable to the success of the Presbyterian scheme, for unless they completed their agreement with Charles, the Scots would not cross the border, the English Royalists would not rise, and the citizens of London would not fight. At Holmby House, Charles was guarded by the regiment of Colonel Graves, who was an ardent Presbyterian, and Graves was under the orders of four Presbyterian commissioners appointed by Parliament. The danger was that Graves, either of his own accord or by order of the commissioners, might remove the King to Scotland or to London.

On May 31, 1647, Cromwell ordered Cornet Joyce, an officer in Fairfax's life-guard, to get together a party of horse, and to prevent the King's removal from Holmby. About midnight on June 2nd, Joyce reached Holmby, and posted his men round the house. Next morning the troopers of the King's guard threw open the gates and fraternised with his men, while

Graves took flight, leaving King and commissioners in Joyce's hands. Cromwell had given no orders for the King's removal, but next day there were rumours that Graves was returning with a strong force to regain possession of the King, and Joyce's men urged him to remove Charles to some place of security in the quarters of the army. Charles, who was offered his choice, selected Newmarket, and leaving Holmby on Friday, June 4th, Joyce and the King reached Hinchinbrook that evening. On Saturday, Joyce was met during his march by Colonel Whalley, whom Fairfax had sent to take command of the King's guard and convey the King himself back to Holmby. But Charles refused to return to what he regarded as his prison, and persisted in going to Newmarket, where the headquarters of the army were now established.

On the same Friday and Saturday, a general rendezvous of the army was held at Kentford Heath, near Newmarket, during which Cromwell arrived from London. At the rendezvous, a full statement of the grievances of the soldiers was presented, and all bound themselves by a solemn engagement not to disband or divide till their rights were secured. A council was instituted, consisting of the general officers, with two officers and two privates chosen from each regiment, which was to negotiate with Parliament on behalf of the soldiers, and to represent the army in political matters. The experiment was a dangerous one, but to limit the functions of the Agitators and to induce them to co-operate with their officers was the only way to bring them under control. In military matters, however, the General and his council of war remained supreme, and in that body Cromwell was the ruling spirit. Adversaries described the Lieutenant-General as the "*primum mobile*," and "the principal wheel" which moved the whole machine. Under his influence subordination and discipline were rapidly restored, and in a few weeks the real direction of the army passed into the hands of the council of war, while the General Council sank into the position of a debating society. No one doubted that this was Cromwell's work. "You have robbed," complained Lilburn in July, "by your unjust subtlety and shifting tricks, the honest and gallant Agitators of all their power and authority, and solely placed it in a thing called a council of war."

From Newmarket, the army advanced toward London. Parliament promised the soldiers all their arrears, and cancelled their offensive declarations. But the soldiers now required guarantees for the future as well as satisfaction for the past. They insisted on the exclusion of the Presbyterian leaders from power, and claimed a voice in the settlement of the nation. A letter to the City of London, signed by all the chief officers, but probably written by Cromwell himself, explained the change in their attitude.

"As Englishmen—and surely our being soldiers hath not stripped us of that interest, though our malicious enemies would have it so—we desire a settlement of the peace of the kingdom and of the liberties of the subject, according to the votes and declarations of Parliament, which, before we took arms, were by the Parliament used as arguments to invite us and divers of our dear friends out; some of whom have lost their lives in this war. Which being now by God's blessing finished, we think we have as much right to demand and desire to see a happy settlement, as we have to our money and the other common interests of soldiers we have insisted upon."

Cromwell asserted that the army had no wish either for a civil or an ecclesiastical revolution, but reiterated the demand for toleration.

"We have said before and we profess it now, we desire no alteration of the civil government. As little do we desire to interrupt, or in the least to intermeddle with, the settling of the Presbyterial government. Nor did we seek to open a way for licentious liberty under pretence of obtaining ease for tender consciences. We profess as ever in these things, when once the State has made a settlement, we have nothing to say but to submit or suffer. Only we could wish that every good citizen, and every man who walks peaceably in a blameless conversation, and is beneficial to the Commonwealth, might have liberty and encouragement; this being according to the true policy of all states, and even to justice itself."

To Cromwell, it is evident, the acquisition of freedom of conscience seemed more important than any possible change in the constitution of

Church or State. The task of formulating the political programme of the army fell to his son-in-law Ireton, who had more definite views than Cromwell as to the constitutional changes needed. Arbitrary power, Ireton asserted in the army's Declaration of June 14th, was the root of all evil. The absolutism of Parliament must be guarded against as well as the absolutism of the King, and parliamentary privilege might become as dangerous to popular liberties as royal prerogative had been. The way to make the rights of the people secure was to make Parliament more really representative. Henceforward the demand for the speedy termination of the existing Parliament was accompanied by demands for equalisation of the constituencies, short Parliaments, and the vindication of the right to petition.

The Long Parliament was not disposed to accept such democratic changes, but it was obliged to temporise. News came that the ten thousand men of the northern army under General Poyntz were on the verge of mutiny, and ready to join the forces under Fairfax. The eleven Presbyterian leaders impeached by the army saved the dignity of the House by a voluntary withdrawal, and negotiations were opened at Wycombe on July 1st. After a fortnight of negotiating, the Agitators murmured at the delay, and urged the immediate resumption of the march on London, and the enforcement of their demands. Cromwell and the higher officers opposed. "Whatsoever we get by a treaty," argued Cromwell, "will be firm and durable. It will be conveyed over to posterity." The friends of the army were daily gaining ground in the House.

"What we and they gain in a free way is better than twice so much in a forced way, and will be more truly ours and our posterity's.... That you have by force I look upon as nothing. I do not know that force is to be used except we cannot get what is for the good of the kingdom without it."

In Cromwell's opinion, it would be sufficient peremptorily to demand certain concessions as a guarantee that the treaty was seriously meant, and to leave the terms of the political settlement for negotiation. Above all things it was essential that the army should be united. "You may be in the right and I in the wrong, but if we be divided I doubt we shall both be in the wrong."

Cromwell's plan was adopted, and the Long Parliament yielded. All preparations for armed resistance were abandoned. Parliament appointed Fairfax commander-in-chief of all the forces in England, including those lately under General Poyntz; it disbanded all the soldiers it had enlisted to oppose Fairfax; it restored the control of the London militia to the old committee, which the army trusted, in place of the exclusively Presbyterian committee appointed in the spring. But if Parliament saw the necessity of yielding, London did not. On July 21st, crowds of citizens signed an engagement for the maintenance of the Covenant, and the restoration of the King on his own terms, though both Houses united in denouncing their engagement. On the 26th, crowds of apprentices and discharged soldiers besieged the Houses and threatened their members with violence unless the command of the City forces were given back to the Presbyterians. The Lords gave way first; the Commons resisted some hours longer, but in the end they too obeyed the mob, and repealed their votes. The rioters also extorted from them a vote inviting the King to London. After this both Houses adjourned till the 30th of July, but before that day came the two Speakers, followed by eight Peers and fifty-seven members of the Commons, had taken refuge with the army, declaring that Parliament was not free, and the army, pledged to restore the freedom of Parliament, was marching on London. The Presbyterians prepared to fight, and placed the forces of the City under the command of Major-General Massey. The eleven impeached Presbyterian leaders took their places in Parliament again, assumed the direction of the movement, and appointed a Committee of Safety. But citizen militia and undisciplined volunteers would have stood a poor chance against the veterans of Naseby. Even the fanatical mob of the City knew it, and when Fairfax arrived at Hounslow with twenty thousand men, their courage fell to zero.

Crowds gathered outside Guildhall, where the City fathers were deliberating whether to fight or yield. "When a scout came in, and brought news that the army made a halt, or other good intelligence, they cried, 'One and all.' But if the scouts brought intelligence that the army advanced nearer to them, then they would cry as loud 'Treat, Treat, Treat.'" On

August 4th, London submitted unconditionally, and two days later the army escorted the fugitive members to Westminster, and made a triumphal progress through the City. The Agitators talked loudly of purging the House of Commons by expelling all members who had sat during the absence of the Speakers, but Cromwell and the officers contented themselves with demanding that the proceedings of the last ten days should be declared null and void. Even this could not be obtained till Cromwell threatened to use force, and drew up a regiment of cavalry in Hyde Park to give weight to his arguments. For the Presbyterians were still a majority in Parliament, though their leaders had now fled to the continent.

The army now rested its hopes on the King rather than on the Parliament. During the march on London it had published its proposals "for clearing and securing the rights of the kingdom, and settling a just and lasting peace." The "Heads of the Proposals," like the Newcastle Propositions, demanded that for the next ten years Parliament should have the control of the militia and the appointment of officers of State, but they were more lenient to the King's party. Royalists were to be for a time incapacitated from office, but their fines were to be reduced, the number of exceptions from pardon diminished, and a general amnesty passed. Besides these temporary measures of security there were to be three permanent changes in the constitution. The religious settlement was to be based on toleration, not on the enforcement of Presbyterianism. No man was to be obliged to take the Covenant, bishops and ecclesiastical officials were to be deprived of all coercive power, and the statutes enforcing attendance at church or use of the Prayer-book were to be abolished. In future the royal power was to be limited by the institution of a Council of State which would share with the King the control of the military forces and the conduct of foreign affairs. Parliaments were to meet every two years, to sit for a limited space of time, and to be elected by more equal constituencies, while the existing Parliament was to end within a year.

Ireton was the chief author of these proposals, but Cromwell was equally eager for an agreement between the army and the King.

"Whatever the world might judge of them," said Cromwell to one of the King's agents, "the army would be found no Seekers of themselves, further than to have leave to live as subjects ought to do and to preserve their own consciences; and they thought no men could enjoy their lives and estates quietly without the King had his rights."

When Charles raised objections to the first draught of the "Proposals," Cromwell and Ireton persuaded the Council of the Army to lower their demands, and to make important alterations in the scheme finally published. If the King accepted it the army leaders assured him that no further concessions should be demanded. And supposing that after he had accepted it Parliament refused its assent, they would purge the Houses of opponents "till they had made them of such a temper as to do his Majesty's business."

Such was the talk amongst the officers, but it soon became evident they had reckoned without their host. The King was little inclined to submit to the permanent restrictions on his royal power which the army demanded, and thought he could avail himself of the quarrel between it and the Parliament to impose his will on both. He avowed it frankly. "You cannot do without me. You will fall to ruin if I do not sustain you," he told the officers, when the "Proposals" were first offered to him. "Sir," answered Ireton, "you have an intention to be the arbitrator between the Parliament and us, and we mean to be it between your Majesty and the Parliament." Another time Charles answered Ireton's remonstrances with the defiant announcement: "I shall play my game as well as I can." "If your Majesty have a game to play," replied Ireton, "you must give us also the leave to play ours."

They could come to no agreement. Charles persisted in his policy of playing off one party against another, confident that his diplomatic skill would secure his ultimate victory. In September, the Parliament once more offered the King the Newcastle Propositions, to which he answered that the "Proposals" of the army offered a better foundation for a lasting peace, and asked for a personal treaty. The advanced party amongst the Independents, headed by Harry Marten and Colonel Rainsborough, urged that Parliament should proceed to the settlement of the kingdom without consulting the King. They compared Charles to Ahab, whose heart God hardened, and to a Jonah who must be thrown overboard if the ship of the state was to come safe to port. Cromwell, backed by Ireton and Vane, argued in favour of a new application to the King, and by eighty-four votes to thirty-four the House decided to draw up fresh propositions. It seemed to Cromwell that the re-establishment of monarchy was the only way to avoid anarchy. Already an officer had been expelled from the Council of the Army for declaring that there was now no visible authority in England but the power of the sword, and Cromwell warned Parliament that men who thought the sword ought to rule all were rapidly growing more numerous amongst the soldiers. He argued that a speedy agreement with the King was necessary, but to persuade the Parliament to reduce its demands proved beyond his power. The new terms it proceeded to draw up showed no sign of any willingness for a compromise. As before, all the leading Royalists were to be excluded from pardon, the establishment of Presbyterianism for an indefinite period was once more insisted upon, and toleration was refused not only to Catholics, but to all who used the liturgy. Cromwell's efforts to limit the duration of Presbyterianism to three or to seven years were unsuccessful. Parliament was as impracticable as the King, and while it was fruitlessly discussing proposals which could produce no agreement, the progress of the democratic movement in the army threatened a new revolution.

Cromwell's negotiations with the King, his speeches in favour of monarchy, his modification of the terms offered by the army to Charles, and his attempt to moderate the terms offered by Parliament, all exposed him to suspicion. While Charles distrusted Cromwell and Ireton because they asked for no personal favours or advantages for themselves, both were freely accused of having made a private bargain with the King for their own advancement. Cromwell, it was said, was to be made Earl of Essex as his kinsman had been, Captain of the King's guard, and a Knight of the Garter; Ireton was to be Lord-Lieutenant of Ireland. Royalists spread these stories in order to sow division between Cromwell and the army; the soldiers swallowed them because they feared the restoration of the monarchy. The pamphleteers of the Levellers, as the extreme Radicals were popularly termed, published broadcast vague charges of treachery and double-dealing against the army leaders. Sometimes Cromwell was described as an honest man led astray by the ambitious Ireton; at other times the two were regarded as confederates in evil, whose occasional differences of opinion were merely a device to throw dust in the eyes of the world. In their appeals to Cromwell there was a touch of surprise and sorrow. "O my once much honoured Cromwell," wrote Wildman, "can that breast of yours—the quondam palace of freedom—harbour such a monster of wickedness as this regal principle?" While Wildman hoped "to waken Cromwell's conscience from the dead," Lilburn, confessing that his good thoughts of Cromwell were not yet wholly gone, threatened to pull him down from his fancied greatness before he was three months older.

These attacks shook the confidence of the soldiers in their chiefs, and fanned the sparks of discontent into a flame. The Agitators, once ardent for an agreement with the King, began to demand the immediate rupture of the negotiations with him. Let the army, said they, take the settlement of the nation into its own hands, since neither their generals nor the Parliament could accomplish it. In October, five regiments of horse cashiered their old representatives as too moderate, elected fresh Agents, and laid their demands before Fairfax.

The existing Parliament was to be dissolved within a year, and in future there were to be biennial parliaments, equal constituencies, and manhood suffrage. Nothing was said of King or House of Lords, but the abolition of both was tacitly assumed. A declaration accompanied this draught constitution, by which freedom of conscience, freedom from impressment, and equality before the law were asserted to be the native rights of every Englishman—rights which no Parliament or Government had power to diminish or to take away. The officers had proposed a more limited monarchy—an adaptation of the old constitution to the new conditions which the Civil War had created. What the soldiers demanded was a democratic republic, based on a written constitution drawn up in accordance with abstract principles new to English politics.

The soldiers asked that their scheme, which they termed "The Agreement of the People," should be at once submitted to the nation for its acceptance. Parliament was to be set aside by a direct appeal to the people as the only lawful source of all political authority. Against this, Cromwell and Ireton protested. The army, they said, had entered into certain engagements in its recent declarations to the nation, and the pledges made in them must be observed. Both declared that unless these public promises were kept they would lay down their commissions, and act no longer with the army. Equally strong were their objections to some of the principles which the "Agreement" contained, and the method in which it was proposed to impose it upon the nation. "This paper," said Cromwell, "doth contain in it very great alterations of the government of the kingdom—alterations of that government it hath been under ever since it was a nation. What the consequences of such an alteration as this would be, even if there were nothing else to be considered, wise and godly men ought to consider." The proposed constitution contained much that was specious and plausible, but also much that was very debatable. And while they were debating it, other schemes equally plausible might be put forward by other parties.

"And not only another and another, but many of this kind. And if so, what do you think the consequences of that would be? Would it not be confusion? Would it not be utter confusion? Would it not make England like Switzerland, one canton of the Swiss against another, and one county against another? And what would that produce but an absolute desolation to the nation? I ask you," he concluded, "whether it be not fit for every honest man seriously to lay that upon his heart?"

Moreover, not only the consequences but the ways and means of accomplishing a thing ought to be considered. Granted that this was the best possible constitution for the people of England, still the difficulty of its attainment was a very real objection.

"I know," said he, "a man may answer all difficulties with faith, and faith will answer all difficulties where it really is; but we are very apt all of us to call that faith which perhaps may be but carnal imagination and carnal reasoning." Faith could remove mountains, "but give me leave to say there will be very great mountains in the way of this."

Cromwell's mention of difficulties called up Colonel Rainsborough, the leader of the democratic party amongst the officers.

"If ever we had looked upon difficulties," cried Rainsborough, "I do not know that ever we should have looked an enemy in the face. Let difficulties be round about you, though you have death before you, and the sea on each side of you and behind you; if you are convinced that the thing is just, I think you are bound in consequence to carry it on; and I think at the last day it can never be answered to God that you did not do it. For it is a poor service to God and the kingdom to take their pay and to decline their work."

"Perhaps," answered Cromwell with quiet dignity, "we have all of us done our parts not affrighted with difficulties, one as well as another, and I hope all purpose henceforward to do so still. I do not think that any man here wants courage to do that which becomes an honest man and an Englishman to do. But we speak as men that desire to have the fear of God before our eyes, and men that may not resolve to do that which we do in the power of a fleshly strength, but to lay this as the foundation of all our actions, to do that which is the will of God."

When it came to a discussion of the details of the Proposals the fiercest debate arose on the question of manhood suffrage.

"Every man born in England," argued Rainsborough, "the poor man, the meanest man in the kingdom," ought to have a voice in choosing those who made the laws under which he was to live and die. It was a natural right, part of every Englishman's birthright, and part of the liberty for which the soldiers had shed their blood. "It was the ground that we took up arms," said one of them, "and it is the ground which we shall maintain."

Ireton answered that to give a vote to men who had no stake in the country would endanger both liberty and property. Logically, he argued, the theory of natural rights implied a claim to property as well as a claim to political power. Cromwell, while agreeing that universal suffrage "did tend very much to anarchy," dismissed abstract principles altogether, and expressed his willingness to assent to a reasonable extension of the franchise.

Next came a struggle on the question of the King and the Lords. Cromwell protested that he had no private pledges to either, and no wish to preserve them, if their preservation was incompatible with the safety of the nation. The democratic party in the council held that both the monarchy and the Upper House must be abolished, and that their retention in any shape was dangerous. Cromwell's view was that at present, considering its public engagements, the army could not with justice and honesty either abolish them or set them aside, and therefore he desired to maintain both so far as it could be done without hazard to the public interest. Some boldly asserted that the power of King and Lords was part of that Babylon which God would destroy, and pleaded their own convictions to that effect as a revelation from heaven. Cromwell replied with a warning against "imaginary revelations." Like them, he said, he believed in the fulfilment of the prophecies in the Bible. "I am one of those whose heart God hath drawn out to wait for some extraordinary dispensations, according to those promises that He hath held forth of things to be accomplished in the later times, and I cannot but think that God is beginning of them." He was inclined to agree with those who held that God would overthrow King and Lords. Yet let them not make those things a rule to them which they could not clearly know to be the mind of God. Let them not say, "This is the mind of God, we must work to it." If it was God's purpose to destroy the power of King and Lords, He could do it without necessitating the army to dishonour itself by breaking its engagements. Let them wait for God's time, and do their plain, immediate duty. "Surely what God would have us do He does not desire we should step out of the way for it."

In these discussions Fairfax was absent or silent. Ireton's readiness in debate and knowledge of constitutional law and political theory made him the spokesman of the superior officers. He had a firm grasp of the principles involved, possessed great logical acuteness, and spoke with clearness, vigour, and even eloquence. But he was too dogmatic and too unconciliatory to convince opponents. With less dialectical skill and much less facility in expressing himself, Cromwell was an infinitely more effective speaker. What distinguished his speeches was an unfailing moderation and good sense which even the visionaries and demagogues whom he combated were forced to acknowledge. Neither religious nor political formulas blinded him to facts. Avowing that the good of the people was the proper end of government, and admitting that all political power was properly derived from the people, he denied the conclusion of the democrats that a republic was the only legitimate government for England. At the very outset of these debates he laid down the rule that in proposing any important political change the first thing to consider was "whether the spirit and temper of the people of this nation are prepared to go along with it." For that reason he declared his preference for monarchy. "In the government of nations that which is to be looked after is the affections of the people, and that I find which satisfies my conscience in the present thing." The particular form of government seemed to him quite unimportant compared with its acceptability to the people. Consider, he argued, the example of the Jews. They were governed successively by patriarchs, by judges, and by kings, and under all these different kinds of government they were happy and contented. Moreover there were things more important than the civil government of a state. Even if you change the government to the best possible kind of government, "it is but a moral thing." Less important, Cromwell meant, than religious freedom. "It is but, as Paul says, dross and dung in comparison with Christ." Why then should they contest so much for merely temporal things? If every man in the kingdom should insist on fighting to realise what he thought the best form of government, "I think the State will come to desolation."

In the background of Cromwell's mind there was always this desire to avoid a new civil war, and this dread of anarchy. It determined him now to put a stop to the spread of insubordination amongst the soldiers, and to limit the political action of the army to a minimum. Without obedience to its officers, he declared, the army would cease to exist. It was intolerable that private men, such as the Agents were, should take upon themselves to issue orders and call a rendezvous of a troop or a regiment. "This way is destructive to the army and to every man in it. I have been informed by some of the King's party that if they give us rope enough we shall hang ourselves." Soldiers must obey their officers: officers must submit to the decisions of Parliament. The army should leave Parliament to decide what government was fittest for the nation, and content itself with requiring that Parliaments should be fairly elected, frequently summoned, and dissolved in due season. As it needed the support of some civil authority, it must own the authority of Parliament. For his own part, he added, he would lay hold of anything, "if it had but the face of authority," rather than have none.

The struggle in the council lasted nearly a fortnight, but in the end Cromwell prevailed. The "Agreement of the People" was converted into a series of proposals to be offered to Parliament, instead of being accepted as a constitution to be imposed on people and Parliament. The demand for universal suffrage became a request for the extension of the franchise. Monarchy and the House of Lords were not to be swept away altogether, but henceforth limited in authority and subordinated to the House of Commons. The old constitution was to be preserved and amended, but not superseded by a new one.

By this time, however, even those officers who were anxious to retain the monarchy had begun to doubt whether it was possible to retain the King. For some weeks past their negotiations with Charles had been completely broken off, and distrust of his sincerity had become general. It was well known that he was intriguing with the commissioners who had lately arrived in England from the Scottish Parliament, and very little was expected from the propositions which the English Parliament was preparing to send to him. The democratic party—the Levellers, as they were now termed—were demanding not only his dethronement, but his punishment. On November 11, 1647, Colonel Harrison, in a committee of the Council of the Army, denounced the King as a man of blood, whom they ought to bring to judgment. All Cromwell said in reply was, that there were cases in which for prudential reasons the shedder of blood might be allowed to escape unpunished. David, for instance, had allowed Joab to escape the penalty due for the murder of Abner, "lest he should hazard the spilling of more blood, in regard the sons of Zeruiah were too strong for him." If the King deserved punishment, he concluded, it was rather the duty of Parliament than the army to do justice upon him. In any case, Cromwell was resolved to keep the King safe from the threatened attempts of the Levellers against his life. "I pray have a care of your guard," he wrote to his cousin, Colonel Whalley, "for if such a thing should be done, it would be accounted a most horrid act."

The same night the King escaped from the custody of Colonel Whalley at Hampton Court, and on November 15th news came that he had reached Carisbrooke Castle in the Isle of Wight. Contemporary pamphleteers and memoir writers often put forward the theory that Cromwell frightened the King into this flight from Hampton Court in order to forward his own ambitious designs. This is the view expressed in the well-known lines of Marvell, which relate how

> *Twining subtle fears with hope*
>
> *He wove a net of such a scope*
>
> *As Charles himself might chase*
>
> *To Carisbrooke's narrow case,*
>
> *That thence the royal actor borne*
>
> *The tragic scaffold might adorn.*

There is no evidence in support of this theory. In the long run, the King's flight was one of the causes of his dethronement and execution, and so of Cromwell's elevation to supreme power. At the moment, it increased Cromwell's difficulties, and added to the dangers which beset the Government. At Hampton Court the King was in the safe hands of Colonel Whalley, Cromwell's cousin, who could be relied upon to observe the orders of the General. At Carisbrooke he was in the hands of Colonel Hammond—a connection indeed of Cromwell's by his marriage with a daughter of John Hampden, but a man as to whose action under "the great temptation" of the King's appeal to his loyalty, Cromwell was painfully uncertain. Cromwell's letters to Hammond prove this. For the next six weeks the question whether Hammond would obey Fairfax and the Parliament, or allow Charles to go where he chose, remained unsettled.

The real cause of the King's flight was his intrigue with the Scottish Commissioners. In October, they had promised him Scotland's assistance in recovering his throne, if he would make satisfactory concessions about religion. But the one thing essential to the completion of the bargain was that Charles should escape from the hands of the army, and be able to treat freely. The plan for the King's flight was arranged early in November. The Scots urged him to take refuge at Berwick; he thought of Jersey, but preferred to remain in England; finally he determined on the Isle of Wight, at the suggestion of one of his attendants who believed Hammond to be a Royalist at heart. Safe in the Isle of Wight, Charles thought he could negotiate with Parliament, Scots, and officers, and accept the terms offered by the highest bidder. If negotiation failed, escape to France would not be difficult.

For six months Charles had succeeded in playing off Parliament against Army, and Army against Parliament. But the result had been to make him thoroughly distrusted by both, and his flight from Hampton Court united them against him. The King had hoped much from the divisions of the army, but simultaneously with his arrival at Carisbrooke Cromwell and Fairfax reduced their troops to obedience again. On November 8th, Cromwell carried a vote for the temporary suspension of the sittings of the Council, and sent Agitators and officers back to their regiments. A week later Fairfax held a general review of the army, dividing it into three brigades, which met at three different places. At each review he solemnly engaged himself to the soldiers to stand by them in securing the redress of their military grievances and the reform of Parliament, exacting from them in return a signed pledge to obey the orders of the General and council of war. At the first rendezvous, which took place near Ware on November 15th, there was some opposition. The Levellers tried to convert it into a general demonstration in favour of the "Agreement of the People." Two regiments came there unsummoned, wearing the "Agreement of the People" in their hats, with the motto, "England's Freedom, Soldiers' Rights." They had driven away their own officers, called on other regiments to do the like, and planned the seizure of Cromwell as a traitor to the cause of the people. But when he rode up to the mutineers none dared to lay hands on him. "Lieutenant-General Cromwell's carriage, with his naked waved sword, daunted the soldiers with the paper in their hats, and made them pluck it out and be subjected to command." One soldier was tried, and shot on the field; others, including several officers, were reserved for the judgment of a future court-martial. On November 19th, Cromwell was able to report to Parliament that the army was very quiet and obedient, and received the thanks of the Commons for his services.

Meanwhile the King sent a message to Parliament from the Isle of Wight, offering various concessions and asking to be admitted to a personal treaty at London. He applied also to the army leaders, urging them to support his request, to which they coldly replied that they were the Parliament's army, and must refer those matters to it. Parliament, equally distrustful of Charles, answered his overtures by drawing up an ultimatum, consisting of four bills, to which his assent was required before any treaty should begin. Their chief demand was the direct control of the militia for the next twenty years, and a share in its control when that period ended. Other constitutional questions might be left to discussion, but they must make sure that the King could never use force to impose his will upon the nation. Driven to extremity by this demand, Charles turned once more to the Scottish Commissioners, who had now arrived at Carisbrooke. He found them ready enough to sacrifice the liberties of Englishmen, and they promised him restoration to all the rights of his crown in return for the three years' establishment of Presbyterianism in England, the rigid suppression of Independents and other heretics, and certain privileges for Scotland and the Scottish nobility. If Parliament refused to disband its forces and to treat with the King in London, an army was to cross the border and replace Charles on his throne (December 27, 1647). "The Engagement," as this treaty was termed, was wrapped in lead and buried in the castle garden till it could be safely smuggled out of the island. The next day the King definitely rejected the ultimatum of the English Parliament, and prepared to effect his escape to the continent.

It was too late. As soon as the King's answer was delivered, his guards were doubled and he was made a close prisoner. The two Houses were well aware that his refusal of their terms was due to some agreement with the Scots, although they were ignorant of its precise nature.

"The House of Commons," wrote Cromwell to Hammond, "is very sensible of the King's dealings and of our brethren's in this late transaction. You should do well, if you have anything that may discover juggling, to search it out, and let us know it. It may be of admirable use at this time, because we shall I hope go upon business in relation to them tending to prevent danger."

On January 3, 1648, the House of Commons voted that they would make no further addresses to the King, and receive no more messages from him. Cromwell and Ireton, who had opposed the resolution to that effect which Marten had brought forward in the previous September, now spoke earnestly in its favour. "It was now expected," said Cromwell, "that the Parliament should govern and defend the kingdom by their own power, and not teach the people any longer to expect safety and government from an obstinate man whose heart God had hardened." In such a policy, he added, the army would stand by the Parliament against all opposition: but if the Parliament neglected to provide for its own safety and that of the nation, the army would be forced to seek its own preservation by other means.

Events had thus driven Cromwell to be the foremost advocate of that policy of completely setting aside the King which he had long so stubbornly opposed. Yet, though convinced that the King could not be trusted, he was not prepared to abandon monarchy. At a conference on the settlement of the government which took place early in 1648, the "Commonwealth's-men," as the republicans were termed, pressed for the immediate establishment of a free commonwealth and the trial of the King. Ludlow noted with great dissatisfaction that Cromwell and his friends "kept themselves in the clouds, and would not declare their judgments either for a monarchical, aristocratic, or democratic government; maintaining that any of them might be good in themselves, or for us, according as Providence should direct us." When he pressed Cromwell privately for the grounds of his objection to a republic, Cromwell replied that he was convinced of the desirableness of what was proposed, but not of the feasibility of it. There is evidence that during the spring of 1648 the Independent leaders discussed a scheme for deposing Charles I., and placing the Prince of Wales or the Duke of York upon the throne. But the unwillingness of the Prince and the escape of the Duke to France frustrated this plan.

While seeking to find some compromise which would prevent a new war, Cromwell endeavoured to unite all sections of the parliamentary party to meet it, if it came. The reunion of the army had already been effected. It was completed in a series of council meetings held at London during December, 1647, in which the officers under arrest for insubordination were pardoned, and a personal reconciliation took place between Cromwell and Rainsborough. In February and March, 1648, Cromwell made conciliatory overtures to the Presbyterians of the City, but as nothing short of the restoration of the King to his authority would content them, the negotiations failed. As little could Cromwell succeed in overcoming the distrust and hostility which the advanced party amongst the Independents now felt towards him. On January 19, 1648, John Lilburn, at the bar of the House of Lords, publicly accused him of high treason. Nor was it only his dealings with the King that made him the object of suspicion. During the last year his political attitude had continually altered. In April, he had urged the army to disband peaceably; in June, he had headed its revolt; in November, he had forced it into obedience to the Parliament again. And besides his apparent inconsistency, he was notoriously indifferent to principles which Levellers and Commonwealth's-men held all-important. To them a republic meant freedom and a monarchy bondage. For him the choice between the two was a question of expediency, and dependent upon circumstances. In open council he had declared that he "was not wedded or glued to forms of government," and in private he was said to have avowed that it was lawful to pass through all forms of government to accomplish his ends. It was not surprising, therefore, that men to whom his opportunism was unintelligible thought self-interest or ambition the natural explanation of his conduct, and that charges of hypocrisy and apostacy were freely made against him.

Through this cloud of detraction Cromwell pursued his way unmoved. Sometimes he answered his accusers with blunt defiance. "If any man say that we seek ourselves in doing this, much good may it do him with his thoughts. It shall not put me out of my way." At other times he referred to these slanders with a patient confidence that justice would be done to him in the end. "Though it may be," he wrote in September, 1647, "for the present a cloud may lie over our actions to those not acquainted with the grounds of them; yet we doubt not but God will clear our integrity from any other ends we aim at but His glory and the public good." Neither loss of popularity, misrepresentations, nor undeserved mistrust could diminish Cromwell's zeal for the cause. "I find this only good," he wrote on his recovery from a dangerous illness in the spring of 1648: "to love the Lord and His poor despised people, to do for them, and to be ready to suffer with them, and he that is found worthy of this hath obtained great favour from the Lord."

Not Cromwell's utterances only but his acts testify to the integrity of his motives. In March, 1648, Parliament settled an estate upon him as a reward for his services, to which he responded by offering to contribute a thousand a year, out of the seventeen hundred it brought in, to be employed in the recovery of Ireland. And so little did he dream of ever becoming himself the ruler of England, that at the very moment when fortune had opened the widest field to ambition, he began negotiations for the marriage of his eldest son to the daughter of a private gentleman of no great influence or position.

CHAPTER X
THE SECOND CIVIL WAR
1648

The Second Civil War broke out in Wales. It began with a revolt of officers and soldiers who had fought zealously for the Parliament throughout the first war. In February, 1648, Colonel Poyer, the governor of Pembroke Castle, refused to hand his charge over to the officer whom Fairfax had appointed to succeed him. In March, he openly declared for the King, and the troops of Colonel Laugharne, followed soon afterwards by their leader, joined Poyer's forces. In April, it became known in London that the Scots were raising an army to invade England, and at the end of the month parties of English Royalists, by Scottish help, seized Berwick and Carlisle. To meet these two dangers Fairfax sent Cromwell to suppress the Welsh insurgents and prepared to march north himself against the Scots.

At the beginning of May, Cromwell left London, taking with him two regiments of horse and three of foot. Poyer was full of confidence. He had won several small victories, and told his men that he would meet Cromwell in fair field, and that he would be himself the first man to charge "Ironsides," adding that if Cromwell "had a back of steel and a breast of iron, he durst and would encounter with him." But before Cromwell reached Wales, Colonel Horton defeated the boastful Poyer at St. Fagans, on May 8th, and when Cromwell arrived the war became a war of sieges. Chepstow was stormed by Colonel Ewer on May 25th, and Tenby surrendered to Colonel Horton at the end of May, but Pembroke Castle held out for over six weeks. Its walls were strong and its garrison desperate. Cromwell had no heavy artillery with him, and though he "scraped up," as he said, a few little guns, and made a breach, his assaults were repulsed with loss. The hostility of the country people and want of provisions added to the difficulties of the besiegers. "It's a mercy," wrote Cromwell to Fairfax, "that we have been able to keep our men together in such necessity, the sustenance of the foot for the most part being bread and water." The besieged, however, were in worse straits, and at last, on the 11th of July, starvation forced Poyer and Laugharne "to surrender themselves to the mercy of the Parliament" and give up town and castle.

Three days before Pembroke fell, Hamilton and the Scottish army crossed the border, and Fairfax was not there to face them. London was seething with discontent: there were riots in the city and in the eastern counties, and mass petitions from Essex, Kent, and Surrey urged Parliament to come to terms with the King and to disband the army. At the end of May a royalist rising broke out in Kent, and the fleet in the Downs declared for the King.

Fairfax collected eight or nine thousand men and set out for Kent. On June 1st, he forced his way into Maidstone, where the main body of the Kentish Royalists had posted themselves, and, after hard fighting in the barricaded streets, mastered the town, and broke up the insurgent army. A part of them, under old Lord Norwich, marched towards London, but found the city gates closed against them, and dispersed. Norwich himself, with five or six hundred horse, crossed the Thames, and called the Royalists of Essex to arms. Ere long four thousand men gathered round him, and Fairfax, leaving detachments to complete the subjugation of Kent, hurried to Essex to suppress this new rising. Norwich threw himself into Colchester, and a bloody battle took place in the suburbs, in which the raw levies of the Royalists repulsed Fairfax's veterans with great loss. The parliamentary general, seeing that he could not carry the town by a *coup de main*, was obliged to sit down to a regular siege, which ultimately developed into a blockade. Forts were built round Colchester, and connected by lines of intrenchments, to cut off all supplies and prevent any escape. The militia of Suffolk and Essex swelled Fairfax's small force of regulars and completed the investment. The besieged fought well and made vigorous sallies, but unless help came from without the end was inevitable. When the siege began, such relief seemed very probable. All over England little local risings were incessantly breaking out which threatened to become general unless they were at once suppressed. In June, there were risings in North Wales, Northamptonshire, and Nottinghamshire. At the beginning of July, Lord Holland and the young Duke of Buckingham gathered about six hundred Cavaliers at Kingston in the hope of relieving Colchester. But they were hunted from place to place by Fairfax's cavalry, and could never stay long enough anywhere to collect their partisans. The few who kept together were captured at St. Neots, in Huntingdonshire, on July 10th. At the end of July, Prince Charles and the revolted ships blockaded the Thames, hoping to persuade London to declare for the King by threatening its trade. But a fleet alone could not relieve Colchester, for Fairfax had occupied Mersea Island and cut off the town from the sea. Moreover, London remained quiet, for, though strongly Presbyterian in feeling, it had no desire to see the King restored unconditionally. The only hope of the besieged lay in the advance of Hamilton and the Scottish army.

In the north of England the Parliament had no force afoot strong enough to stop the Scots from marching southwards. Major-General Lambert, the commander-in-chief in the northern counties, with three or four regiments of regular horse and the local levies of Yorkshire and Lancashire, more than held his own against the English Royalists under Langdale and Musgrave, defeating them in the field and reducing the garrison of Carlisle to extremities. But when Hamilton advanced to relieve his allies, Lambert could only fall back, stubbornly skirmishing, into north Yorkshire, leaving the Scots to overrun Cumberland and the north. He, too, was hampered by risings in his rear, for early in June Pontefract Castle had been surprised by the Royalists, and later in the month Scarborough had declared for the King. On the 8th of July, when Hamilton entered England, he brought with him no more than ten thousand or eleven thousand men, but additional forces followed later, and including the English Royalists under Langdale and Musgrave he had, by the next month, about twenty-four thousand men under his command. He marched slowly in order to give time for his reinforcements to come up, and spent some time in besieging Appleby and other northern castles. It was only about the middle of August that he resumed his advance and determined to push south through Lancashire.

Meanwhile, Cromwell was hurrying north to Lambert's aid. Even before Pembroke fell he had sent a portion of his horse northwards. As soon as it surrendered, he set out at once with the rest of his horse and the infantry. His men had not been paid for months, but his iron discipline kept them from plundering. The most part of his foot were shoeless and in rags, but boots were provided to meet them at Leicester. Marching by way of Gloucester and through the midlands, Cromwell reached Leicester on

August 1st, Nottingham on August 5th, and joined Lambert near Knaresborough in the West Riding on Saturday, August 12th. Some regiments had to be left to besiege Pontefract and Scarborough, so that their united forces came to no more than about eight thousand five hundred men, of whom about three thousand were horse. But three quarters of this army were old soldiers, and, as one of Cromwell's officers wrote, it was "a fine, smart army, fit for action."

Cromwell had hitherto been under the impression that the Scots intended to advance through Yorkshire, and, relieving Pontefract on their way, to march straight for London. He now learnt that Hamilton had chosen the Lancashire route, and was already on his way through that county. Accordingly, on Sunday, August 13th, he set out to cross the hills which separate Lancashire from Yorkshire, and to attack the invaders. On Monday night, he quartered at Skipton; on Tuesday night, at Gisburn. On Wednesday, he marched down the valley of the Ribble into Lancashire. Two courses were now open to him. He might cross by Hodder Bridge to the southern bank of the Ribble, and seek to bar Hamilton's advance southwards by placing himself somewhere in his path; or he might keep along the northern bank of the river and engage Hamilton somewhere near Preston itself. Cromwell chose the second course, and he did so with a full consciousness of the importance of the choice. "It was thought," he wrote, "that to engage the enemy to fight was our business," and to march straight upon Preston was more likely to bring about a battle because it seemed probable that Hamilton would stand his ground there. There was also a second reason. If he put himself to the south of Hamilton, a defeat would throw Hamilton back upon his supports in Westmoreland and on the road to Scotland. If he defeated Hamilton at Preston, he might be able to drive him southwards, separating him from his supports, and cutting off his line of retreat. Under such circumstances, a defeat would lead to the annihilation of the Scottish army instead of merely forcing it to retire to Scotland. It was for these reasons, and not by any happy accident, that Cromwell adopted the second plan. As he explained a couple of years later, "Upon deliberate advice we chose rather to put ourselves between their army and Scotland." All Wednesday, therefore, he continued his march down the northern bank of the Ribble, and camped his army for the night at Stonyhurst, about nine miles from Preston.

Meanwhile, Hamilton's army was marching through Lancashire as carelessly and loosely as if Cromwell were fifty miles away. Hamilton himself, with ten thousand foot and perhaps fifteen hundred horse, was at Preston. The Earl of Callendar and General Middleton, with the bulk of the Scottish horse, were at Wigan, fifteen miles ahead of the infantry, while thirty miles in the rear, at Kirby Lonsdale, in Westmoreland, lay Major-General Monro, with about three thousand veteran horse and foot drawn from the Scottish army in Ulster, and two or three thousand English Royalists under Sir Philip Musgrave. Between Cromwell and Preston, covering Hamilton's flank, was Sir Marmaduke Langdale's division of English Royalists, numbering three thousand foot and six hundred horse. Hamilton had been warned of the enemy's approach by Langdale, but discredited his information, and believed he was threatened merely by some Lancashire militia forces.

Early on Thursday, the 17th of August, Cromwell fell upon Langdale's division with tremendous vigour, and beating his foot from hedge to hedge drove them towards Preston. Langdale sent pressing appeals to Hamilton, but the Duke gave him no adequate support. Instead of helping him, he drew the Scottish foot out of Preston and to the south of the Ribble, in order to facilitate their junction with the cavalry at Wigan. To defend Preston, he kept merely a couple of brigades of foot, and the fifteen hundred or sixteen hundred horse of his rearguard. Against forces so divided, Cromwell's attack was irresistible. At nightfall on Thursday, Preston was in his possession, and not only the town but the bridge over the Ribble, and the second bridge over the Darwen, a mile or so to the south of it. His whole army was solidly planted between Hamilton and Scotland. Langdale's division had ceased to exist, and of Hamilton's two brigades of foot hardly a man had escaped. A thousand had fallen in the fight, Cromwell had four thousand prisoners, and his cavalry had chased Hamilton's flying horse ten miles on the road to Lancaster.

In the Scottish camp there was great distraction and depression. Hamilton's forces were still superior in number to Cromwell's, for he had six or seven thousand foot on the south side of the river, who had scarcely fired a shot, besides Middleton and the vanguard of cavalry at Wigan. But the Duke, who had shown plenty of personal courage, was weak and irresolute in council. Major-General Baillie, who commanded his foot, urged him to make a stand where he was until Middleton and the horse rejoined them. The Earl of Callendar, Hamilton's second in command, proposed that the foot should march away as soon as it was dark, to join Middleton, and Callendar's proposal was accepted. It involved the abandonment of Hamilton's train, for they had no horses left to draw the waggons; and all the ammunition except what the men carried in their flasks fell into Cromwell's hands. All night the Scottish infantry marched. "Our march," says one of them, "was very sad, the way being exceeding deep, the soldiers both wet, hungry, and weary, and all looked on their business as half ruined." They had lost many stragglers when they arrived at Wigan. On Friday morning, Cromwell, leaving the Lancashire militia to guard Preston and his prisoners, set out in pursuit of Hamilton with three thousand foot and twenty-five hundred horse. The fighting on Friday was mainly between the horse of the two armies. While the Scottish infantry were marching to Wigan to join Middleton, Middleton was marching to Preston to join them, and as he went by a different road they failed to meet. On reaching the camp of the infantry, he found nothing but deserted fires and a few stragglers, and turned back to follow Hamilton's track to Wigan. Cromwell's horsemen were at his heels all the way, "killing and taking divers," though Colonel Thornhaugh, who commanded Cromwell's van, was killed by a Scottish lancer.

Hamilton's army, when the horse joined, drew up on the moor, north of Wigan, as if to give battle, but, judging the ground disadvantageous, Hamilton retreated into the town before Cromwell came up. "We lay that night in the field," says Cromwell, "close by the enemy, being very dirty and weary, and having marched twelve miles of such ground as I never rode in my life, the day being very wet." There was no rest, however, for the Scots in Wigan. Their commanders resolved to make another night march to Warrington, intending to break down the bridge, and put the

Mersey between themselves and their pursuer. On Saturday, Cromwell's cavalry found the Scottish foot posted in a good position at Winwick, about three miles from Warrington.

"We held them in dispute," wrote Cromwell, "till our army came up, they maintaining the pass with great resolution for many hours, ours and theirs coming to push of pike and very close charges, which forced us to give ground; but our men by the blessing of God quickly recovered it, and charging very home upon them, beat them from their standing. We killed about a thousand of them, and took, as we believe, about two thousand prisoners."

This was the last stand the Scots made. When Cromwell reached Warrington the same Saturday evening, General Baillie and the rest of the Scottish infantry surrendered as prisoners of war. Hamilton and Callendar, with two or three thousand horse escaped into Cheshire, intending to join Lord Byron who was in arms for the King, but their fate was not long delayed. Cromwell sent Lambert with four regiments of horse in pursuit, and called on the neighbouring counties to send all the horses they could muster after the fugitives.

"They are so tired, and in such confusion, that if my horse could but trot after them I could take them all. But we are so weary we can scarce be able to do more than walk after them. My horse are miserably beaten out—and I have ten thousand of them prisoners."

Skirmishing incessantly with the country people and the local militia, Hamilton made his way as far as Staffordshire, party after party of his followers dropping off by the way, either to surrender or to escape in disguise. With the few who remained, he capitulated to Lambert at Uttoxeter, on Friday, August 25th. On the Monday following, Colchester surrendered to Fairfax, and the Second Civil War was practically over.

After the capitulation at Warrington, Cromwell turned northwards again as soon as his soldiers could march. Monro and his six thousand men were still undisposed of, and he feared an attack from them upon the forces left at Preston. Colonel Ashton, who commanded at Preston, had under his charge prisoners more in number than his troops, and like Henry V. at Agincourt Cromwell had ordered Ashton to put the prisoners to the sword if he were attacked. But nothing was farther from Monro's mind than an advance. On the news of the defeat at Preston, he retreated at once, marched through Durham, and re-entered Scotland. Garrisons were left in Berwick and Carlisle, which Cromwell summoned as soon as he came up, and when they refused to surrender he made a formal application to the Scottish Committee of Estates for their restoration. To give force to his demand he marched his army across the Tweed, protesting at the same time that he had no quarrel with the Scottish nation. If he entered Scotland it was simply to overthrow the faction which had instigated the late invasion.

"We are so far from seeking the harm of the well affected people of Scotland, that we profess as before the Lord, that we shall use our endeavours to the utmost that the trouble may fall upon the contrivers and authors of this breach, and not upon the poor innocent people, who have been led and compelled into this action, as many poor souls now prisoners to us confess."

A revolution in Scotland facilitated Cromwell's policy. The rigid Presbyterians of the west country, who abhorred any union with Episcopalians and Malignants, and cared more for the Kirk than the Crown, had risen in arms and seized Edinburgh. Argyle and his Highlanders backed them, and on September 26th the Hamiltonian faction, who formed the Committee of Estates, agreed to send Monro's force back to Ireland, to disband their men, and to give up power to their rivals. Argyle's party was only too glad to come to terms with Cromwell, and to procure the support of his army against their opponents, till they could organise a substantial force of their own. Orders were sent for the immediate surrender of Carlisle and Berwick, and Cromwell came to Edinburgh to treat with Argyle. "Give assurance," demanded Cromwell, "that you will not admit or suffer any that have been active in or consenting to the engagement against England, to be employed in any public place or trust whatsoever. This is the least security I can demand." There was nothing the rival faction would more willingly do, and by an Act of the Scottish Parliament "the Engagers," as Hamilton's partisans were called, were permanently excluded from political power.

Cromwell left three regiments in Scotland for a few weeks to secure the new government, and returned with the bulk of his army to England. Scarborough and Pontefract still remained to be captured, but the Second Civil War was over. Some of Cromwell's friends amongst the Independent leaders blamed his agreement with Argyle, and saw no security for England in the predominance of a bigoted Presbyterian faction at Edinburgh. They thought that Cromwell should either have exacted more substantial guarantees for future peace, or divided power between the two parties, so that they would balance each other, and be incapable of injuring England. Cromwell answered that the one hope of future peace between the two nations lay in creating a good understanding between English Independents and Scotch Presbyterians, and that he had taken the only course which could produce it.

"I desire from my heart—I have prayed for—I have waited for the day to see—union and right understanding between the godly people—Scots, English, Jews, Gentiles, Presbyterians, Anabaptists, and all. Our brothers of Scotland—sincerely Presbyterians—were our greatest enemies. God hath justified us in their sight—caused us to requite good for evil—caused them to acknowledge it publicly by acts of State and privately, and the thing is true in the sight of the Sun.... Was it not fit to be civil, to profess love, to deal with clearness with them for the removing of prejudices; to ask them what they had against us, and to give them an honest answer? This we have done and no more: and herein is a more glorious work in our eyes than if we had gotten the sacking and plunder of Edinburgh, the strong castle, into our hands, and made a conquest from the Tweed to the Orcades; and we can say, through God, we have left such a witness amongst them, as, if it work not yet, by reason the poor souls are so wedded to their Church government, yet there is that conviction upon them that will undoubtedly have its fruit in due time."

He came back to England with the confident hope that peace with Scotland was henceforth secure.

CHAPTER XI
CROMWELL AND THE KING'S EXECUTION
1648–1649

While Fairfax and Cromwell were fighting the armies raised in the King's name, the Parliament was once more negotiating with Charles I. In spite of the vote for no addresses, passed on January 17, 1648, April was not over before both Houses were discussing the reopening of negotiations. Petition after petition came from the City demanding a personal treaty with the King, and the House of Lords echoed the demand. The Lords were so zealous for a peace that when Hamilton and the Scots invaded England they refused to join the Lower House in declaring them enemies. The Commons, more cautious, insisted that the King should accept certain preliminaries before any treaty began, and refused to allow him to come to London to treat. At last the two Houses arrived at a compromise, and on August 1st it was agreed that there should be a personal treaty with Charles in the Isle of Wight. The Commissioners of Parliament met the King at Newport on September 18th, a couple of days before Cromwell entered Scotland. Charles consented to annul his former declarations against the Parliament, and to admit that they had undertaken the war "in their just and lawful defence." He promised the establishment of the Presbyterian system for three years, and a limited Episcopacy afterwards. He even offered the control of the militia for twenty years and the settlement of Ireland in such fashion as Parliament should think best. The question whether these concessions were a sufficient basis for lasting peace is one on which modern historians have differed as much as contemporary politicians did. It is certain that the King was not sincere in making them. "To deal freely with you," wrote Charles to one of his friends, "the great concession I made this day—the Church, militia, and Ireland—was made merely in order to my escape.... My only hope is, that now they believe I dare deny them nothing, and so be less careful of their guards." The Presbyterian leaders argued and haggled in the hope of obtaining the permanent establishment of Presbyterianism, but the question whether any treaty would bind the King they neglected to take into account.

Meanwhile a dangerous excitement was spreading in the army. From an agreement between the Presbyterians and the Royalists, an Independent army had much to fear. The first result of the treaty would be a general disbanding. To be dismissed with a few shillings in his pocket, but without security for his arrears, or indemnity for his acts during the war, was the most a soldier could expect. If any sectary who had fought for the Parliament hoped that it would give him freedom to worship as his conscience dictated, the act against heresy and blasphemy, passed in May, 1648, had shown the futility of his hopes. Whether Episcopacy or Presbyterianism gained the upper hand, toleration would be at an end as soon as he laid down his arms. Add to this, that the soldiers were firmly convinced that the proposed treaty afforded no security for the political liberties of the nation. Once restored to his authority, Charles would, either by force or by intrigue, shake off the restrictions the treaty imposed, and rear again that fabric of absolutism, which it had cost six years' fighting to overthrow. The renewal of the war had heightened their distrust of Charles, and embittered their hostility to him. The responsibility for the first Civil War had been laid upon the King's evil counsellors; the responsibility for the second was laid upon the King himself. It was at his instigation, said the officers, that conquered enemies had taken up arms again, old comrades apostatised from their principles, and a foreign army invaded England. In a great prayer-meeting held at Windsor before they separated for the campaign, they pledged themselves to bring this responsibility home to the King. "We came," wrote one of them, "to a very clear resolution, that it was our duty, if ever the Lord brought us back again in peace, to call Charles Stuart, that man of blood, to an account for the blood he had shed, and mischief he had done to the utmost, against the Lord's cause and people in these poor nations." They were equally determined to punish the King's instruments. At the close of the first war, the army had shown itself more merciful than the Parliament, but the second war made it fierce, implacable, and resolute to exact blood for blood. Fairfax's execution of Lucas and Lisle, two royalist leaders taken at Colchester, "in part of avenge for the innocent blood they have caused to be spilt," was a sign of this change of temper.

Cromwell shared this vindictive feeling towards the authors of the second war. When he took Pembroke, he excepted certain persons from the terms of the capitulation and reserved them for future punishment.

"The persons excepted," he wrote to Parliament, "are such as have formerly served you in a very good cause; but being now apostatised, I did rather make election of them than of those who had always been for the King; judging their iniquity double, because they have sinned against so much light, and against so many evidences of Divine Providence going along with and prospering a just cause, in the management of which they themselves had a share."

He was equally exasperated against those who had promoted the Scottish invasion.

"This," he said, "is a more prodigious treason than any that hath been perfected before; because the former quarrel was that Englishmen might rule over one another, this to vassalise us to a foreign nation. And their fault that appeared in this summer's business is certainly double to theirs who were in the first, because it is the repetition of the same offence against all the witnesses that God hath borne."

The moral he drew from his victory at Preston was that Parliament should use it to protect peaceable Christians of all opinions, and punish disturbers of the peace of every rank.

"Take courage," he told them, "to do the work of the Lord in fulfilling the end of your magistracy, in seeking the peace and welfare of this land—that all that will live peaceably may have countenance from you, and they that are incapable, and will not leave troubling the land, may speedily be destroyed out of the land. If you take courage in this God will bless you, and good men will stand by you, and God will have glory, and the land will have happiness by you in despite of all your enemies."

When Cromwell returned from Scotland, he found the Parliament preparing to replace the King on his throne, and to content itself with banishing some dozen of the royalist leaders. Regiment after regiment of Fairfax's army was presenting its general with petitions against the treaty and demands for the punishment of the authors of the war. Cromwell's troops imitated their example, and in forwarding their petitions to Fairfax, their leader expressed his complete agreement with his soldiers.

"I find," he wrote, "a very great sense in the officers ... for the sufferings and ruin of this poor kingdom, and in them all a very great zeal to have impartial justice done upon all offenders; and I do in all from my heart concur with them, and I verily think they are things which God puts into our hearts."

On November 20, 1648, the army in the south sent Parliament a "Remonstrance," demanding the rupture of the negotiations, and the punishment of the King as "the grand author of all our troubles." Cromwell approved of this declaration, and told Fairfax he saw "nothing in it but what is honest, and becoming honest men to say and offer." It would have been better, he thought, to wait till the treaty was concluded, before making their protest, but now that it had been made he was prepared to support it. The Newport treaty seemed to him to be a complete surrender to Charles. "They would have put into his hands," he said later, "all that we had engaged for, and all our security would have been a little bit of paper." No one knew better than Cromwell that a mere protest would not stop the Parliament, and he was ready to use force if necessary. The arguments by which he justified its employment are fully stated in his letter to his friend, Robert Hammond, whose scruples he sought to overcome.

Was it not true that the safety of the people was the supreme law? Was it not certain that this treaty would undo all that had been gained by the war, and make things worse than before the war began? If resistance to authority was lawful at all, was it not as lawful to oppose the Parliament as it was to oppose the King?

"Consider," he urged, "whether this army be not a lawful power called by God to oppose and fight against the King upon some stated grounds; and being in power to such ends, may not oppose one name of authority for those ends as well as another name,—since it was not the outward authority summoning them that by its power made the quarrel lawful, but the quarrel that was lawful in itself."

These, however, were but "fleshly reasonings," and there were higher arguments. "Let us look into providences; surely they mean somewhat. They hang so together; have been so constant, so clear, unclouded."

The victories God had given could not be meant to end in such a sacrifice of His cause and His people as "this ruining hypocritical agreement." "Thinkest thou in thy heart that the glorious dispensations of God point to this?" The determination of the army to prevent the treaty was also God's doing. "What think you of Providence disposing the hearts of so many of God's people this way? We trust the same Lord who hath framed our minds in our actings is with us in this also." There were difficulties to be encountered and enemies not few—"appearance of united names, titles, and authorities"; yet they were not terrified, "desiring only to fear our great God that we do nothing against His will."

Briefly stated, Cromwell's argument was that the victories of the army, and the convictions of the godly, were external and internal evidence of God's will, to be obeyed as a duty. It was dangerous reasoning, and not less dangerous that secular and political motives coincided with the dictates of religious enthusiasm. Similar arguments might be held to justify not merely the temporary intervention of the army, but its permanent assumption of the government of England. Practical good sense and conservative instincts prevented Cromwell from adopting the extreme consequences of his theory; with most of his comrades the logic of fanaticism was qualified by no such considerations.

As Parliament continued the treaty without attending to their Remonstrance, the army determined to employ force. On December 1st, officers sent by Fairfax seized Charles at Newport and removed him to Hurst Castle in Hampshire. The next day, Fairfax and his troops occupied London. Undeterred, the House of Commons resolved by 129 votes to eighty-three that the King's answers were a ground to proceed upon for the settlement of the kingdom. The same evening, the commanders of the army and the leaders of the parliamentary minority held a conference to decide what was to be done. On their march, the officers had declared their intention of dissolving the Long Parliament, and constituting the faithful minority a provisional government until a new Parliament could meet. But now, in deference to the wishes of their friends in Parliament, they resolved, instead, to expel the Presbyterian majority from the House, and to leave the Independent minority in possession of the name and authority of a Parliament. On December 6th, accordingly, Colonel Pride and a body of musketeers beset the doors of the House of Commons, seized some members as they sought to enter, and turned others back by force. The same process continued on the 7th, till forty-five members were under arrest, and some ninety-six others excluded.

Cromwell arrived at London on the night after "Pride's Purge" began, and took his seat next day amongst the fifty or sixty members who continued to sit in the House. Like the rest of the officers, he had contemplated a forcible dissolution and the calling of a new Parliament. But seeing that a different plan had been adopted by his friends on the spot, he did not hesitate to accept it. He said, "that he had not been acquainted with this design, but since it was done he was glad of it, and would endeavour to maintain it."

On the question of the King, a difference of opinion between Cromwell and the bulk of the officers soon showed itself. He approved of their seizure of Charles, and had no doubt of the justice of bringing him to trial. But he doubted the policy of the King's trial and condemnation, if any other satisfactory expedient could be devised to secure the rights of the nation. It might be that the King's deposition would be sufficient, or that he would at last make the concessions which he had hitherto refused. Of the discussions which went on in the council of officers during the next three weeks very little is known. There are vague rumours of a great division of opinion amongst them, of one party sternly insisting on the King's punishment, of another willing to be content with his deposition or imprisonment. We get glimpses of Cromwell negotiating with lawyers and judges about the settlement of the nation, inspiring a final attempt to come to terms with Charles, and arguing that it would be safe to spare the King's life, if he would accept the conditions now offered him. All these attempted compromises failed. The King preferred to part with his life rather than with his regal power, and unless he yielded no constitutional settlement was possible. So the military revolution, for a moment arrested in its progress, moved inevitably forward, and Cromwell went with it.

On December 23rd, Charles was brought to Windsor. "The Lord be with you and bless you in this great charge," wrote Cromwell to the governor, sending him therewith minute instructions for the safe-keeping of his captive. On the same day, the House of Commons appointed a committee "to consider how to proceed in the way of justice against the King." "If any man," Cromwell is reported to have said, "had deliberately designed such a thing, he would be the greatest traitor in the world, but 'the Providence of God' had cast it upon them."

Five days later an ordinance was introduced erecting a tribunal to try the King, to consist of three judges and a jury of 150 commissioners. On January 2, 1649, the ordinance was transmitted to the Lords, with a resolution declaring that "by the fundamental laws of this kingdom it is treason in the King of England for the time being to levy war against the Parliament and the kingdom of England." The unanimous rejection of this ordinance, and the discovery that the judges would refuse the part assigned to them, did not make the Commons draw back. A new ordinance was brought in, creating a court of 135 commissioners, who were to act both as judge and jury, and omitting the three judges. Fresh resolutions declared the people the original of all just power, the House of Commons the supreme power in the nation, and the laws passed by the Commons binding without consent of King or Lords. This ordinance, or, as it was now termed, act, was passed on January 6, 1649. It set forth that Charles Stuart had wickedly designed totally to subvert the ancient and fundamental laws of this nation, and in their place to introduce an arbitrary and tyrannical government; that he had levied and maintained a cruel war against Parliament and kingdom; and that new commotions had arisen from the remissness of Parliament to prosecute him. Wherefore that for the future "no chief officer or magistrate whatsoever may presume to imagine or contrive the enslaving or destroying of the English nation, and to expect impunity for trying or doing the same," the persons whose names followed were appointed to try the said Charles Stuart. On the 19th of January, the King was brought from Windsor to St. James's, guarded by troops of horse.

Ever since the eighth, the commissioners for the King's trial had been meeting in the Painted Chamber to settle their procedure. But nearly half of those named refused to accept the duty laid upon them. Some had fears for their own safety; some, political objections; others objected to the constitution or authority of the court. Algernon Sidney told his colleagues that there were two reasons why he could not take part in their proceedings. First, the King could not be tried by that court; secondly, that no man could be tried by that court. "I tell you," answered Cromwell, with characteristic scorn of constitutional formulas, "we will cut off his head with the crown upon it."

Nevertheless, the question of their authority was a question to which the court was bound to agree upon an answer. If a story told at the trial of the Regicides may be trusted, the commissioners were still at a loss for a formula on the morning of the 20th of January, when the trial began. As they sat in the Painted Chamber, news was brought that the King was landing at the steps which led up from the river.

"At which Cromwell ran to the window, looking on the King as he came up the garden; he turned as white as the wall ... then turning to the board said thus: 'My masters, he is come, he is come, and now we are doing that great work that the whole nation will be full of. Therefore I desire you to let us resolve here what answer we shall give the King when he comes before us, for the first question he will ask us will be by what authority and commission we do try him?' For a time no one answered. Then after a little space, Henry Marten rose up and said, 'In the name of the Commons in Parliament assembled and all the good people of England.'"

About one o'clock the court adjourned to Westminster Hall. At the upper or southern end of the Hall, a wooden platform had been constructed, covering all the space usually occupied by the Courts of Chancery and King's Bench. A wooden partition rising about three feet above the floor of this platform divided the court itself from the body of the Hall. On the lower side of this partition, running across the Hall from side to side, was a broad gangway fenced in by a wooden railing, and a similar gangway ran right down the Hall to the great door. Along the sides of the gangways, with their backs to the railings, stood a line of musketeers and pikemen, whose officers walked up and down the vacant space in the middle of the passages. The mass of the audience stood within the railed spaces between the sides of the Hall and the gangways, but on each side of the court itself, and directly overlooking it, were two small galleries, one above the other, reserved for specially favoured spectators. At the back of the court, immediately under the great window, sat the King's judges, about seventy in number, ranged on four or five tiers of benches which were covered with scarlet cloth. They wore their ordinary dress as officers or gentlemen. In the back row, on each side of the scutcheon bearing the arms of the Commonwealth of England, sat Cromwell and Harry Marten. In the centre of the front row of the judges, at a raised desk, sat Serjeant John Bradshaw, the president of the court, and on each side of him his assistants, Lisle and Say, dressed in black lawyer's gowns. About the middle of the floor of the court was a table where the two clerks were seated, and on the table lay the mace and the sword of State. In the front of the court, at the very edge of the platform, were three compartments, somewhat like pews, the backs of which were formed by the low partition separating the court from the Hall. In the central one were a crimson-velvet arm-chair, and a small table covered with Turkey carpet, on which were an inkstand and paper. Here sat the King, and in the partition on his right were the three lawyers who were counsel for the Commonwealth. The King had his face turned towards the president and his back to the crowd in the body of the Hall. As the floor of the court was higher than the floor of the Hall, the spectators stood, as it were, in the pit of a theatre, but the partition somewhat intercepted their view of the interior of the court. Yet they could see the King's head and shoulders above it.

Charles kept his hat on his head, and showed no sign of respect to the court.

"The prisoner," says the official account, "while the charge was reading, sat down in his chair, looking sometimes on the High Court, and sometimes on the galleries, and rose again, and turned about to behold the guards and spectators, and after sat down, looking very sternly, and with a countenance not at all moved, till these words '*Charles Stuart to be a tyrant*,' traitor, etc., were read; at which he laughed, as he sat, in the face of the court."

Throughout the trial, as the King's judges had anticipated, he declined to admit the jurisdiction of the court. On each of the three days when he appeared before it, on the 20th, the 22d, and the 23rd of January, he maintained his refusal to plead. "Princes," he had said in a declaration published in 1629, "are not bound to give an account of their actions but to God alone," and he now consistently repeated that "a king cannot be tried by any superior jurisdiction on earth." What excited more sympathy, however, was his association of the rights of his subjects with his own, and his claim to be defending both against the arbitrary power of the army.

"It is not my case alone," he said; "it is the freedom and liberty of the people of England; and do you pretend what you will, I stand more for their liberties. For if power without law may make laws, may alter the fundamental laws of the kingdom, I do not know what subject he is in England that can be sure of his life, or anything that he calls his own."

On Tuesday, the 23rd, after Charles had for a third time refused to plead, the court adjourned to the Painted Chamber, and the more determined members resolved to treat the King as contumacious, and proceed to pronounce judgment against him. Others opposed this course, and the next two days were spent in hearing evidence at private meetings of the court in the Painted Chamber—partly in order to gain time whilst the recalcitrant members of the court were being converted. One after another, a number of witnesses deposed that they had seen the King in arms against the Parliament. One had seen the royal standard set up at Nottingham. Another had seen the King at Newbury, in complete armour with his sword drawn, and had heard him exhort a regiment of horse to stand by him that day, for that his crown lay upon the point of the sword. A third swore that he heard Charles encourage his soldiers to strip and beat their prisoners when Leicester was stormed. Documents were also brought to prove the King's invitations to foreign forces to enter England. At length, on the evening of Thursday, the 25th, a vote that the court would proceed to sentence Charles Stuart to death was procured, and on the morning of the 26th, sixty-two commissioners agreed to the terms of the sentence which their committee had drawn up. It was resolved, however, that the King should be brought before the court to hear his sentence, instead of being condemned in his absence, and this was doubtless done in order to give him a chance to plead, in case he should repent of his contumacy.

On the afternoon of Saturday, January 27th, sixty-seven commissioners took their seats in Westminster Hall, headed by Bradshaw, who had now donned a scarlet gown in which to deliver sentence. Once more Charles refused to plead, requesting that before sentence was given he might be heard before the Lords and Commons assembled in the Painted Chamber. He had something to say, he declared, which was "most material for the welfare of the kingdom and the liberty of the subject.... I am sure on it, it is very well worth the hearing." It was afterwards rumoured that he meant to propose his own abdication, and the admission of his son to the throne upon such terms as should have been agreed upon. The court after a brief deliberation refused the request, and Bradshaw, after setting forth the prisoner's crimes and exhorting him to repentance, ordered the clerk to read the sentence. The King strove to speak. "Your time is now past," replied Bradshaw, and bade the clerk read on. After the sentence was read, all the commissioners stood up to testify their assent. Once more Charles endeavoured to obtain a hearing. "Sir, you are not to be heard after sentence," was the answer. He still struggled to be heard. "Guard, withdraw your prisoner," ordered the president. "I am not suffered to speak," cried the King. "Expect what justice other people will have."

As the King was led from the Court, the soldiers gave a great shout, crying fiercely, "Execution, execution!" Others, it was said, reviled him as he passed by them, and blew their tobacco smoke in his face. But outside, in the street, as he went from Westminster to Whitehall, "shop-stalls and windows were full of people, many of whom shed tears, and some of them with audible voices prayed for the King." It was clear that the feeling of the people was on the King's side, and that consideration, if no other, might well have induced the army leaders even at the last to draw back. But even had they wished it, the army would not have permitted them to do so. Moreover, Cromwell all through the trial never wavered or hesitated, and his influence kept the Regicides together. When the King's judges came to be tried for their own lives, some strove to represent themselves as acting under coercion. One said that Cromwell and Ireton laid hold of him and compelled him to take his place in the court; others described Cromwell as forcing recalcitrant judges to sign the death-warrant, and bearing down the little minority who wished the King to be heard after sentence had been pronounced. Colonel Ingoldsby boldly declared that Cromwell seized his hand and guided his pen, though the truth is that Ingoldsby's signature shows no signs of constraint. Many such legends circulate in contemporary literature, fictitious in themselves, yet all testifying to a well-founded popular impression. Cromwell had made up his mind that the King must die, and when his mind was made up he was inflexible. Against that will, all efforts to save the King were futile. Fairfax was applied to by Prince Charles, but while steadfastly refusing to take any part in the trial, he remained in all other respects a passive tool in the hands of his council of officers. The Dutch ambassadors appealed to Parliament, but what remained of Parliament was helpless or obdurate.

The commissioners of the Scottish Parliament presented public protests and made private appeals to the leaders of the army. They argued with Cromwell, telling him that the Covenant obliged both nations to preserve the King's person, and that to proceed to extremities against him was to break the league between England and Scotland. Cromwell answered them by a discourse on the nature of the regal power, asserting that a breach of trust in a king ought to be punished more than any other crime. As to the Covenant, its end was the defence of the true religion; if the King was the greatest obstacle to the establishment of the true religion, they were not bound to preserve him. "It pledged them," he added, "to bring to condign punishment all incendiaries and enemies to the cause, and were small offenders to be punished and the greatest of all to go free?"

Meanwhile, during Sunday and Monday, Charles prepared himself for death. He spent much time in prayer with Bishop Juxon, burnt his papers, distributed the small remains of his personal property, and took leave of his children. As he feared that the army would make the Duke of Gloucester king, he charged him in simple language not to take his "brother's throne."

"Sweetheart," said Charles, taking the child upon his knee, "now they will cut off thy father's head [upon which words the child looked very steadfastly upon him]; mark, child, what I say: They will cut off my head, and perhaps make thee a king; but mark what I say: You must not be a king so long as your brothers Charles and James do live; for they will cut off your brothers' heads when they can catch them, and cut off thy head, too, at the last; and therefore I charge you do not be made a king by them."

At which the child, sighing, said, "I will be torn in pieces first." What Charles said to his daughter, the Lady Elizabeth herself related:

"He wished me not to grieve and torment myself for him, for it would be a glorious death that he should die, it being for the laws and liberties of this land, and for maintaining the true Protestant religion. He told me he had forgiven all his enemies, and hoped God would forgive them also, and commanded us and all the rest of my brothers and sisters to forgive them. He bid me tell my mother that his thoughts had never strayed from her, and that his love should be the same to the last."

Then, striving to console her, he bade her again "not to grieve for him, for that he should die a martyr, and that he doubted not but the Lord would settle his throne upon his son, and that we should all be happier than we could have expected to have been if he had lived."

Monday night the King slept at St. James's. Two hours before the dawn of the 30th of January, he rose up, and, calling to his servant Herbert, bade him dress him with care. "Let me have a shirt more than ordinary," said he, "by reason the season is so sharp as probably may make me shake, which some will imagine proceeds from fear. I would have no such imputation; I fear not death. Death is not terrible to me. I bless my God I am prepared."

About ten o'clock, Colonel Hacker came to fetch the King to Whitehall. Attended by Herbert and Juxon, he walked through St. James's Park. A guard of halberdiers surrounded him, and companies of foot were drawn up on each side of his way. "The drums beat, and the noise was so great as one could hardly hear what another spoke." It was a cold, frosty morning, and the King walked, as his custom was, very fast, and calling to his guard "in a pleasant manner," told them to march apace. When he reached Whitehall, he was kept waiting in his bedchamber for two or three hours, perhaps in order to give Parliament time to pass an act forbidding the proclamation of any new king. During part of this time, he prayed with Juxon, and at the bishop's urging ate a mouthful of bread and drank a glass of claret. About half-past one, Hacker came again to summon the King to the scaffold. In the galleries and the Banqueting House, through which Charles followed him, men and women had stationed themselves to see the King go by. As he passed "he heard them pray for him, the soldiers not rebuking any of them, seeming by their silence and dejected faces afflicted rather than insulting."

From the middle window of the Banqueting House, Charles stepped out upon the scaffold. He was dressed in black from head to foot, but not in mourning, and wore the George and the ribbon of the Garter. The scaffold was covered with black cloth, and from the railings round it, which were as high as a man's waist, black hangings drooped. In the middle of the scaffold lay the block, "a little piece of wood, flat at bottom, about a foot and a half long," and about six inches high. By it lay "the bright execution axe for executing malefactors," which had been procured from the Tower— probably the very axe which had beheaded Strafford. Near the block stood two masked men; both were dressed in close-fitting frocks,—like sailors, said one spectator; like butchers, said another. One of them wore a grizzled periwig and seemed by his grey beard an old man. Immediately round the foot of the scaffold stood ranks of soldiers, horse and foot, and behind them a thronging mass of men and women. Other watchers filled the windows and the roofs of the houses round.

Seeing that his voice could not reach the people, Charles addressed himself to the persons on the scaffold, some fourteen or fifteen in number. He must clear himself, he said, as a man, a king, and a Christian. To encroach on the liberties of the people had never been his intent. The Parliament began this unhappy war, not himself. "But for all this," he continued, thinking of Strafford, "God's judgments are just. An unjust sentence that I suffered to take effect is now punished by an unjust sentence upon me."

Then the King forgave the causers of his death, and stated in a few words his conception of the cause for which he died.

"For the people, I desire their liberty and freedom as much as anybody whomsoever; but I must tell you that their liberty and freedom consists in having government, in those laws by which their life and goods may be most their own. It is not their having a share in government; that is nothing pertaining to them.... If I would have given way to have all changed according to the power of the sword, I needed not to have come here; and therefore I tell you (and I pray God it be not laid to your charge) that I am the martyr of the people."

O horrible Murder

But lo a Charg is drawne, a day is set

The Silent Lamb is brought, the Wolves are met;

And where's the Slaughterhouse? Whitehall must be,

Lately his Palace, now his Calvarie

And now ye Senators, is this the thing

So oft declard Is this your glorious King?

Religion vails her self; and Mourns that she

Is forc'd to own such Horrid Villanie.

When he had done, the King put his long hair under his cap, helped by Juxon and the grey-bearded man in the mask, and spoke a few words with Juxon. He took off his cloak and doublet, gave his George[1] to the bishop, and bade the executioner set the block fast. Then, as he stood, he said two or three words to himself, with hands and eyes lifted up, and lying down, placed his neck on the block. For a moment he lay there praying; his eye shining, said one of those who watched, as brisk and lively as ever he had seen it. Suddenly, he stretched forth his hands, and with one blow the grey-bearded man severed his head from his body. It was now, noted another spectator, precisely four minutes past two.

The other masked man took the King's head, and without a word held it up to the people. A groan broke from the thousands round the scaffold,— "such a groan," writes Philip Henry, "as I never heard before, and desire I may never hear again." Thereupon he saw two troops of horse, one marching towards Westminster, the other towards Charing Cross, roughly dispersing the crowd, and was glad to escape home without hurt.

The King's body was placed in a plain wooden coffin, covered with a black-velvet pall, then, after embalming, enclosed in an outer coffin of lead, and conveyed to St. James's. His servants wished to bury him at Westminster, in Henry the Seventh's Chapel, amongst his ancestors, but this was denied, because "it would attract infinite numbers of people of all sorts thither, which was unsafe and inconvenient." Windsor seemed safer, and the Parliament authorised Herbert to bury his master there, allowing

five hundred pounds for the expenses of the funeral. Leave was given to the Duke of Richmond, the Earl of Southampton, and two other noblemen to attend it. They selected a vault in St. George's Chapel, where Henry VIII. and Jane Seymour were interred, and laid the King's body there on Friday, the 9th of February. No service was read over him, for the governor would not allow Juxon to use the service in the Prayer-book, saying that the form in the Directory was the only one authorised by Parliament. To the mourners, however, it seemed that heaven gave a token of their dead sovereign's innocence.

"This is memorable," writes Herbert, "that at such time as the King's body was brought out of St. George's Hall the sky was serene and clear; but presently it began to snow, and fell so fast, as by that time they came to the west end of the royal chapel, the black velvet pall was all white, the colour of innocency, being thick covered with snow."

England mourned, but the army and its partisans rejoiced. At last the blood shed in the Civil War was expiated by the death of its author. "Blood defileth the land," quoted Ludlow, "and the land cannot be cleansed of the blood that is shed therein, but by the blood of him that shed it." The publicity and formality of the proceedings against the King, which seemed to most men an insulting mockery of justice, was to the Regicides themselves a source of exultation. "We did not assassinate, nor do it in a corner," said Scot. "We did it in the face of God, and of all men." A tradition, supported by some contemporary stories, tells that Cromwell himself came by night to see the body of the dead King in the chamber at Whitehall, to which it had been borne from the scaffold. He lifted up the coffin lid, gazed for some time upon the face, and muttered "Cruel necessity." A royalist poet represents him as haunted on his death-bed by "the pale image" of the martyred monarch. Poetical justice required such retribution, but history knows nothing of Cromwell's repentance. He had been one of the last men of his party to believe the King's death a necessity, but having persuaded himself that it was a just and necessary act he saw no reason for remorse. It seemed to him that England had freed itself from a tyrant "in a way which Christians in after times will mention with honour, and all tyrants in the world look at with fear."

CHAPTER XII
THE REPUBLIC AND ITS ENEMIES
1649

The execution of Charles I. was followed by the abolition of monarchy. On February 6, 1649, the House of Commons voted that the House of Lords was useless and dangerous, and that it ought to be abolished. On February 8th, it resolved that the office of a king was unnecessary, burdensome, and dangerous to the liberty, safety, and public interest of this nation. Acts abolishing both followed, and on May 19th a third Act established the English Republic. "England," it declared, "shall henceforth be governed as a Commonwealth, or a Free State, by the supreme authority of this nation, the representatives of the people in Parliament, and by such as they shall appoint and constitute as ministers under them for the good of the people." Henceforth all writs were to run in the name of the Keepers of the Liberty of England, and the Great Seal was to bear the picture of the Parliament with the legend, "In the first year of Freedom by God's blessing restored."

Exactly what they meant by "a Free State" the founders of the Republic did not explain. Hobbes and Harrington agreed in defining the new government as an oligarchy. A pamphleteer praised it as an aristocracy. But the principles on which it was ostensibly based were the principles of democracy. In their resolutions of January 4, 1649, the House of Commons had declared that the people were, under God, the original of all just power, and had based their claim to override the Lords on that ground. In their declaration of the reasons for establishing a republic, they asserted that kings were officials, instituted by agreement amongst the people they governed, whom the people had therefore a right to dethrone in case of misgovernment. Milton, who became one of the Secretaries of the Council of State, echoed the same principles. In his *Tenure of Kings and Magistrates*, he asserted "that all men were naturally born free, being the image and resemblance of God Himself," and anticipated Rousseau in tracing the origin of government to a social contract. Yet, in spite of democratic professions, the Republic was simply the rule of the Long Parliament under a new name. All the power which the King and the three estates of the realm had formerly possessed, the little remnant of the House of Commons claimed as its own. All the checks which the existence of King and Lords, or the share of the Church in legislation, had once imposed, were now swept away. The one new institution established was simply a further development of that system of government by committees which the Civil War had made necessary. The Council of State was neither a senate nor a cabinet; it possessed no power either to balance or to control the Parliament, but was only an annually elected committee, to which the Parliament had entrusted executive and administrative duties. Of the forty-one persons composing it, all but ten were members of the Parliament itself.

Thus the Long Parliament possessed an authority which no political assembly in England has ever possessed before or since. Its power of legislation was unlimited. It exercised the executive power indirectly through the Council, and directly through its own resolutions. By interference with private suits, and by the appointment of committees with quasi-judicial functions, it also exercised the judicial power. Its sovereignty was undivided and uncontrolled.

"This was the case of the people of England at that time," said Cromwell, eight years later, "the Parliament assuming to itself the authority of the three estates that were before. It had so assumed that authority that if any man had come and said, 'What rules do you judge by?' it would have answered, 'Why, we have none. We are supreme in legislature and judicature.'"

What made this authority still more burdensome was that there was no prospect of its ever ending. Instead of sitting for about seven months in the year, as Parliaments do now, it sat all the year round, never taking more than three or four days' holiday. Moreover, by the Act of May 11, 1641, it could not be adjourned, prorogued, or dissolved, save by its own consent, and though the King, who had passed the act, was dead, it was held to be still in force. So, in Cromwell's phrase, the country was governed by "a perpetual Parliament always sitting."

Although the claims of the Long Parliament had reached their highest, the theory on which they rested had ceased to be in accordance with facts. "The Commons of England in Parliament assembled," said the resolution of the House on January 4, 1649, "*being chosen by and representing the people*, have the supreme power in this nation." But the House was never less representative than at the moment when it passed this vote. By the expulsion of royalist members during the war, and of Presbyterians in 1648, it had been, as Cromwell said, "winnowed, and sifted, and brought to a handfull." When the Long Parliament met in November, 1640, it consisted of about 490 members; in January, 1649, those sitting, or at liberty to sit, in the House were not more than ninety. Whole districts were unrepresented. In the list of sitting members given in a contemporary pamphlet, there were none from the counties of Herefordshire, Hertfordshire, Cumberland, and Lancashire, or from any borough within their limits. Wales was represented by three persons, and London by but a single citizen. In later years, a few readmissions and a few new elections swelled the total of sitting members to about 125, but at no date between 1649 and 1653 was the Long Parliament entitled to say that it represented the people. Its power rested not on popular consent, but on the support of the army, and on the superstitious reverence which Englishmen paid even to the shadow of a Parliament.

Politically the all-important question was how long the army would continue to maintain this remnant of the Long Parliament in power. The agreement between the two covered a fundamental difference in their political views. The army regarded the maintenance of the existing assembly as a temporary expedient. The Parliament looked upon itself as a legitimate sovereign with an indefeasible right to rule. By a Free State, the army meant a democracy, and could not understand a republic without republican institutions. Above all it demanded that the new State should be based on a written constitution defining the rights of the governed and the powers of the government. In the Agreement of the People, drawn up in January, 1649, it sketched the outlines of the republic it desired. The Long Parliament was to come to an end in April, 1649. All ratepayers assessed to the relief of the poor, and every man not a menial servant or a pauper, were to have votes. Electoral districts were to be made more equal. Parliaments were to be elected every two years, and not to sit for more than six months in the year, and a Council of State was to hold power when they were not sitting. If the State chose, it might provide for the maintenance of a national Church, but with the exception of Popery and prelacy, all forms of Christianity were to be tolerated. Finally, as a safeguard against arbitrary power, certain fundamental rights were enumerated with which no government might interfere: freedom from impressment, equality before the law, and freedom of worship.

The constitutional scheme of the army was presented to the Parliament on January 20, 1649. They did not ask that it should be imposed on the nation by law, but that it should be tendered to the nation for acceptance. It was to be circulated, somewhat as a petition, amongst the people for signatures, and if most of the supporters of the cause approved of it, steps were to be taken to give it effect. The Parliament received the Agreement with thanks, and laid it aside.

April, 1649, passed and they showed no sign of dissolving. Their feeling on the subject of a new Parliament was well expressed by Harry Marten in 1650. Marten compared the Commonwealth to the infant Moses. When Moses, he said, was found amongst the bulrushes and brought to Pharaoh's daughter, she took care to find out the child's mother, and to commit him to her to nurse. The Commonwealth was an infant, of weak growth and very tender constitution; nobody was so fit to nurse it as the mother who brought it forth, and till it had obtained more years and vigour they should not trust it to other hands.

In 1649, there was much to be urged in favour of this view. At home and abroad the young Republic was surrounded by enemies. In England it was threatened by Royalists, Presbyterians, and Levellers; in Europe it had no friends. The execution of Charles I. had excited universal horror amongst foreigners. There was indeed no prospect of the general league of European potentates to punish regicide, for which Royalists hoped, but both governments and peoples were hostile. In Russia, the Czar imprisoned English merchants and confiscated their goods. In Germany, Sweden, and Denmark, ministers preached sermons denouncing the English sectaries, and proving that there was no necessary connection between Protestantism and king-killing. In the United Provinces, where republicans might have expected sympathy, public opinion was equally incensed against them. The States-General addressed Charles II. as King, condoled with him on the death of his father, and allowed Rupert to equip his fleet in Dutch ports. They refused to give audience to Strickland, the English agent in Holland, and declined to recognise the new State. In May, 1649, a special ambassador from England, Dr. Dorislaus, was murdered by Scottish Royalists at The Hague, and though the Dutch Government promised redress, popular feeling secured the escape of the murderers. Much of this hostility was due to the influence of the Stadtholder, William II., whose marriage with Mary, daughter of Charles I., had made the House of Orange the one firm friend of the House of Stuart. William II. helped his brother-in-law with money and advice, and would have done more if he had been able. But Holland, the richest and most powerful of the seven provinces, was opposed to the warlike schemes of the Stadtholder and wished to remain at peace with England.

In France, the King's death made every Englishman unpopular. The war with Spain and the distractions of France itself prevented Mazarin from assisting Charles II., but he would not recognise the Republic. The relations of England and France grew rapidly worse. The French Government forbade the importation of English draperies; the English replied by prohibiting French wines, woollen goods, and silks. French privateers and even government ships attacked English commerce, and during 1649 and 1650 took English shipping to the amount of five thousand tons, and goods worth half a million. Naturally English merchants made reprisals on French trade. Diplomatic intercourse came to a stop; one French agent was ordered to leave England, a second was turned back at the coast, and a third was dismissed almost as soon as he arrived in the country.

The hostility of France made Spain comparatively friendly. It did not recognise the Republic, but its ambassador kept up unofficial intercourse with the Council of State, and its Government maintained a real neutrality between English parties. It waited till the permanence of the new government should be assured, and in the meantime declined to help a claimant whose chances of restoration seemed precarious. Cottington and

Hyde, the ambassadors whom Charles II. sent to Spain, were received with coldness, and their petitions for assistance rejected. On the other hand, Ascham, the agent of the Commonwealth, was murdered by English Cavaliers as soon as he reached Madrid (May 27, 1650), and only one of his murderers was punished. "I envy those gentlemen," said the Spanish prime minister, "for having done so noble an action." Political necessity might force Spain to preserve friendly relations with the Commonwealth, but the feeling of subjects and rulers alike was as hostile as that of the French.

In England itself, the reaction which began when the King became a captive was increased by the manner of his death. Ten days after the execution, there appeared in print the *Eikon Basilike*—the portraiture of King Charles in his solitude and sufferings. The book was really written by Dr. Gauden, but no Cavalier doubted that it contained the King's thoughts and feelings set down by his own hand. It inspired Royalists with more fervid loyalty; converted the wavering, and touched even the indifferent. The mob began to believe that Charles had been the best of monarchs, and the meekest of martyrs. He was no longer the perfidious tyrant of politicians, but the man with the mild voice and mournful eyes whom dramatists were to glorify. Milton complained that the people, "with a besotted and degenerate baseness of spirit, except some few who yet retain in them the old English fortitude and love of freedom, are ready to fall down flat and give adoration to the image and memory of this man, who hath offered at more cunning fetches to undermine our liberties and put tyranny into an art, than any British king before him." In his *Eikonoklastes*, he undertook to shatter the idol of "the inconstant, irrational, and image-doting rabble," but failed altogether.

For the moment, the royalist party was too weak to be a serious danger. In Holland and in France, a crowd of ruined noblemen and battered soldiers waited impatiently for the chance of striking another blow against their conquerors. Already Montrose was enlisting men in Northern Europe for a fresh descent on Scotland. In his lines to the dead King, he had promised to avenge his death.

"I'll sing thine obsequies in trumpet sounds,

And write thine epitaph in blood and wounds."

Other exiles, with an eye to profit as well as vengeance, took to privateering. From the Irish ports, from the Isles of Man, Jersey, and Scilly, issued swarms of privateers, who infested the Channel and plundered English merchantmen. Nor were more distant seas secure. A few months later Prince Rupert, with what was left of the royal fleet, took a number of prizes in the Atlantic, made a sudden raid into the Mediterranean, intercepted homeward-bound ships off the Azores, and even spread havoc in West Indian waters. "We plough the seas for a subsistence," wrote one of his officers, "poverty and despair being our companions, and revenge our guide."

At home, however, the Royalists were crushed and subdued. Some of their leaders were prisoners; others had suffered under the Republic's High Court of Justice. As a rule, the penalties inflicted on the defeated party were limited to pecuniary fines. Early in the war, the Parliament had resolved to sequestrate all the property of those in arms against it. Subsequently it adopted the plan of compounding with delinquents; that is, allowing a Royalist to redeem his estate on paying a certain proportion of its value. These compositions varied in amount from one-half to one-tenth of the capital value of the property, and were determined according to the position and the criminality of the owner. Under this system, large sums were raised to pay the expenses of the war, but it was less effective as a means of raising revenue than as a method of punishing Royalists. A country gentleman who had melted his plate and felled his oaks to succour the King found himself forced to raise money when money was scarce and land had immensely fallen in value. The fixing of his fine was a long and cumbrous process, and till it was fixed his estate was under sequestration. If he failed to pay his instalments at the right time, or was found to have understated his property, there came a re-assessment of the fine, or a fresh sequestration of the estate. He might long as fervently as ever to see the day when the King would enjoy his own again, but, disarmed and impoverished as he was, he could do little to bring it nearer. Yet many Cavaliers were willing to risk their lives again in the attempt. This section of the party maintained an active correspondence with the exiled Court, and by 1650 a central royalist council was established with agents in every county. But the most sanguine plotters admitted that without some assistance from abroad the party in general was "too extremely awed" to take up arms.

In England their possible allies against the government were the Presbyterians and the Levellers. The Presbyterians were numerous, rich, and powerful. Their strength lay in London, in the large towns, and in Lancashire, but most of the middle classes and the bulk of the beneficed clergy belonged to their party. The Presbyterian clergy had protested loudly against the King's trial; many of them preached against the Republic, and some were bold enough to pray for Charles II. They condemned the Commonwealth as "an heretical democracy," and refused the engagement to be faithful to it which Parliament imposed. But beyond this passive resistance few of them went. Cordial co-operation between Presbyterians and Royalists was impossible, for the desires of the parties differed widely. What the Presbyterians wanted was a constitutional monarchy on the basis of the terms offered the King in the Newport treaty; what the Royalists wanted was the restoration of monarchy as it had existed before the war began. One party demanded the establishment of some form of Presbyterianism, the other the maintenance of Episcopacy. In 1648, the distrust and apathy of the Presbyterians had prevented the success of the Royalists, and the same cause prevented their union now. The Royalists distrusted the Presbyterians quite as much. To men like Hyde, they seemed traitors and rebels, whose penitence was hollow, and whose principles were as fatal to monarchy and religion as those of the Independents. By depriving Charles of his kingly power they had made it possible for the Independents to deprive him of his life. A Royalist summed up the share of the two parties by saying that the Independents cut off the King's head, but the Presbyterians brought him to the block. Adversity might draw Presbyterians and Royalists together; but not till hatred of military rule and dread of anarchy had effaced the memories of the war was their joint action possible.

As little prospect was there of the union of the Levellers with the Royalists. Under the name of Levellers two distinct parties were included, neither of which, however hostile to the existing government, was favourable to monarchy. A small section, calling themselves the true Levellers, demanded sweeping social changes. Without these, said they, the Republic is a mockery. "Unless we that are poor have some part of the land to live upon freely as well as the gentry, it cannot be a free Commonwealth." At present, they asked for the right to establish themselves on the commons and waste lands, but they dreamed of a socialistic republic in which there would be no private property in land, no buying or selling, and neither rich nor poor.

The majority of the Levellers demanded political changes only, and protested they had no desire "to level men's estates, destroy property, or make all things common." What they wanted was to limit the powers of the Government and extend the rights of the individual. The three chief points in their programme were manhood suffrage, annual Parliaments, and complete religious liberty. Their complaint was that the revolution of 1648 had stopped too soon, and that the Republic was not an absolute democracy.

The socialists were harmless dreamers whose doctrines fell on stony ground, but the teaching of the democrats bore abundant fruit. Lilburn, their spokesman, was an effective pamphleteer, a vigorous orator, and a party leader of singular pertinacity and courage. In his struggle with the Government he gave voice not only to the aspirations of his own party, but to the feelings of all the opponents of the Republic. The Government seized his pamphlets, threw him in prison, and put him on trial for treason. It only increased his popularity. When "honest John" denied the right of the sword to dictate laws, and demanded the liberty which was the birthright of every Englishman, no London jury would agree to convict him. He was imprisoned time after time, but it was impossible to suppress him till Parliament passed an act for his banishment (December, 1651).

With so many enemies around them, the founders of the Republic had to deal with a task of extraordinary difficulty. But all the machinery of government was in their hands, and although their supporters were a minority, energy and enthusiasm compensated for lack of numbers. The Council of State consisted of country gentlemen of military or political experience, with a few lawyers, a few merchants, besides three or four professional soldiers. It contained a number of able men, and several statesmen, than whom, as Milton says of Vane, better Senators ne'er held the helm of Rome when the Roman Senate beat back Pyrrhus and Hannibal. The system of governing through committees and boards made it possible to add to each of the bodies entrusted with the management of a department a certain number of outsiders of special knowledge or skill. The administrative business of the Republic was consequently far better conducted than that of the Long Parliament or the monarchy. Royalist pamphleteers represented the men in power as universally corrupt and self-seeking; but with some few exceptions they were men of high character and great disinterestedness. To a foreign observer, hostile rather than friendly, they seemed worthy to exercise power, however defective their title to it might be.

"Not only are they powerful by sea and land," wrote one of Mazarin's agents, "but they live without ostentation, without pomp, and without mutual rivalry. They are economical in their private affairs and prodigal in their devotion to public affairs, for which each man toils as if for his private interest. They handle large sums of money, which they administer honestly, observing a strict discipline. They reward well and punish severely."

The pecuniary resources of the Republic were far greater than any of the Stuarts had ever possessed. The revenue of Charles I., in 1633, was estimated at £618,000. The revenue of the Republic, in 1649, from monthly assessments, customs, excise, fines from delinquents, and sales of confiscated lands amounted to about two millions. But the demands upon the revenue were greater still. The safety of the seas and the possibility of a foreign war made the reorganisation of the navy an immediate necessity. Accordingly, Warwick's commission as Lord High Admiral was revoked, and the command of the fleet given to three Generals at Sea, Blake, Deane, and Popham. In place of Warwick, the Admiralty Committee of the Council of State exercised a general supervision over naval affairs, but the building of ships, the care of their crews, and all the practical management of the navy were given to a Board of Navy Commissioners taught by service at sea what a fighting fleet required. During the next three years, forty-one new men-of-war were added to the navy, which was further increased by hired merchantmen. The sailors were better fed, better paid, and better cared for than they had been under Charles I., and, moreover, their zeal was stimulated by giving them a third of all the prizes they took. Invasion rapidly became an impossibility, and the dominion of the seas a reality instead of an empty claim.

The army of the Commonwealth, if small for the tasks before it, was amply sufficient to suppress rebellion or prevent invasion. The twenty-one thousand men of the "New Model" had swollen to a host of double that size. The standing army, in 1649, amounted to forty-four thousand men, of whom twelve thousand were destined for the reconquest of Ireland. In character and composition it differed little from the "New Model." The uniform had become universal, and henceforth redcoat and soldier were synonymous. As the pay of the troops was high, and discharged with comparative regularity, it was no longer necessary to raise recruits by pressing. For the officers the army had become a career, and few retired, unless disabled or cashiered. Officers of all grades were inspired by a certain corporate feeling, and accustomed to act together in politics. But between officers and privates a serious divergence of opinion was beginning to reveal itself. The agitation of the Levellers had found a ready response in the lower ranks of the army. Many of the soldiers demanded, like Lilburn, the immediate realisation of the democratic Republic. Others wanted the re-establishment of the Council of Agitators and the abolition of martial law. As in 1647, reluctance to serve in Ireland and the question of arrears of pay swelled the discontent.

Lilburn seized the opportunity to attack the council of officers, and Cromwell as its guiding spirit. He and his disciples denounced the Lieutenant-General as a tyrant, an apostate, and a hypocrite. "You shall scarce speak to Cromwell about anything," says one of their pamphlets, "but he will lay his hand on his breast, elevate his eyes, and call God to record. He will weep, howl, and repent, even while he doth smite you under the fifth rib."

Personal abuse had no effect on Cromwell, but he felt the danger with which this agitation threatened the Republic. Tenaciously attached to the existing social order, he regarded the teaching of the Levellers as calculated to overthrow authority and destroy property. In one of his later speeches he sums up his views on the levelling movement. The distinction between class and class was the corner-stone of society. "A nobleman, a gentleman, a yeoman, that is a good interest of the land and a great one." But the "levelling principle" tended to reduce all the orders and ranks of men to an equality. Consciously or unconsciously it aimed at that, "for what was the purport of it but to make the tenant as liberal a fortune as the landlord?" The preaching of such a doctrine was a danger to the State "because it was a pleasing voice to all poor men, and truly not unwelcome to all bad men."

When it came to propagating levelling views in the army, and inciting soldiers to disobey their officers, Cromwell's way with the ringleaders was short and sharp. In March, 1649, Lilburn and three other incendiaries were brought before the Council of State.

"I tell you," said Cromwell, thumping the council table, "you have no other way to deal with these men but to break them, or they will break you; yea, and bring all the guilt of the blood and treasure shed and spent in this kingdom upon your heads, and frustrate and make void all that work that, with so many years' industry, toil, and pains you have done; and therefore I tell you again, you are necessitated to break them."

Lilburn and his friends went to the Tower, but the effervescence amongst the soldiers still continued. At Salisbury, in May, 1649, three of the regiments selected to go to Ireland broke into open mutiny, and declined to march till the liberties of England were secured. Their watchword was "England's freedom, soldiers' rights," and they expected other regiments to join them. But Cromwell and Fairfax left them no time to gather strength. Hurrying from London to Oxfordshire by forced marches, the two generals fell on the mutineers at Burford, took four hundred prisoners, and scattered the rest. Little blood was shed. Three non-commissioned officers were shot; the rest of the mutineers were told that they deserved to be decimated;

nevertheless, they were re-embodied in the ranks, and shipped off to Ireland.

Cromwell did not limit himself to the soldier's task of striking down the enemies of the cause; he laboured with equal zeal to conciliate doubtful supporters and regain lost friends. Many Independents were willing to accept the Republic, now it was established, if they could do so without approving the method by which it had been brought into being. Cromwell was probably the author of the compromise by which these men were induced to take their seats in the Council of State side by side with the authors of the late revolution. Equally conciliatory was his attitude on the question of the House of Lords. To fanatical republicans like Ludlow, it was a proof of his want of principle that he objected to the abolition of that institution, and wished to retain it as a purely consultative body. In reality, his natural conservatism disinclined him to make more constitutional changes than necessity required, and he sought to keep the support of those few peers who had hitherto stood by the cause. In April, 1649, Cromwell even made overtures to the Presbyterians. He offered, as he had offered in 1647, to consent to the establishment of the Presbyterian system, if there were toleration for men of other creeds who "walked peaceably." He was willing to consent to the readmission of the members excluded by Pride's Purge, if they would promise fidelity to the Republic. But the Presbyterians refused his offers.

Of these attempted compromises there is little trace in history, but Cromwell's letters show his efforts to convert individuals. Robert Hammond and Lord Wharton had once been his comrades in the struggle, but now, as Cromwell put it, they had reasoned themselves out of the Lord's service. To win them back, it was to faith rather than to reason that he appealed, for that was the way he had quieted his own scruples.

"It were a vain thing," he told Wharton, "to dispute over your doubts, or undertake to answer your objections. I have heard them all, and I have rest from the trouble of them, and of what has risen in my own heart, for which I desire to be humbly thankful. I do not condemn your reasonings. I doubt them."

Pride's Purge and the King's execution stuck in Wharton's throat. He condemned the illegality by which the Republic had been established and the character of some of the men concerned.

"It is easy," replied Cromwell, "to object to the glorious actings of God, if we look too much upon instruments. Be not offended at the manner; perhaps there was no other way left. What if God accepted their zeal as he did that of Phineas, whom reason might have called before a jury?" But above all, "what if the Lord have witnessed His approbation and acceptance to this also—not only by signal outward acts, but to the heart too?"

To Cromwell this union of the outward sign with the inward conviction was something far above argument. The logic of events was the only convincing logic. It was the answer that he had given to Hammond's doubts in 1648. "Fleshly reasonings ensnare us"; let us see what the purpose of God is, as it is made manifest in events. For as nothing happened but because God willed it should happen, so what men termed events were to the Christian "dispensations," "manifestations," "providences," "appearances of God." There was no such thing as fate—"that were too paganish a word." There was no such thing as chance. Every battle was "an appeal to God"—Cromwell often uses that phrase as a synonym for fighting. Victory or defeat was not an accident; it was the working of "the Providence of God in that which is falsely called the chance of war." Therefore each successive triumph of his cause was a fresh proof of its righteousness. His victories in Ireland became a justification of the Republic. "These," he told the Speaker, "are the seals of God's approbation of your great change of government."

That there was something fatalistic in this belief cannot be denied. Cromwell himself once owns that he was inclined to make too much of "outward dispensations." But the confidence in his cause which this creed gave was the source of his power over his followers.

"In the high places of the field," said one of them, "as at Dunbar, Worcester and elsewhere, when he carried his life in his hand, did not his faith then work at a more than ordinary rate? Insomuch that success and victory was in his eye, when fears and despondencies did oppress the hearts of others, and some good men too."

Whatever happened to himself, the Cause could not fail. "The Cause is of God, and it must prosper." It was not for the sake of the Cause, but for the sake of his doubting friends that he strove to persuade them. "The Lord hath no need of you," he tells one. "The work needs you not, but you it," he tells another. The fear in his mind was only this: "what if my friend should withdraw his shoulder from the Lord's work through false, mistaken reasonings?" To serve in that work in any station was "more honour than the world can give or show." "How great is it," he cries, "to be the Lord's servant in any drudgery!" How little, then, it matters whether a man is called an apostate or a tyrant, or what reproaches that service brings, what estrangements, what vigils, or what labours. "Let us all be not careful what men will make of these actings. They, will they, nill they, shall fulfill the good pleasure of God, and we shall serve our generations. Our rest we expect elsewhere: that will be durable."

Therefore, when others faltered and fell behind, Cromwell (in Marvell's phrase) "marched indefatigably on." Fortunate was the Republic that in its hour of need it had such a servant. More fortunate would it have been had its rulers realised that the Cause which Cromwell served was not a form of government, but ideal ends compatible with any form. He had sought to find religious and civil liberty in a monarchy; he sought it now in a republic; he was to seek it hereafter in a government which was neither. At present it seemed to him inseparable from the life of the Republic.

CHAPTER XIII
IRELAND
1649–1650

The Second Civil War had its counterpart in Ireland, where in May, 1648, Lord Inchiquin and the Munster Protestants threw off obedience to the Parliament and hoisted the royal standard. Ormond returned again to Ireland in September, 1648, and by January, 1649, he succeeded in uniting Anglo-Irish Royalists and Confederated Catholics in a league against the adherents of the Parliament. In vain Rinuccini, the Papal Nuncio, opposed the league. The freedom and equality promised to the Catholic religion, the independence promised to the Irish Parliament, allured many even of the clergy to Ormond's support. They called on the Irish soldiers to fight for God and Cæsar under his banners, and engaged to supply him with an army of twenty thousand men. In February, 1649, Rinuccini left Ireland.

The King's execution further swelled the royalist ranks; for whilst a portion of the Ulster Presbyterians openly declared for Ormond, and proclaimed Charles II., the rest threw off all semblance of obedience to the Parliament. Only Owen Roe and the Ulster Irish, dissatisfied with the terms of the treaty, stood aloof from the coalition, and, negotiating first with Ormond, then with the parliamentary officers, maintained for some time a neutral attitude. In Londonderry, Sir Charles Coote still held out for the Parliament, Colonel Monk held Dundalk, and Colonel Michael Jones, ever vigilant and energetic, maintained himself in Dublin. Jones had been made Governor of Dublin, in June, 1647, when Ormond gave it up to the Parliament. He had won a signal victory over the Irish at Dungan's Hill in August, 1647, and could be trusted to fight to the last. But unless help came from England, the preservation of these last strongholds was only a question of months.

It was not merely a question whether Ireland should be separated from England, for it was certain that Ireland in royalist hands would be used as a basis for an attack upon England. The young King's messengers announced his speedy coming to Ireland, and nothing but the lack of money hindered his journey. Already Prince Rupert, with a squadron of eight ships, was in the harbours of Munster. It was at this juncture that the Council of State nominated Cromwell to command in Ireland (March 15, 1649). The speech which Cromwell made to the officers of the army a week later showed his appreciation of the crisis. "Your old enemies," he told them, "are again uniting against you." Scotland had proclaimed Charles II.; a great party in England was ready to co-operate with the Scots; all parties in Ireland were joined together "to root out the English interest there and set up the Prince of Wales." "If we do not endeavour to make good our interest there, and that timely, we shall not only have our interest rooted out there, but they will in a very short time be able to land forces in England, and put us to trouble here." All the national pride of an Englishman rose up at the thought of Scottish or Irish interference.

"I confess," he continued, "I have often had these thoughts with myself which perhaps may be carnal and foolish: I had rather be overrun by a Cavalierish interest than a Scotch interest, I had rather be overrun by a Scotch interest than an Irish interest, and I think that of all this is the most dangerous.... If they shall be able to carry on their work they will make this the most miserable people in the earth, for all the world knows their barbarism.... The quarrel is brought to this state: that we can hardly return to that tyranny which formerly we were under the yoke of, but we must at the same time be subject to the kingdom of Scotland or the kingdom of Ireland for the bringing in of the king. It should awaken all Englishmen."

At bottom, as Cromwell truly said, the quarrel was a national quarrel, and the question was whether the growth of English freedom should be checked by Irishmen and Scotchmen, seeking, for their own ends, to replace the

Stuarts on the throne they had lost. There was little real danger of this so long as the army remained united. "There is more cause of danger from disunion amongst ourselves than by anything from our enemies.... I am confident we doing our duty and waiting upon the Lord, we shall find He will be as a wall of brass round about us, till we have finished that work that He has for us to do." But with all this faith in divine assistance, Cromwell did not underestimate the difficulty of reconquering Ireland, and left nothing undone that was necessary to secure success.

Cromwell refused to accept the command until he was certain of adequate support from the Government, and after accepting it (March 30th) declined to lead his soldiers across the sea until he was provided with money for their payment. Parliament entrusted him for three years with the combined powers of Lord-Lieutenant and Commander-in-chief, granting him a salary for the two posts of about thirteen thousand pounds a year, and giving him an army of twelve thousand men, well officered and well equipped. The organisation of his army, the collection of ships to transport it, and, more than all, the difficulty of raising money to maintain it, delayed his start for more than four months, and it was not till August 13th that Cromwell landed at Dublin.

If Ormond had been a great commander, or if Owen Roe had abandoned his neutrality in March instead of in August, every English garrison might have been taken before Cromwell's coming. Inchiquin, Ormond's lieutenant, took Dundalk and Drogheda in July, and Ormond himself blockaded Jones in Dublin. But Cromwell reinforced Jones with three regiments from England, and on August 2nd the garrison of Dublin surprised Ormond's camp at Rathmines, and defeated him with a loss of five thousand men. "An astonishing mercy," wrote Cromwell, "so great and seasonable that we are like to them that dreamed." Its result was that Ormond could bring together no army which was sufficient to face Cromwell in the field, and was driven to rely on fortresses to check the invader till he could gather fresh forces. Into Drogheda, the first threatened, Ormond threw the flower of his army. Cromwell stormed Drogheda on September 10th, and put the twenty-eight hundred men who defended it to the sword. "I do not think thirty of the whole number escaped with their lives," he wrote. Then sending a detachment to the relief of Londonderry, he turned his march southwards, and on October 11th took Wexford by storm. Some fifteen hundred of its garrison and its inhabitants fell in the streets and in the market-place, and, as at Drogheda, every priest who fell into the hands of the victors was immediately put to death.

At Drogheda the order to spare none taken in arms had been deliberately given by Cromwell after his first assault had been repulsed. At Wexford the slaughter was accidental rather than intentional. Cromwell showed no regret for this bloodshed. He abhorred the indiscriminating cruelties practised by many English commanders of the time in Ireland, and no general was more careful to protect peaceable peasants and non-combatants from plunder and violence. "Give us an instance," he challenged Catholic clergy, "of one man, since my coming into Ireland, not in arms, massacred, destroyed, or banished, concerning the massacre or the destruction of whom justice has not been done or endeavoured to be done." But when towns were taken by storm, the laws of war authorised the refusal of quarter to their defenders, and on this ground Cromwell justified his action at Drogheda and Wexford. He justified it both on military and political grounds. He had come to Ireland not merely as a conqueror, but as a judge "to ask an account of the innocent blood that had been shed" in the rebellion of 1641, and "to punish the most barbarous massacre that ever the sun beheld." Of the slaughter at Drogheda he wrote:

"I am persuaded that this is a righteous judgment of God upon those barbarous wretches, who have imbrued their hands in so much innocent blood, and that it will tend to prevent the effusion of blood for the future; which are the satisfactory grounds of such actions, which otherwise cannot but work remorse and regret." Of Wexford he said: "God, by an unexpected providence, in His righteous justice brought a just judgment upon them, causing them to become a prey to the soldiers who in their piracies had made preys of so many families, and with their bloods to answer the cruelties which they had exercised upon the lives of divers poor Protestants."

Cromwell, in short, regarded himself, in Carlyle's words, as "the minister of God's justice, doing God's judgments on the enemies of God!" but only fanatics can look upon him in that light. His justice was an imperfect, indiscriminating, human justice, too much alloyed with revenge, and, as St. James says, *Ira viri non operatur justitiam Dei*. Politically these massacres were a blunder—their memory still helps to separate the two races Cromwell wished to unite. From a military point of view, however, they were for a short time as successful as Cromwell hoped, in saving further effusion of blood.

"It is not to be imagined," wrote Ormond, "how great the terror is that those successes and the power of the rebels have struck into this people. They are so stupefied, that it is with great difficulty that I can persuade them to act anything like men towards their own preservation."

Trim and Dundalk were abandoned by their garrisons, Ross opened its gates as soon as a breach was made in its walls, and Ormond's English Royalists deserted in scores. But, in November, when Cromwell attacked Waterford, the spell was broken. Its stubborn resistance and the tempestuous winter weather obliged him to raise the siege, for the hardships of Irish campaigning had thinned his army, and a large part of it were "fitter for an hospital than the field." Michael Jones, Cromwell's second in command, died of a fever, and Cromwell himself fell ill.

Meanwhile, the inherent weakness of the coalition which Ormond had built up revealed itself. Between the Munster Protestants, whom Inchiquin had induced to declare for the King in 1648, and their Catholic Irish allies there was a gulf which no temporary political agreement could bridge over. Before Cromwell left England, he had opened secret negotiations with some of the commanders in Munster, and his intrigues now bore fruit. In October, Cork expelled Ormond's garrison, and in November, Youghal, Kinsale, Bandon, and several smaller places hoisted the English flag. Thus, by the close of 1649, all the coast of Ireland, from Londonderry to Cape Clear, with the sole exception of Waterford, was in Cromwell's hands: "a great longitude of land along the shore," wrote Cromwell, "yet hath it but little depth into the country."

The task of the next campaign was the extension of English rule inland. After wintering in the Munster ports, Cromwell led his army against the fortresses in the interior of Munster. Cashel, Cahir, and many castles fell in February, and Kilkenny, the seat of the Irish Catholic Confederation, capitulated at the end of March.

More and more the war became a purely national war between Celts and English. The last of Inchiquin's Protestant officers made terms with Cromwell. On the other hand, the Ulster army of Owen Roe stood no longer neutral, and though Owen Roe himself died in November, 1649, his Celtic soldiers fought for the freedom of their race with unsurpassable courage and devotion. Owen's nephew, Hugh O'Neill, defended Clonmel against Cromwell, and repulsed with enormous loss his attempt to storm it. The Ironsides confessed that they had found in Clonmel "the stoutest enemy this army had ever met in Ireland," but though the garrison escaped by a skilful night march, the town itself was obliged to surrender (May 10, 1650).

By this time war between England and Scotland was imminent. Cromwell's recall had been voted by the Parliament in January, and a fortnight after the fall of Clonmel he sailed for England, leaving his lieutenants to complete the conquest of Ireland. Ireton, who remained as President of Munster and commander-in-chief, captured Waterford (August 10th), but failed before Limerick, while Coote in the north defeated Owen Roe's old army at Scarrifholis (June 21st). There was no longer any Irish army in the field, and the war became a war of sieges and forays. At the end of 1650, Ormond left Ireland in despair. His successor, Clanricarde,—distrusted and disobeyed as Ormond had been,—could neither unite the Irish factions for the last struggle, nor combine the scattered bands who still held out in their bogs and mountains. The nobility still clung to the House of Stuart, but the clergy turned for help to the Catholic powers, and offered to accept the Duke of Lorraine as Protector of the Irish nation, if he would come to their defence with his army. In June, 1651, Ireton again besieged Limerick, and after a siege of five months the city yielded to famine and treachery. Ireton himself died of plague fever in November, 1651, but his successors, Ludlow and Fleetwood, completed the subjugation of the country. Galway, the last city to resist, surrendered to Coote in May, 1652. During the year, the last Irish commanders capitulated, and their soldiers entered Spanish or French service.

So ended the twelve years' war. The contest had been unequal, but the failure of the Irish to regain their independence was due not so much to the greater strength and wealth of England, as to their own divisions. As a contemporary Irish poet wrote:

> *"The Gael are being wasted, deeply wounded,*
>
> *Subjugated, slain, extirpated,*
>
> *By plague, by famine, by war, by persecution.*
>
> *It was God's justice not to free them,*
>
> *They went not together hand in hand."*

Ireland was devastated from end to end, and a third of its population had perished during the struggle. Plague and famine, said an English officer, had swept away whole counties, and in some places "a man might travel twenty or thirty miles, and not see a living creature, either man, or beast, or bird." "As for the poor commons," said another, "the sun never shined upon a nation so completely miserable."

It was not very difficult for Cromwell and the English Republic to subdue a divided nation, but the task which lay before them now was less easy. It remained to effect a settlement which would secure order, restore prosperity, prevent future rebellions, and extinguish the feuds of race and creed. In the last years of the Republic and during the Protectorate, first under Lord-Deputy Fleetwood and then under Henry Cromwell, this reorganisation of Irish government and society was carried out. The main lines of the Cromwellian settlement of Ireland had been determined by the Long Parliament. In all essentials the parliamentary policy towards Ireland was simply a return to the traditional policy which, since the close of the Tudor period, all English governments had more or less consistently pursued. Colonisation, conversion, and the impartial administration of justice were the aims of Cromwell just as they had been the aims of Strafford.

The basis of the settlement was therefore a great confiscation of Irish land, and the substitution of English for Irish landowners. Parliament had announced this policy in 1642, when it voted that two million five hundred thousand acres of Irish land should be set aside for the repayment of the "adventurers" who advanced money for the reconquest of Ireland. The pay of the soldiers employed against the Irish and the reimbursement of the merchants who supplied provisions and other necessaries were provided for in this way. By 1653, the debt which the Parliament owed these three classes of creditors amounted to over three and a half millions. Accordingly, in August, 1652, Parliament passed an Act confiscating the estates of all Catholic landholders who had taken part in the rebellion. The leaders and originators were to lose all their land, others two thirds, some one third, according to the degree of their guilt. The rich Catholic burgesses of Waterford, Kilkenny, and other large towns shared the same fate, but the Munster Protestants who had revolted in 1648 were merely fined two years' income. In 1653 it was decreed that even those persons to whom a portion of their estates was theoretically left should be transplanted to Connaught, and receive there the proportion of land to which they were entitled. In most cases they received inferior land, in some cases nothing, and in all cases the removal entailed great suffering. Even a still more sweeping scheme for the transplantation of all classes of native Irish was for a time under consideration, but in the end few but landholders were actually transplanted. Artificers and labourers were allowed to remain behind, partly because their guilt was held to be less, partly because it was difficult to remove them, and because their services were needed by the new owners of the soil. Finally, the confiscated lands were surveyed, divided into different classes, and distributed by lot amongst the soldiers and the creditors of the government.

By 1656, the process was practically completed, and two thirds of the land of Ireland had passed to its new owners.

Cromwell himself thoroughly approved of the principles of confiscation and colonisation. "Was it not fit," he asked, "to make their estates defray the charges who had caused all the trouble?" "It were to be wished," he told Parliament when announcing his capture of Wexford, "that an honest people would come to plant here." Accordingly he wrote to New England inviting "godly people and ministers" to leave their homes in America and establish themselves in Ireland. But with the details of the land settlement effected during his Protectorate, Cromwell had little to do, though sometimes he intervened in favour of persons harshly treated by the Irish government. Thus he saved Peregrine Spenser, the grandson of the poet, from transplantation, not for the sake of the *Faery Queene*, but for the sake of Edmund Spenser's *Dialogue on the State of Ireland*. Moreover, it was largely due to the Protector that the scheme for universal transplantation was reduced to more moderate limits.

The ecclesiastical policy of Cromwell and the Puritans was the traditional English policy of suppressing Catholicism in Ireland and propagating Protestantism. The difference consisted in the consistent vigour with which that policy was now pursued. Under the Stuarts the laws had forbidden the Catholic worship, but the government had often connived at its exercise. Charles, in his struggle with the Parliament, had promised the Catholics at one time toleration, at another equal rights. Cromwell, as soon as he arrived in Ireland, announced that the old laws would be rigidly enforced. Catholicism, he declared, had no right to exist in Ireland at all, the priests were mere intruders; for their own ends they had instigated the rebellion; they poisoned the flocks they professed to feed with their "false, abominable, anti-Christian doctrine and practices." Liberty of conscience, in the narrowest sense of the word, Irish Catholics might enjoy, for they were not to be forced to attend Protestant churches, but of liberty of worship they were to have none. "I meddle not with any man's conscience," wrote Cromwell to the Governor of Ross. "But if by liberty of conscience, you mean a liberty to exercise the mass, I judge it best to exercise plain dealing and to let you know where the Parliament of England have power, that will not be allowed of." "As for the people," he declared, "what thoughts they have in matters of religion in their own breasts I cannot reach, but shall think it my duty, if they walk honestly and peaceably, not to cause them in the least to suffer for the same." Under the Protector's government, therefore, priests were hunted down, and either imprisoned or exiled. Some were transported to Spain, others shipped off to Barbadoes, and a sort of penal settlement was established in the island of Innis-boffin.

From persistency in these repressive measures, and from the active preaching of Protestantism, Cromwell hoped for the conversion of the Irish. He thought he saw signs of it even during his campaign. "We find the people," he wrote, "very greedy after the word, and flocking to Christian meetings, much of that prejudice which lies upon people in England being a stranger to their minds. I mind you the rather of this because it is a sweet symptom if not an earnest of the good we expect." During the Protectorate, the English governors of Ireland made great efforts to propagate Protestantism. Independent congregations were founded in most of the great towns, and preachers invited over. In 1654, the commissioners in whose hands the government was, appealed to New England for ministers. "Sir," began one of their letters, "we being destitute of helpers to carry on the work of the Lord in holding forth the gospel of Christ in this poor nation, being informed that the Lord hath made you faithful and able in the work, we hereby desire you to come over and help us."

"Assiduous preaching," argued Cromwell, "together with humanity, good life, equal and honest dealing with men of different opinion," would in the end convert the Irish to Protestantism. The government also hoped much from the spread of education. In 1650, Parliament endowed Trinity College with the lands of the Archbishopric of Dublin and the Dean and Chapter of St. Patrick's. Trinity was reorganised and filled with Independent divines, while the appointment of a number of professors, the establishment of a public library, and the foundation of a second college were also projected. When Archbishop Ussher died, the officers of the Irish army bought his books to be the nucleus of the intended library.

Like Strafford, Cromwell believed that the impartial administration of justice would make the Irish people good subjects and attach them to English rule.

"We have a great opportunity," he wrote, "to set up a way of doing justice amongst these poor people, which, for the uprightness and cheapness of it may exceedingly gain upon them, who have been accustomed to as much injustice, tyranny, and oppression from their landlords, the great men, and those that should have done them right, as

I believe any people in that which we call Christendom.... If justice were freely and impartially administered here, the foregoing darkness and corruption would make it look so much the more glorious and beautiful, and draw more hearts after it."

In the newly conquered country the obstacles which made the reform of the Law so difficult in England, could more easily be overcome. "Ireland," Cromwell said, "was as a clean paper, and capable of being governed by such laws as should be found most agreeable to justice; which may be so impartially administered as to be a good precedent even to England itself."

Some improvement in these respects there certainly was. The Irish judges appointed by Cromwell were capable and honest, and one of the chief-justices, John Cooke, was a zealous law-reformer. But no improvement in the administration of the laws could reconcile Irishmen to English rule while the laws themselves were so little "agreeable to justice." Justice combined with forfeiture and proscription, and without equal laws, was a legal fiction which had no healing virtue.

Equally futile was the attempted conversion of the Irish. The struggle against England had made Irish nationality and Catholicism identical terms, and a faith associated with spoliation and foreign conquest could make no progress in the hearts of the conquered. The only permanent result of Cromwell's zeal was an increase in the number of Protestant Nonconformists in Ireland. Some nominal converts from Catholicism were made. A few landowners professed themselves Protestants in order to obtain a temporary respite from transplantation, and a good many Irish women who had married English soldiers passed as Protestants in order to elude the laws against the intermarriage of soldiers and papists. But converts of this kind usually relapsed, and the mixture of the two races, which the government could not prevent, profited Catholicism, not Protestantism. The failure of the policy of conversion entailed the partial failure of the policy of colonisation as well. The families of the greater landowners established by the confiscations remained English and Protestant. The families of the smaller landowners—of the ex-soldiers who became yeomen and small farmers—tended to become Catholic in creed and Irish in feeling. "How many there are," lamented a pamphleteer in

1697, "of the children of Oliver's soldiers in Ireland who cannot speak one word of English. This comes of marrying Irish women instead of English."

In the main, Cromwell's Irish policy followed the lines which Tudor and Stuart statesmen had laid down. In one respect, however, he was more original and more enlightened than either his predecessors or his successors. Strafford's economic policy had aimed at making the Irish rich, but also at keeping Ireland economically subject to England and preventing Irish manufactures or products from competing with those of England. No such jealousy of Irish trade warped Cromwell's policy. Its fundamental principle was that the English colony were to be regarded simply as Englishmen living in Ireland, and entitled to the same rights as Englishmen living in England. "I would not," said a speaker in the Parliament of 1657, "have our own people oppressed because they live in Ireland." Accordingly, in the levy of any general tax on the three countries, care was taken that their respective shares should be equitably assessed. The same customs and excise were paid in Ireland as in England, and Ireland enjoyed equal rights with regard to foreign and colonial trade. However, as the native Irish and the Catholics were excluded from the corporate towns which were the seats of commerce and manufactures, the benefit of this trade was almost exclusively reaped by the English colony. Cromwell's object was to secure the prosperity of what he called "the interest of England newly begun to be planted in Ireland." If it were overtaxed, or in any other way overburdened, "the English planters must quit the country," and then, as he warned his second Parliament, "that which hath been the success of so much blood and treasure, to get that country into your hands, what can become of it, but that the English must needs run away for pure beggary, and the Irish must possess the country again?"

With free trade, Cromwell also gave the English colonists in Ireland representation in the Parliament of the Three Nations. The Long Parliament had projected the legislative union of England, Scotland, and Ireland, and had fixed the number of their representatives, but it was left to Cromwell to call the first united Parliament. The "Instrument of Government" allotted Ireland thirty members, leaving the Protector to fix the particular constituencies by which these members were to be returned, and thirty representatives of Ireland sat accordingly in the Parliaments of 1654, 1656, and 1659. As Catholics and persons who had taken part in the rebellion were excluded from voting, the members for Ireland consisted entirely of officers and officials representing the English colony. "I am not here," said one of them in 1659, "to speak for Ireland, but for the English in Ireland."

Outside the ranks of the new colonists, the union of the English and Irish Parliaments found few cordial supporters. The older English colony preferred a separate Parliament for Ireland. It would be impossible, argued one of their spokesmen in 1659, for the Irish to get their grievances redressed, if they had to come over to England and apply to the English Parliament for the purpose. "I pray that they may have some to hear their grievances in their own nation, seeing they cannot have them heard here." In 1659, the republican opposition in Richard Cromwell's Parliament, moved largely by the fact that the Irish members were staunch Cromwellians, urged their exclusion from the House. Ireland, Vane argued, was only a province, and had no right to a voice in the government of the mother country. "They are still in the state of a province, and you make them a power not only to make laws for themselves, but for this nation; nay, to have a casting vote for aught I know in all your laws." The attempted exclusion of the members from Ireland failed in 1659, but at the Restoration, the legislative union with Ireland was the first thing to go. No law was required to repeal it, for it had never received the King's assent, and no voice was raised in its defence. English conservatism and Irish provincialism were too strong, and Cromwell's imperial scheme went to the limbo reserved for policies too wise for their generation.

The natural consequence of the termination of the legislative union was the loss of the commercial equality which had accompanied it. The English colonists were no longer treated as Englishmen domiciled in Ireland, but as strangers and rivals. The Navigation Act of Charles II. excluded them from American and colonial trade, while two other acts followed, prohibiting the export of Irish cattle and provisions to England. Finally, in the reign of William III. the Irish woollen manufacture was destroyed, and the ruin of Irish commerce and agriculture was completed.

It was only Cromwell's policy towards the English colony in Ireland which was reversed; his policy towards the native Irish was still pursued.

So far as his policy coincided with the traditional policy of England towards Ireland it was maintained; so far as it was wiser and more original it was abandoned. Carlyle draws a picture of Ireland as it might have been if the "ever blessed restoration" had not "torn up" Cromwell's system "by the roots." "Ireland under this arrangement," he holds, "would probably have grown up into a sober, diligent, drab-coloured population, developing itself most probably into some sort of Calvinistic Protestantism." It is a baseless dream. Even in Cromwell's lifetime it was evident that his scheme for the conversion of the Irish was doomed to failure. After his death the proscription of Catholicism and the hopeless attempt to force Protestantism on a reluctant people were still continued, nor were they abandoned till 1829. The new proprietors whom Cromwell had established still kept their hold, and only a very small proportion of the confiscated estates— nominally one third, in reality much less—returned to their old possessors at the Restoration. So the Cromwellian land settlement survived its author, to be his most permanent monument, and to be also, as Mr. Lecky writes, "the foundation of that deep and lasting division between the proprietary and the tenants which is the chief cause of the political and social evils of Ireland."

CHAPTER XIV
CROMWELL AND SCOTLAND
1650–1651

The execution of the King destroyed the alliance which Cromwell had established between Argyle and the Independents. Argyle would have been glad to preserve it, but his power depended on the clergy and the middle classes, both deeply incensed with the sectaries who had dared to kill a Scottish king. The day after the news of the King's death reached Edinburgh, Charles II. was there proclaimed King, not of Scotland only, but of Great Britain and Ireland. The Scottish envoys in England protested against the late revolution, denouncing the establishment of toleration or any other change in the fundamental laws of the kingdom, and demanding that Charles II., "upon just satisfaction given to both kingdoms," should be placed upon his father's throne. The Long Parliament retorted by expelling the envoys and declaring that their protest laid "the grounds of a new and bloody war." Henceforth indeed the war took a new character,—it was no longer a constitutional but a national struggle. Scotland like Ireland was attempting to dictate to England the form of government which it should choose, and thus the English contest for self-government inevitably widened into a contest for the supremacy of the British Isles.

Nothing delayed war between Scotland and England but the difficulty of effecting an agreement between Charles and the Scots. Except on their own terms the Presbyterians would not fight for him, and till no other way of regaining his crown was left Charles would not accept their terms.

The Scottish Commissioners demanded that he should not only accept the Covenant and the Presbyterian system for Scotland, but pledge himself to impose them on England and Ireland. As he declined to force Presbyterianism on those two kingdoms without the consent of their parliaments the negotiations were broken off in May, 1649, and while Charles prepared to join Ormond in Ireland, Montrose was commissioned to call the Scottish Royalists once more to arms.

In September, 1649, Charles landed at Jersey on his way to Ireland, but Cromwell's victories checked his further progress. Before the year ended, it was evident that if he was to be restored it must be by Scottish hands, and in February, 1650, he returned to Holland. Necessity left him no choice. "Indeed," wrote a Scottish agent from Jersey, "he is brought very low; he has not bread both for himself and his servants, and betwixt him and his brother not one English shilling." Negotiations began again at Breda in March, 1650. The Scots required him to take both Covenants, to impose Presbyterianism on England and Ireland, and to disavow both Ormond and Montrose. Charles struggled hard to modify these conditions, and the treaty by which he agreed to them was not signed till he was actually on his voyage. He hoped that when he came to Scotland his presence would win concessions from the Covenanters, and a royalist party would gather round him. But he found himself treated more as a captive than a king. English Royalists who had accompanied him from Holland were ordered to leave the country, Scottish Royalists were excluded from his army and his Court, and when he reached Edinburgh he saw, fixed over the tower of the Tolbooth, and fresh from the hangman's hands, the head of Montrose.

The diplomacy of the King had sacrificed his noblest champion. Instead of holding Montrose back till the negotiations ended, he had urged him to immediate action. "Your vigorous proceeding," he wrote, "will be a good means to bring them to such a moderation ... as may produce a present union of that whole nation in our service." When the Scottish envoys at Breda demanded the abandonment of Montrose, Charles agreed to order him to disband his troops with a secret promise of their indemnity. But the countermands came too late. Knowing that Charles was treating with the Covenanters, and that he was in danger of disavowal, Montrose still resolved to spend his life for the King's service. In March, 1650, he arrived in the Orkneys with a little body of Danish and German mercenaries. In April, with about twelve hundred men and forty horse, he advanced through Caithness to the south of Sutherland. There, at Carbisdale, on April 27th, Major Strachan, with two hundred and fifty of David Leslie's disciplined cavalry, fell upon him in his march south, scattered his handful of horsemen, and cut to pieces his foreign infantry. Montrose escaped from the rout, and wandered amongst the hills till starvation obliged him to seek shelter. Macleod of Assynt gave him up to the Scottish Government, and on May 21st he was hanged at the market-cross in the High Street of Edinburgh.

About the time of Montrose's death, Cromwell returned to England. Parliament had voted that both Fairfax and Cromwell should command against the Scots, the one as General, the other in his old post as Lieutenant-General. But when Fairfax found that the Council of State meant to invade Scotland, he laid down his commission. The best refutation of the theory that Cromwell sought to undermine Fairfax in order to obtain his post is the vigour with which he endeavoured to persuade him to keep it. It was morally certain, urged Cromwell, that the Scots meant to invade England. War was unavoidable. "Your excellency will soon determine whether it is better to have this war in the bowels of another country than our own." But nothing could overcome Fairfax's repugnance to an offensive war. Human probabilities, he repeated, were not sufficient ground to make war upon our brethren, the Scots. The truth was, he had long been dissatisfied with the results of the revolution in which events had given him so prominent a part, and seized any plausible excuse for retirement. As he persisted, his resignation was accepted, and on the 26th of June, 1650, Cromwell became, by Act of Parliament, Captain-General and Commander-in-chief of all the forces of the Commonwealth. "I have not sought these things," he wrote to a friend; "truly I have been called unto them by the Lord, and therefore am not without some assurance that He will enable His poor worm and weak servant to do His will."

At the end of July, Cromwell entered Scotland with an army of 10,500 foot and 5500 horse. His old comrade, David Leslie, to whom the Scots had given the command, could bring about eighteen thousand foot and eight thousand horse to meet him, but as Leslie's soldiers were much inferior in quality, he stood resolutely on the defensive. Marching along the coast and drawing supplies mainly from the English fleet, Cromwell found the Scottish army intrenched between Leith and Calton Hill. A month passed in marches around Edinburgh, in fruitless skirmishes, and unsuccessful attempts to draw the Scots from their unassailable fastnesses. Leslie took no risks, and met each move with unfailing skill. At the end of August, victuals grew scarce in the English camp and disease was rife. With a "poor, shattered, hungry, discouraged army," Cromwell fell back on Dunbar, intending to fortify the town to be used as a magazine and basis of operations, and to await reinforcements from Berwick. Leslie, pressing hard on his heels, occupied Doon Hill, which overlooks Dunbar, and seized the passes between Dunbar and Berwick. Thanks to his knowledge of the country he had again outmanœuvred Cromwell, and the Scots boasted that they had Cromwell in a worse pound than the King had had Essex in Cornwall.

Cromwell owned the greatness of the danger.

"We are," he wrote, "upon an engagement very difficult. The enemy hath blocked up our way at the pass at Copperspath, through which we cannot get without almost a miracle. He lieth so upon the hills that we know not how to come that way without great difficulty, and our lying here daily consumeth our men, who fall sick beyond imagination."

His sixteen thousand men were reduced now to eleven thousand, and some officers proposed that the foot should be shipped on the fleet, while the horse endeavoured to cut their way through the enemy. But their General remained, as he expressed it, "comfortable in spirit and having much hope in the Lord."

Leslie's original plan was to fall on Cromwell's rear as he tried to force his way along the road to Berwick, but the parliamentary committee in his camp ordered him to descend the hill and bar Cromwell's route. Seeing that Cromwell did not continue his march, he believed he was shipping his guns, and perhaps part of his infantry, and thought all he had to do was to prevent the escape of the enemy. Accordingly, on September 2nd, Leslie moved his army from the Doon hill to the gentle slopes at its foot, intending to attack the next day. His left was covered in flank, and to some extent in front too, by the steep ravine of the Brock burn, which ran obliquely from the hill to the sea and separated the positions of the two armies. His infantry were posted in the centre, with their backs to the hillside. On the right, where the ground was more level and open, he had massed two-thirds of his cavalry. Leslie had twenty-two thousand men to Cromwell's eleven thousand, and told his soldiers they would have the English army, alive or dead, by seven next morning.

When Cromwell examined the new position of the Scots, he saw that his opportunity had come at last. Leslie's left, shut in between the hill and the ravine, was practically useless, and his centre, cramped by the hill in its rear, had too little room to manœuvre. Both Cromwell and Major-General Lambert agreed that if the Scottish right were beaten their whole army would be endangered.

That evening, in answer to Leslie's movement, Cromwell drew up his forces along the line of the ravine and about Broxmouth House, as if his sole purpose was to stand on the defensive. The night was stormy and wet, and after one or two alarms the Scots were convinced that he did not mean to attack. Just before dawn Cromwell pushed a strong body of horse and foot across the ravine, and under cover of a false attack on their left massed all the troops he could against their right and their centre. Lambert and Fleetwood, with six regiments of horse, attacked the Scottish right, while Monck, with about three thousand or four thousand foot, engaged their centre, supported by the fire of Cromwell's guns from the other side of the ravine. The Scots were taken unprepared, but as soon as they could get into battle order numbers told. Charging, with the slope in their favour, the Scottish lancers broke one of Lambert's regiments, and Monk's division was repulsed and forced to give ground. At this critical moment, Cromwell himself came up with the reserve, consisting of three regiments of foot and one of horse. His own regiment of horse fell on the flank of the Scottish cavalry, Lambert's troopers charged again, and after a short, sharp struggle the Scottish right wing was broken through and through. Simultaneously Cromwell's and Pride's foot regiments furiously assailed the advancing Scottish infantry, and "at push of pike did repel the stoutest regiment the enemy had," while all along the line the English foot, once more advancing, drove back the Scots. Some of Leslie's infantry stood stubbornly, but a cavalry charge on their exposed flank completed their discomfiture. At Cromwell's direction, the flank attack became more and more pronounced, till the Scottish centre was rolled up from right to left; and, penned in the triangle between the hill and the ravine, the Scottish infantry became a helpless mob, unable either to fight or fly.

"Horse and foot," says one of Cromwell's officers, "were engaged all over the field and the Scots all in confusion. The sun appearing upon the sea I heard Noll say, 'Now let God arise, and His enemies shall be scattered,' and following us as we slowly marched I heard him say, 'I profess they run,' and then was the Scots army all in disorder and running, both right wing and left and main battle. They routed one another after we had done their work on their right wing."

Three thousand men fell in the battle, and ten thousand were taken prisoners. While Leslie collected the shattered remnant of his army at Stirling, Cromwell occupied Edinburgh and Leith, and all the eastern portion of the Scottish Lowlands. Edinburgh Castle held out, and the southwest was still in arms.

After Dunbar, as before it, Cromwell's strongest wish was not a conquest but an agreement which would restore peace between the two nations.

"Give the State of England," he wrote to the Committee of Estates, "that satisfaction and security for their peaceable and quiet living beside you, which may in justice be demanded from those who have, as you, taken their enemy into their bosom, whilst he was in hostility against them."

He had opened his campaign with manifestos protesting the affection of England for the Scots, and demonstrating their error in supporting the Stuarts. These overtures the leaders of the Independents urged him to renew. They regarded it as a fratricidal war. The grim Ireton expressed the fear that Cromwell had not been sufficiently forbearing and long-suffering. Subtle St. John drew a distinction between Scots and Irish, reminding him that although the Irish were atheists and papists to be ruled with a rod of iron, the Scots were truly children of God, and he must still endeavour to heap coals of fire on their heads. Cromwell, whose heart "yearned after the godly in Scotland," began now a new set of expostulations, directed particularly to the ministers whose influence had frustrated his appeals to the nation. He charged them with pretending a reformation and laying the foundation of it in getting worldly power for themselves; with perverting the Covenant to serve secular ends; with claiming infallibility for their doctrine just as the Pope did. Their claim to control the civil government he dismissed with few words. "We look on ministers as helpers of, not lords over, God's people." Then he refuted with like vigour the claim of the Kirk to prohibit dissent in order to prevent heresy.

"Your pretended fear lest error should step in, is like the man who would keep all wine out of the country, lest men should be drunk. It will be found an unjust and unwise jealousy to deprive a man of his natural liberty upon a supposition he may abuse it. When he doth abuse it, judge."

Finally, he rebuked them for their hypocrisy and their blindness. Was it not hypocritical "to pretend to cry down all Malignants, and yet to receive and set up the head of them, and to act for the kingdom of Christ in his name?" Was it not blindness to shut their eyes to the meaning of their late defeat? God had given judgment in their controversy at Dunbar, and they refused to see it. "Did not you solemnly appeal and pray? Did not we do so too? And ought not you and we to think with fear and trembling of the hand of the great God in this mighty and strange appearance of his?"

Either events or Cromwell's arguments produced their effect in the Scotch camp. There were great searchings of heart amongst devout Presbyterians, and a schism broke out in the army. Rigid Covenanters renounced worldly alliances and compliance with an ungodly monarch. "I desire to serve the King faithfully," said Colonel Ker, "but on condition that the King himself be subject to the King of Kings." Colonel Strachan, after some negotiation with Cromwell, laid down his commission. Ker, with three or four thousand Westland Whigs, refused obedience to the Committee of Estates, and tried to wage war independently. But attempting to surprise Lambert, at Hamilton, in Lanarkshire, on December 1st, he was taken prisoner, his force scattered, and the whole of the south-west fell into Cromwell's power.

More lasting was the division amongst the clergy. One party, headed by Gillespie and Guthry, published a Remonstrance repudiating the idea of fighting for Charles II. till he had proved his fitness to be a covenanted king, and condemning those who had closed their eyes to his insincerity. The Remonstrants, as they were termed, would have no alliance with either Malignants or Engagers. The other party, laxer in its moral views, and moved more by national than religious feeling, was ready to accept the compromises which the necessities of the State demanded. When Parliament passed resolutions allowing Malignants and Engagers to fight in the national ranks, it consented to their employment on a simple profession of penitence. For the next ten years the quarrels of Resolutioners and Remonstrants made up Scotland's ecclesiastical history.

Cromwell had foreseen the political consequences of Dunbar. "Surely," he predicted, "it's probable the Kirk has done their do. I believe their King will set up upon his own score now." The prediction now came true. Charles had suffered great humiliations since he came to Scotland. He had submitted to all conditions and sworn many kinds of oaths. He had been obliged to declare his sorrow for his father's hostility to the work of reformation and his mother's love of idolatry. He had seen the Scottish ranks purged of Royalists, and had been forbidden to approach the army that was fighting in his name. At last, events had brought the Parliament round to his policy. From the date of his coronation at Scone on January 1, 1651, Charles was King of Scotland in fact as well as name. Partly driven by necessity, because the ecclesiastical divisions had deprived him of his strongest supporters, partly lured by hope, because Charles offered to marry his daughter, Argyle fell in with the King's policy. But each stage in its development diminished his influence. First he had to share his power with Hamilton and his partisans, and then the repeal of the Act of Classes put an end to it altogether by allowing even Montrose's adherents to hold office.

Thus within a year from his landing in Scotland Charles had succeeded in combining both Royalists and Presbyterians in support of his cause. His hopes were never higher. It seemed possible to effect a similar combination between the Presbyterians and Royalists in England. In March, 1651, the English Government detected a plot for a rising in Lancashire which was to be helped by troops from Scotland, and isolated insurrections which broke out in Norfolk (December, 1650) and in Cardiganshire (June, 1651) proved the reality of these conspiracies. If a Scottish army entered England, the general royalist rising of 1648 might be repeated, and perhaps with a different issue.

The campaign of 1651 began late. During the winter, Blackness and Tantallon castles were captured, and in February there was an advance on Stirling which the tempestuous weather frustrated. In the spring, Cromwell's illness delayed operations. The hardships of Irish campaigning had impaired his health. "I grow an old man, and feel the infirmities of age marvellously stealing upon me," he wrote to his wife on the day after Dunbar; but he never spared himself, and in February, 1651, he fell ill of an intermittent fever brought on by exposure. Three successive relapses brought him to the verge of the grave, and more than once his life was despaired of. Parliament in alarm sent him two of the best physicians of the day, and advised him to remove to England for change of air. In June he was sufficiently recovered to take the field, and found Leslie's army posted on the hills south of Stirling. "We cannot come to fight him except he please, or we go upon too manifest hazards," wrote Cromwell, "he having very strongly laid himself, and having a very great advantage there."

Unable to attack or to lure Leslie from his position, Cromwell resolved to turn it. The English fleet commanded the sea, and it was easy to throw Lambert and four thousand men across the Forth into Fife. Leslie sent Sir John Brown against him with a like force, but Lambert annihilated Brown's force at Inverkeithing on July 20th. Cromwell poured more troops across the water till he had fourteen thousand men in Fife, and then taking their command himself he marched on Perth, which fell after a siege of twenty-four hours (August 2nd).

The capture of Perth cut off Leslie from his supplies, and severed his communications with the north of Scotland. But the way to England was left open, and confident that English Royalists would flock to his banner Charles and his whole army marched for the border. Cromwell had foreseen the movement, and was well aware that it might alarm the English Government. But he justified his strategy with sober confidence.

"We have done," he said, "to the best of our judgment, knowing that if some issue were not put to this business it would occasion another winter's war, to the ruin of your soldiery, for whom the Scots are too hard in respect of enduring the winter difficulties of this country, and to the endless expense of the treasury of England in prosecuting this war. It may be supposed we might have kept the enemy from this by interposing between him and England; which truly I believe we might, but how to remove him out of this place without doing what we have done, unless we had a commanding army on both sides the river of Forth, is not clear to us; or how to answer the inconveniences aforementioned we understand not."

He bade them be of good courage and collect what forces they could to check the march of the Scots.

"Indeed we have this comfortable experience from the Lord, that the enemy is heart-smitten by God, and whenever the Lord shall bring us up to them, we believe the Lord will make the desperateness of this counsel of theirs to appear, and the folly of it also. When England was much more unsteady than now, and when a much more considerable army of theirs unfoiled invaded you, and we had but a weak force to make resistance, at Preston, upon deliberate advice, we chose rather to put ourselves between their army and Scotland; and how God succeeded that is not well to be forgotten."

Charles entered England by Carlisle, and marched through Lancashire and along the Welsh border, hoping to gather recruits from those districts during his progress. Cromwell, leaving Monk to secure Scotland, sent his cavalry under Lambert and Harrison to pursue the King, and followed himself through Yorkshire with the infantry. As he went, he was joined by the forces of the counties through which he passed, and all over England the new county militia rushed to arms. For, however much they might detest the Republic, Englishmen hesitated to assist a Scottish invader.

In Lancashire, distrust of Malignants prevented the Presbyterians from taking up arms, though the Earl of Derby raised a little army amongst the Cavaliers. On the 22nd of August, Charles reached Worcester with less than sixteen thousand men, worn out by marching, and halted to rest and collect his adherents. A few devoted gentlemen made their way to his standard, but the people remained apathetic, and three days later Derby's levies were routed at Wigan by Colonel Lilburn. By this time the net was closing round the King. Cromwell, joining Lambert and Harrison, had established himself at Evesham, and blocked the road to London with thirty thousand men. His superior numbers enabled him to divide his forces, and to attack Worcester from both sides. Lambert and Fleetwood, with eleven thousand men, crossed to the west bank of the Severn, and prevented the retreat of the Royalists into Wales, whilst Cromwell, with the bulk of the army, remained on the east bank and pushed close up to the city. On September 3rd, the anniversary of Dunbar, Fleetwood's force advanced upon Worcester from the south-west. Between it and Worcester lay the river Teame, a tributary of the Severn, held by a royalist division, which had broken the bridges. Cromwell threw a bridge of boats across the Severn, just above the mouth of the Teame, and fell on the flank of the Scots with four of his best regiments. "The Lord General did lead the van in person, and was the first man that set foot on the enemy's ground." Under cover of Cromwell's attack, Fleetwood threw a similar bridge across the Teame, and his infantry poured across to co-operate with Cromwell. Outnumbered, but fighting stubbornly, the Scots gave way. "We beat the enemy from hedge to hedge," wrote Cromwell, "till we beat him into Worcester."

Charles, who watched the battle from the tower of the cathedral, seeing that the great part of Cromwell's army was engaged on the western bank, sallied forth with every man he could muster to crush the force left on the eastern side. For three hours the struggle lasted. At first the Scots gained ground, but Cromwell, recrossing the river, put himself at the head of his men, and drove the enemy back in confusion into the city. His soldiers entered at their heels, and storming their "Fort Royal" turned its guns on the streets. "My Lord General did exceedingly hazard himself, riding up and down in the midst of the fire; riding himself in person to the enemy's foot to offer them quarter, whereto they returned no answer but shot." In the end, what was left of the foot laid down their arms, while the horse fled through the north gate, and took the road to Scotland. But not a single regiment or troop reached their home. The militia, which beset the bridges and highways, gathered up prisoners in hundreds, and the country people hunted down stragglers with merciless ferocity. Half the nobility of Scotland were amongst the prisoners.

Amongst the few who escaped was the young King. The Parliament threatened all who sheltered Charles with the penalties of high treason, and promised one thousand pounds to any person who gave him up. Troopers scoured the roads to find him, and officials at all the ports were warned to watch for "a tall man above two yards high, with hair a deep brown near to black." But, though Englishmen would not fight for Charles, they would not betray him, and of the scores he trusted not one proved false. Sometimes hiding in an oak tree, sometimes in a "priest's hole," disguised now as a countryman in an old worn leathern doublet and green breeches, and now as a serving-man in grey homespun, Charles wandered through the south-west searching for a ship. At last he found one at Brighton, and landed safe in France on October 22nd.

For Scotland, Cromwell's victory marked the end of independence. The absence of Leslie's army left no force in Scotland capable of giving battle to Monk's six thousand veterans, and there was no fortress in Scotland which could resist his artillery. Monk captured Stirling on August 14th, and the seizure of the Committee of Estates at Alyth on August 28th deprived the national defence of its head, and destroyed the last relic of a national government. Dundee was stormed and sacked on September 1st. Montrose, Aberdeen, Inverness, and other towns fell without a blow. In February, 1652, the Orkneys were occupied, and in May, Dunottar Castle, the last fortress to hold out, surrendered. Argyle, who had refused to follow Charles into England, endeavoured to maintain an independent position in the West Highlands, but in August he too was forced to give in his adhesion to the English Government, and the subjugation of Scotland was completed. An English garrison of twelve thousand or fourteen thousand men, and strong fortresses built at Leith, Ayr, Inverness, and Inverlochy, kept henceforth the conquered country in submission. In spite of the general discontent no effort to throw off the English yoke had any chance of success. In 1653, the war with Holland emboldened the Highlanders to take arms again, and a rising began which was headed first by the Earl of Glencairn, afterwards by General Middleton. The insurgents made forays into the Lowlands, but were never strong enough to do much more, and their own disputes ruined their cause. Monk returned to his command in Scotland in May, 1654, wasted the Highland glens with fire and sword, defeated Middleton's forces, and by the end of the year put an end to the insurrection.

The policy of the Long Parliament and of the Protector toward Scotland resembled in its aim their policy toward Ireland. In each case the object was to make the conquered country into an integral part of a British empire. But the measures adopted to attain this object differed considerably in the two countries. In Scotland there was no general confiscation of the lands of the vanquished, and no far-reaching alteration in the framework of society. The Scottish Royalists were treated much as the English Cavaliers had been. The Long Parliament confiscated the estates of those who had invaded England in 1648 and 1651, but the Protector adopted a more moderate policy, imposing the penalty of forfeiture only on twenty-four leaders, and fining minor offenders. A few English officers were given grants of the forfeited lands, but most of their revenue was devoted to public purposes. Hence the Scottish confiscations, although they ruined many of the nobility and gentry, left the bulk of the nation untouched.

In Scotland there was no proscription of the national religion, but the national Church lost a portion of its independence, and was deprived of all power to check or control the civil government. In 1653, the General Assembly—"the glory and strength of our Church upon earth," as a Presbyterian minister termed it—was forcibly dissolved, but local synods and presbyteries were allowed to meet. The English Government deprived the Church courts of their coercive jurisdiction over non-members, and protected the formation of Independent congregations. It appointed commissioners to visit the universities, punished ministers who preached against it, and decided disputes about appointments to vacant livings. But it interfered little in the internal affairs of the Church, and held the balance tolerably even between Remonstrants and Resolutioners. Though deprived of its political power and much of its independence, the Scottish Church was not unprosperous. "These bitter waters," says Robert Blair, "were sweetened by the Lord's remarkably blessing the labours of His faithful servants. A great door and an effectual was opened to many."

As in Ireland so in Scotland the separate national Parliament ended, and was replaced by representation in the Parliament of Great Britain. The incorporating union, which James I. had unskilfully attempted, the Long Parliament decreed, and the Protector realised. In 1652, commissioners sent by the Long Parliament extorted a reluctant consent to the principle of the union, but the details were still unsettled when Cromwell became Protector. By the "Instrument of Government," Scotland was assigned thirty members in the British Parliament, and the Protector's ordinances completed the work. English statesmen regarded the union as a generous concession. It was intended by the Parliament, says Ludlow,

"to convince even their enemies, that their principal design was to procure the happiness and prosperity of all that were under their government," and "was cheerfully accepted by the most judicious amongst the Scots, who well understood how great a concession it was in the Parliament of England to permit a people they had conquered to have a part in the legislative power."

In reality, both ecclesiastical and national feeling were arrayed against it. "As for the embodying of Scotland with England," said Robert Blair, "it will be as when the poor bird is embodied in the hawk that has eaten it up." With few exceptions all classes regarded the incorporating union with hostility and aversion.

The Protector hoped to reconcile Scotland to the union by the material benefits which accompanied it. Absolute freedom of trade between the two countries, proportionate taxation, and a better system of justice were promised. Nor were these empty words. Tenures implying vassalage and servitude and heritable jurisdictions were abolished. Popular courts-baron were set up, English justices of the peace introduced, the fees of the law courts diminished, and new judges appointed who administered the laws without fear or favour. Even Scots admitted the improvement in the administration of justice. "There was good justice done," says Burnet. "To speak truth," adds Nichol, "the English were more indulgent and merciful to the Scots, than the Scots to their own countrymen and neighbours, and their justice exceeded the Scots' in many things."

The civil administration of Scotland was in the hands, at first, of parliamentary commissioners, and, after 1655, of a Scottish Council of Nine appointed by the Protector, which included two Scots. Under their vigorous rule, such order was maintained as Scotland had never known before. The Highlands were tamed by the English garrisons, and the mosstroopers of the border hunted down and punished. A man, boasted one of the English officials, might ride all through Scotland with a hundred pounds in his pocket, and nothing but a switch in his hand.

The class which benefited most by these reforms was the middle class. "The towns," wrote Monk to Cromwell, "are generally the most faithful to us of any people in this nation." In 1658, Cromwell, describing to his Parliament the condition of Scotland, exulted over the improvement which English rule had produced.

"The meaner sort," he said, "live as well and are likely to come into as thriving a condition under your government, as when they were under their own great lords, who made them work for their living no better than the peasants of France. I am loath to speak anything which may reflect upon that nation; but the middle sort of people do grow up into such a substance as makes their lives comfortable, if not better than before."

Burnet, in his description of the Cromwellian régime in Scotland, goes so far as to say, "we always reckon those eight years of usurpation a time of great peace and prosperity." But this is an evident exaggeration. The devastation and loss caused by the long wars had produced widespread poverty. "I do think," admitted the Protector, "the Scots nation have been under as great a suffering, in point of livelihood and subsistence outwardly, as any people I have yet named to you. I do think truly they are a very ruined nation." The weak point of English rule was the heavy taxation which the necessity of maintaining so large an army in Scotland caused.

Baillie's letters are full of complaints of the burden of taxation. "A great army in a multitude of garrisons bides above our heads, and deep poverty keeps all estates exceedingly under; the taxes of all sorts are so great, the trade so little, that it is a marvel if extreme scarcity of money end not soon in some mischief." The English Government had originally imposed a land tax of ten thousand pounds per month on Scotland, but this was levied with such difficulty that it was finally reduced to six thousand pounds. And in the year of Cromwell's death, England had to remit to Scotland a contribution of over £140,000 towards the expenses of the military government which held Scotland in obedience.

Scots in general regarded the benefits which English rule conferred as too dearly purchased at the cost of heavy taxes and national independence. In Ireland, for weal or woe, the Cromwellian conquest left an ineffaceable mark on the national history. In Scotland, on the other hand, all that Cromwell had done, or tried to do,—union, law-reform, and freedom of trade,—vanished when the Restoration came. But the aims of his policy were so just that subsequent statesmen were compelled to follow where he led. The union and free trade came in 1707, and the abolition of hereditary jurisdictions in 1746.

CHAPTER XV
THE END OF THE LONG PARLIAMENT
1651–1653

When the Parliament received the news of Worcester, they voted Cromwell four thousand pounds a year, gave him Hampton Court for a residence, and sent a deputation to present their thanks. On September 12th, he made a triumphal entry into London. Hugh Peters, the army chaplain, professed to perceive a secret exultation in his bearing, and whispered to a friend that Cromwell would yet make himself king. But Whitelocke recorded that "he carried himself with great affability, and in his discourses about Worcester would seldom mention anything of himself, but mentioned others only, and gave, as was due, the glory of the action to God." From his despatch, it was evident that Cromwell regarded the "crowning mercy" of Worcester not only as the consummation of the work of war, but as a call to take in hand and accomplish the tasks of peace. It should provoke the Parliament, he told the Speaker,

"to do the will of Him who has done His will for it and for the nation—whose good pleasure it is to establish the nation and the change of government, by making the people so willing to the defence thereof, and so signally blessing the endeavours of your servants in this late great work."

For in spite of its victories the government of the Commonwealth was essentially a provisional government, and acquiesced in, rather than accepted by, the nation. Even its adherents felt that something more permanent and more constitutional must be established in its place, now that the Civil War was over. In a conference between officers and members of Parliament, which Cromwell brought about soon after his return to London, this feeling plainly appeared. The lawyers were all for some monarchical form of government. Some suggested that the late King's third son, the Duke of Gloucester, now twelve years old, should be made king. The soldiers would not hear of anything that smacked of monarchy. "Why," asked Desborough, "may not this as well as other nations be governed in the way of a republic?" Cromwell said little, and seemed more anxious to learn what others thought, than to express his own views. He agreed with the lawyers that "a settlement of somewhat with monarchical power in it" would be most effectual. He knew that a strong executive power was needed either for the tasks of peace or war, but doubted whether a return to the Stuart line was possible. He agreed with the soldiers that a new Parliament was an immediate necessity, but, as in 1649, he held that it would be more honourable and more expedient to induce the Long Parliament to dissolve itself. Publicly and privately he used all his influence to persuade the House to do so. "I pressed the Parliament," he says, "as a member to period themselves, once and again and again, and ten, nay, twenty times over." But, in spite of "a long speech made by his Excellency," it was only by two votes that the House resolved to fix a date for its dissolution, and then the date named was three years distant (November 3, 1654). Cromwell was obliged to resign himself to the delay, and do what he could for the settlement of the nation through the instrumentality of the existing Parliament. The task which was now before him was more difficult than fighting the Irish or the Scots; more was expected of him, and his power was less.

"Great things," said a letter to Cromwell, "God has done by you in war, and good things men expect from you in peace: to break in pieces the oppressor, to ease the oppressed of their burdens, to release the prisoners out of bonds, and to relieve poor families with bread."

For some months after Worcester, petitions were often addressed directly to the General and the Army instead of to the Parliament. But all power was in the hands of the Parliament, and as dangers grew more remote, this body grew less amenable to the influence of the man who had saved it. Of the sixty or seventy members who habitually took part in its proceedings, the ablest were also members of the Council of State, absorbed in the daily business of administration, and with little energy left for the consideration of far-reaching legislative plans. Of the rest, many were engrossed by local affairs, others occupied with their farms and their merchandise, many building up fortunes by speculating in confiscated lands. Some few were notoriously corrupt, but partisanship and favouritism were more general evils than corruption. Vane complained to Cromwell that some of his colleagues were so obstructive, that "without continual contestation they will not suffer to be done things that are so plain that they ought to do themselves." "How hard and difficult a matter it was," said Cromwell himself, "to get anything carried without making parties, without practices indeed unworthy of a Parliament."

Yet difficult though it was, Cromwell and the officers succeeded in inspiring the Parliament with some portion of their own energy. Politically, the most pressing measure was the grant of an amnesty to the conquered Royalists. So long as they were liable to punishment and confiscation for acts done during the last ten years, the wounds of the Civil War could never be healed. In February, 1652, Cromwell at last persuaded Parliament to pass an act of pardon for all treasons committed before the battle of Worcester, but it was unhappily clogged with exceptions and restrictions which robbed it of much of its efficacy. More than once during the divisions on the bill, Cromwell was teller against these restrictions, and bigoted republicans afterwards thought he did so from sinister motives. He contrived that delinquents should escape due punishment, wrote Ludlow, "that so he might fortify himself by the addition of new friends for the carrying on his designs." To Cromwell it seemed an act of political expediency. It was necessary, he held, to be just to Royalists as well as Puritans, to unbelievers as well as believers; perhaps even more necessary.

"The right spirit," he added, "was such a spirit as Moses had and Paul had—which was not a spirit for believers only, but for the whole people."

Next in importance to a general amnesty came the Reform of the Law—a phrase which, in the minds of those who used it, meant not simply legal changes, but social reforms in general. There was much need of both. The Civil War had ruined its thousands; society was disorganised by its consequences: the relations of landlord and tenant, of debtor and creditor, were complicated by unforeseen calamities; the prisons of London were crammed with poor debtors, and the country swarmed with beggars. For the lawyers it was the best possible of worlds, and they were never more prosperous or more unpopular.

"We cannot mention the Reformation of the Law," said Cromwell to Ludlow in 1650, "but the lawyers cry out we mean to destroy property, whereas the law as it is now constituted serves only to maintain the lawyers, and to encourage the rich to oppress the poor." "Relieve the oppressed," he urged Parliament in his Dunbar despatch; "reform the abuses of all professions, and if there be any one that makes many poor to make a few rich, that suits not a Commonwealth."

Parliament had done something already to meet these complaints. In November, 1650, it had passed an act ordering that all legal proceedings and documents should be henceforth in English, besides an earlier act for the relief of poor prisoners. Now it boldly appointed twenty-one commissioners, chosen outside its own body, with Matthew Hale at their head, "to consider the inconveniencies of the Law—and the speediest way to remedy the same," and to report their proposals to a Committee of the House itself (January 17, 1652). The commissioners fell roundly to work, and presented in the next few months drafts of many good bills, some of which became law during the Protectorate, and others in the present century. They even took in hand the task of codification, and drew up "a system of the Law" for the consideration of Parliament.

During this same period the reorganisation of the Church was also attempted. The Long Parliament had passed acts for the augmentation of livings, for the punishment of blasphemy, and for the propagation of the Gospel in Wales and Ireland. But it had abolished Episcopacy without replacing it by any other system of Church government, and it had ejected royalist clergymen without providing any machinery for the appointment of fit successors. In London, in Lancashire, and in a few other districts, there were voluntary associations of ministers on the Presbyterian model, but throughout the greater part of England, the Presbyterian organisation decreed in 1648 had never been actually established. The Church was a chaos of isolated congregations, in which a man made himself a minister as he chose, and got himself a living as he could. The reduction of this chaos to order seemed so difficult a problem, and beset with so many controversial questions, that Parliament hesitated to undertake it.

John Owen, once Cromwell's chaplain in Ireland, took the duty on himself, and on February 10, 1652, he and fourteen other ministers presented to Parliament a comprehensive scheme for the settlement of the Church. The House answered by referring it to a committee appointed to consider the better propagation of the Gospel, of which committee Cromwell was the most important member. Owen's scheme, like the Agreement of the People, proposed the continuance of a national Church with tolerated dissenting bodies existing by its side. The Church was to be controlled by two sets of commissioners, partly lay and partly clerical: local commissioners, who were to determine the fitness of all candidates seeking to be admitted as preachers; itinerant commissioners, who were to move from place to place ejecting unfit ministers and schoolmasters. On the limits of the toleration to be granted to dissenters, the committee was split into two sections. The scheme proposed that the opponents of the essential principles of the Christian religion should not be suffered to promulgate their views. When pressed to define what these principles were, Owen and his friends produced a list of fifteen fundamentals, the denial of which was to disqualify men from freedom to propagate their opinions. Cromwell thought these limitations too restrictive, and wished for a more liberal definition of Christianity. "I had rather," he emphatically declared, "that Mahometanism were permitted amongst us, than that one of God's children should be persecuted." It was in consequence of these debates that Milton, in May, 1652, addressed to Cromwell the sonnet in which he adjured him to remember that "peace hath victories no less renowned than war."

"New foes arise

Threatening to bind our souls with secular chains;

Help us to save free conscience from the paw

Of hireling wolves whose gospel is their maw."

But Milton did not share Cromwell's belief in the necessity of an Established Church, and it was Vane, not Cromwell, whom he praised as the statesman who knew the true bounds of either sword, and had learnt what severed the spiritual from the civil power. By the time the sonnet to Vane was written, ecclesiastical controversies had fallen into the background; the short period of peace and reform was over; Cromwell and Vane alike were forced to turn their attention to the problems of foreign policy and the tasks of war.

When Cromwell left England in the summer of 1649, all the world seemed hostile to the Republic. Worcester made Great Britain once more a power in Europe, and foreign States began to seek the friendship of the Republic, or at least to fear its enmity.

This great change was chiefly due to Cromwell's victories. "Truth is," wrote Bradshaw to Cromwell after Dunbar, "God's blessing upon the wise and faithful conduct of affairs where you are gives life and repute to all other attempts and actions upon the Commonwealth's behalf." Much, too, was due to the successes of Blake. By the spring of 1652, the navy had swept royalist privateers from the British seas and the Mediterranean, and reduced, one after another, all the colonies or dependencies which refused to submit to the Republic. Rupert's fleet, blockaded in Kinsale by Blake from May to November, 1649, could do nothing to help Ormond in capturing Dublin and Londonderry, or to hinder Cromwell's progress in Ireland. When Rupert escaped he made his way to Lisbon, and under the protection of the King of Portugal refitted his ships and captured English merchantmen. In March, 1650, Blake appeared off the mouth of the Tagus, and kept Rupert's ships cooped up there for the next six months. At last, in October, 1650, during Blake's absence, Rupert put to sea, and entering the Mediterranean began to plunder and burn English merchantmen. Blake captured or destroyed most of his ships off Malaga and Cartagena, and with the two which were left him Rupert took refuge in Toulon. Next came the turn of the islands, which were the headquarters of the royalist privateers. In May, 1651, Sir John Grenville surrendered the Scilly Islands to Blake, just in time to prevent their falling into the hands of a Dutch fleet sent to punish Grenville's attacks on Dutch commerce. The Isle of Man fell in October. In December, Blake captured Jersey and Guernsey, where Sir

George Carteret had carried on the business of piracy on a larger and still more lucrative scale than Grenville. Finally, in January, 1652, Sir George Ayscue's fleet reduced Barbadoes and the West Indian islands, while in March, Virginia and Maryland gave in their submission. Lords of all the territories the Stuarts had ruled, and with a stronger army and fleet than they had ever possessed, the republican leaders were free to intervene in European politics.

The Thirty Years' War had ended with the Treaty of Westphalia in 1648. France and Spain were still fighting, but with no great vigour, the one distracted by the civil wars of the Fronde, the other weak from misgovernment and the decay of its trade. Each wanted the help of England, but while Spain had recognised the Republic in December, 1650, France still delayed, and while Spain had allowed Blake to victual his fleet in Spanish ports, France gave shelter to Rupert's ships in its harbours, and allowed him to sell his prizes there. Not only French privateers but French men-of-war attacked English commerce in the Levant; and in France Charles gathered around him the exiled Royalists, and plotted against the peace of the Republic. At the moment, even religious as well as political motives favoured an alliance with Spain. In the Spanish dominions, there were no Protestants left to be persecuted, but the Huguenots of Southern France, relying upon the tradition of English policy which had existed since the Reformation, still looked to their co-religionists in England for support. The wars of the Fronde supplied a second motive for intervention, and to support the last defenders of political freedom in France against the encroachments of a centralising monarchy was a cause which naturally appealed to enthusiastic republicans. When Condé and the Frondeurs of Guienne applied to England and Spain for help against Mazarin, Spain responded at once, and a strong party in the English Council of State was ready to return a favourable answer. Whether the Spanish or the French party in that body would gain the upper hand depended largely on the decision of Cromwell. Ever since Worcester, and indeed earlier, foreign diplomatists had turned their attention to the General, reported his casual utterance, and striven to divine his intentions.

People who believed that the Republic would seek to propagate republican institutions abroad regarded Cromwell as the destined instrument of that policy. "If he were ten years younger," Cromwell was rumoured to have said, "there was not a king in Europe he would not make to tremble," and that as he had better motives than the late King of Sweden he believed himself capable of doing more for the good of nations than the other did for his own ambition. Marvell hailed him on his return from Ireland as a deliverer,—one whose future conquests should mark a new era in the history of all oppressed nations.

> *"A Cæsar he ere long to Gaul,*
>
> *To Italy a Hannibal,*
>
> *And to all states not free*
>
> *Shall climacteric be."*

Cromwell's acts, however, showed no trace of the revolutionary zeal attributed to him. He revealed himself at his first appearance in foreign politics as a keen and realistic statesman, more anxious to extend his country's trade and his country's territory than to spread republican principles in foreign parts. The only sentimental consideration which seemed to move him was sympathy for oppressed Protestants. He refused the proposals which Condé's agents made to him immediately after Worcester, but he did not hesitate to send one emissary to Paris to negotiate with De Retz, and another to ascertain the real condition of the south of France. The question how to improve the position of the Huguenots was the one which interested him most, and it soon appeared evident that to effect this by an understanding with the French Government would be easier than to attempt armed intervention in their favour. From the beginning, therefore, Cromwell showed a preference for the French rather than the Spanish alliance. In the spring of 1652, he and two other members of the Council of State opened a secret negotiation with Mazarin for the cession of Dunkirk. Its garrison was hard pressed by the Spaniards, and the opinion was that the French Government, being unable to relieve it, would rather see it in English than Spanish hands. In April, five thousand English soldiers were collected at Dover, to be embarked for Dunkirk at a moment's notice. But Mazarin refused to pay the price demanded for the

English alliance, and while he hesitated and haggled, the partisans of a Spanish alliance gained the upper hand in the English Council and the negotiation was broken off. As France continued its refusal to recognise the Republic unconditionally, it became necessary to use force. In September, 1652, Blake swooped down on a French fleet sent to revictual Dunkirk, took seven ships, and destroyed or drove ashore the rest, with the result that the besieged fortress surrendered to the Spaniards the next day. At last, in December, 1652, an ambassador arrived in London announcing, in the name of Louis XIV., that the union which should exist between neighbouring states was not regulated by their form of government, and formally recognising the Commonwealth.

Ere this took place, England had become involved in a war with Holland. The two Protestant Republics seemed created by nature for allies. England had helped the Dutch to establish their freedom, and Holland had ever been the chosen refuge of Puritan fugitives. But ever since 1642, dynastic and commercial causes had driven the two states farther apart. The marriage of William II. with Mary, daughter of Charles I., had secured the support of the Stadtholder to Charles I. and Charles II., and neutralised the good will of the Dutch republicans. With the death of William II., in October, 1650, and the practical abolition of the office of Stadtholder, the republican party gained the ascendancy, and better relations seemed possible. Six months later, the Commonwealth sent St. John and Strickland to The Hague to offer on behalf of England, not merely a renewal of the old amity, but "a more strict and intimate alliance and union, whereby there may be a more intrinsical and mutual interest of each in other than hath hitherto been, for the good of both." The Dutch were willing to make a close commercial alliance, but would go no farther, and negotiations were broken off without any discussion of the "coalescence," or political union, which the English ambassadors were empowered to propose. After this failure the commercial rivalry of the two nations became more acute. "We are rivals," a member of the Long Parliament once said, "for the fairest mistress in the world—trade." In March, 1651, the Dutch made a treaty with Denmark, which damaged English trade in the Baltic. In October, England passed the Navigation Act, which at one stroke barred Dutch commerce with the English colonies, deprived Dutch fishermen of their market in England, and threatened to destroy the Dutch carrying trade. The United Provinces sent ambassadors to negotiate for its repeal, but other questions arose which complicated the situation still further. There were old disputes about the acknowledgment of the sovereignty of England in the British seas, the salute due to the English flag, and the right to exact tribute for permission to fish. There was a new dispute about the rights of neutrals. England, practically at war with France, claimed the right of seizing French goods in Dutch ships, whilst the Dutch put forward the principle that the flag covered the cargo. Memories of the Amboyna Massacre, and demands for compensation for old misdeeds of the Dutch in the East Indies, put fresh obstacles in the way of agreement. Then on May 12, 1652, came a chance collision between Blake and Tromp, off Dover, and the two Republics were at war.

To Cromwell, nothing could have been more unwelcome than this war with the Dutch. He thought England in the right on the questions at issue between the two states, and when Parliament sent him to investigate the causes of the fight, he came back convinced that the fault lay with Tromp and not with Blake. But the war threatened to frustrate for ever the scheme of a league of Protestant powers which Cromwell cherished in his heart. "I do not like the war," he declared to the representatives of the Dutch congregation in London; "I will do everything in my power to bring about peace." In every attempt made to come to terms with the Dutch, Cromwell headed the peace party, and the negotiations through unofficial agents, which began in the summer of 1652, were inspired by him.

At first, the result of the war was favourable to England. The Dutch had an enormous commerce and a comparatively small navy; England had a large navy and comparatively little commerce. "The English," said a Dutchman, "were attacking a mountain of gold, while the Dutch were attacking a mountain of iron." Individually, the English men-of-war were stronger vessels than the Dutch, and armed with heavier guns. Moreover, English naval operations were under the direction of one body, whilst the Dutch were managed by five distinct admiralty boards. Added to this, the geographical position of England gave it the command of the route by which Dutch fleets approached their own shores, and while Blake and Ayscue were free to attack as they chose, the Dutch admirals were generally hampered by the task of defending large convoys of merchantmen. In November, 1652, however, Tromp defeated Blake off Dungeness, and for more than two months the command of the Channel passed to the Dutch. It was not regained till Blake and Monk defeated him in a three days' fight off Portland, in February, 1653. Meanwhile, in the Mediterranean, one English squadron had been defeated off Elba, and another was blockaded in Leghorn; the Baltic was closed to English commerce, Denmark was about to ally itself with Holland to maintain the exclusion, and 1652 closed gloomily for the Commonwealth.

A still stronger argument for peace was provided by the internal condition of England. The war put a stop to all reforms; instead of progress there was a retrograde movement. The army cost a million and a half a year, the navy nearly a million; three hundred thousand pounds were required to build new frigates, and there was a deficit of about half a million. To meet this expenditure, the Long Parliament fell back on the old plan and confiscated the estates of about 650 persons, and applied the proceeds to the maintenance of the navy. Most of the persons thus sentenced to beggary were insignificant people who had done nothing deserving such a punishment. The healing policy which Cromwell had advocated was definitely abandoned, and he was full of indignation at the injustice he witnessed. "Poor men," he afterwards said, "were driven like flocks of sheep by forty in a morning to confiscation of goods and estates, without any man being able to give a reason why two of them should forfeit a shilling."

The reorganisation of the Church ceased to make any progress. Parliament discussed some of the proposals of Cromwell's committee, but did nothing. One of its last acts was to decline to continue the powers of the Commissioners for the Propagation of the Gospel in Wales, appointed some three years earlier. To Cromwell, this refusal seemed a deliberate discouragement of "the poor people of God in Wales," and a clear proof that men zealous for the spread of religion had little to hope from the Parliament. "That business," he said, "to myself and officers was as plain a trial of their spirits as anything." As to the reform of the law, it appeared equally hopeless. Hale's bills lay neglected on the table of the House, or, like that for the registration of all titles to land, were swamped by floods of talk in committee.

"I will not say," said Cromwell of the Parliament, "that they were come to an utter inability of working reformation, though I might say so in regard to one thing—the Reformation of the law, so much groaned under in the posture it is now. That was a thing we had many good words spoken for, but we know now that three months together were not enough for the settling of one word 'Incumbrances.'"

The army grew more and more impatient. In August, 1652, the council of officers presented a petition to Parliament demanding that "speedy and effectual means" should be taken for carrying out a long list of reforms specified. But for Cromwell they would have included in it the demand for an immediate dissolution. The House gave the officers good words in plenty, and told them that the things they asked for were "under consideration," but months passed and there were only a few feeble indications of activity. In October, meetings began between the officers and the leading members of Parliament.

"I believe," affirmed Cromwell, "we had at least ten or twelve meetings, most humbly begging and beseeching of them that by their own means they would bring forth those good things which had been promised and expected; that so it might appear that they did not do them by any suggestion from the army, but from their own ingenuity: so tender were we to preserve them in the reputation of the people."

Whitelocke relates an interview between himself and Cromwell, in which the latter dwelt on the pride, ambition, and self-seeking of the members of Parliament, their engrossing all places of honour and profit for themselves and their friends, their delays, their factions, their injustice and partiality, and their design to perpetuate themselves in power. It was necessary, continued Cromwell, that there should be some other authority strong enough to restrain and curb the exorbitances of a body which claimed supreme power and was so unfit to rule. Whitelocke hoped that the Parliament would mend its ways, and thought it would be hard to create such an authority. "What if a man should take upon him to be king?" asked Cromwell. All Whitelocke could answer was, that if Cromwell were to take upon himself that title the remedy would be worse than the disease, and that his best plan was to make terms with Charles II.

These conferences came to nothing, and in January, 1653, the impatience of the army grew uncontrollable. The officers held regular meetings at St. James's, sent a circular letter to the armies in Ireland and Scotland, appealed to their fellow soldiers to stand by them, and drew up threatening addresses to Parliament. Most of the council of officers would be content with nothing less than an immediate dissolution, and were ready to effect it by force. Cromwell opposed any resort to violence, and succeeded, though with difficulty, in holding them back. To a friend, he complained that he was pushed on by two parties to do an act, "the consideration of the issue whereof made his hair to stand on end." Major-General Lambert headed one party, eager to be revenged on the House for depriving him of the Lord Deputyship of Ireland. The other was headed by Major-General Harrison, an honest man, "aiming at good things," but too impatient to obtain them "to wait the Lord's leisure."

Meanwhile Parliament, thoroughly alarmed by the rising agitation, took up once more the "Bill for a New Representative," and began to press it forward in earnest. They determined what the constituencies should be, and fixed the qualification for the franchise. By the middle of April, the bill was nearly through committee, and required nothing but a third reading to make it law. In the hands of the parliamentary leaders, however, it had become a scheme for perpetuating themselves in power. The bill was to be a bill for recruiting the numbers of the House, and the present members were to keep their seats without the necessity of re-election. They would be the sole judges of the validity of the votes given, and the eligibility of the persons chosen. Nor was it only at the next election that this system of recruiting was to be adopted; it was to be applied also to all future Parliaments.

To this ingenious scheme the officers of the army had many objections. One was, that the right of election was too loosely defined, and that its interpretation was entrusted to men in whom they had no confidence. They insisted on a political as well as a pecuniary qualification for the franchise, and complained that neutrals and men who had deserted the cause would be able to vote. To put power into the hands of such men, was to throw away the liberties of the nation.

Equally objectionable was the system of election proposed. It gave the people no real right of choice, but only a seeming right. Leicestershire might be tired of Haslerig, and Hull have lost confidence in Vane, yet both must continue to be represented by the men they had chosen in 1640. Lancashire would cease to be unrepresented, but the members it elected might be kept out by the veto of men who had practically elected themselves. Though the army was prepared to restrict the franchise and limit the choice of the electors, it was not prepared to acquiesce in so complete a mockery of representative government.

To Cromwell and the constitutional theorists amongst the officers, there was another insurmountable objection to the bill. What they disliked most in the rule of the Long Parliament was the union of legislative and executive power in the hands of a body possessing unlimited authority and always in session. They wanted short Parliaments, sitting for not more than six months in the year, and limited in their power as well as in their duration. What the bill offered instead of the perpetuation of the Long Parliament, was a succession of perpetual Parliaments, sitting all the year round, following each other without any interval, and exercising the same arbitrary power which the Long Parliament had exercised.

"We should have had fine work then," said Cromwell.... "A Parliament of four hundred men, executing arbitrary government without intermission, except some change of a part of them; one Parliament stepping into the seat of another, just left warm for them; the same day that the one left, the other was to leap in.... I thought, and I think still, that this was a pitiful remedy."

For these reasons, the officers resolved to prevent the passage of the bill at any cost. The whole future of the Cause seemed to depend on the issue.

"We came," said Cromwell, "to this conclusion amongst ourselves: That if we had been fought out of our liberties and rights, necessity would have taught us patience, but to deliver them up would render us the basest persons in the world, and worthy to be accounted haters of God and His people."

Cromwell became reluctantly convinced that if persuasion failed, it was his duty to use force.

The only hope of an honourable ending of the Long Parliament lay in its acceptance of a compromise. At a conference with some members on April 19, 1653, Cromwell and the officers proposed an expedient which they thought would answer: Let the Parliament drop the bill, dissolve itself at once, and appoint a provisional government. Let the members "devolve their trust to some well affected men, such as had an interest in the nation, and were known to be of good affection to the Commonwealth," and leave these men "to settle the nation." "It was no new thing," said the officers, "when this land was under the like hurlyburlies," and they proved it by historical precedents. The members demurred and argued, but in the end they promised to think it over and meet the officers for another conference next day. Vane and others pledged themselves, in the meantime, to suspend further proceedings on the Bill for a New Representative, and the officers separated hopefully.

Another parliamentary leader, Sir Arthur Haslerig, whose authority with the House was equal, if not superior, to Vane's, had come up from the country resolved to defeat the compromise. He told his fellow members vehemently that the work they went about was accursed, and that it was impossible to devolve their trust. When the House met next day, it adopted Haslerig's view, called for the bill, and proceeded to push it through its last stage regardless of protests. They meant then to adjourn to November, so that it would be impossible to amend or repeal the act; to leave the Council of State to carry on the government, and to make Fairfax General, instead of Cromwell.

News came to Cromwell at Whitehall that the House was proceeding with all speed upon the Bill fora New Representative. Till a second and a third messenger confirmed the tidings, he could not believe "that such persons would be so unworthy." Then he hurried down to the House, dressed as he was, not like a general or a soldier, but like an ordinary citizen, "clad in plain black clothes with grey worsted stockings," and sat down, as he used to do, "in an ordinary place." For a quarter of an hour he sat still, listening to the debate, until the Speaker was about to put the question whether the bill should pass. Cromwell turned to Major-General Harrison, whispered "This is the time I must do it," and, rising in his place, put off his hat and addressed the House. At first, and for a good while, he spoke in commendation of the Parliament, praising its labours and its care for the public good. Then he changed his note, and told the members of their injustice, their delays of justice, their self-interest, and other faults. As his passion grew, he put his hat on his head, strode up and down the floor of the House, and, looking first at one, then at another member, chid them soundly, naming no names, but showing by his gestures whom he meant. These were corrupt, those scandalous in their lives, that man fraudulent, that an unjust judge. "Perhaps you think," he said, "that this is not parliamentary language; I confess it is not; neither are you to expect any such from me. You are no Parliament, I say you are no Parliament. I will put an end to your sitting." "Call them in," he cried, turning to Harrison, and at the word Harrison went out and brought back twenty or thirty musketeers of Cromwell's own regiment from the lobby. Only a show of force was needed. Cromwell pointed to the Speaker in his chair, and said to Harrison, "Fetch him down." The Speaker refused to leave the chair unless he were forced. "Sir," said Harrison, "I will lend you my hand," and putting his hand in Lenthall's he helped him to the floor. Sidney, who sat next the chair that day, declined to move. "Put him out," ordered Cromwell; so Harrison and an officer laid their hands on his shoulders and led him towards the door. Then, looking scornfully at the mace on the table, Cromwell exclaimed, "What shall we do with this bauble?" and, calling a soldier, said, "Here, take it away."

After the mace and the Speaker were gone, all the members left the House. As they went out, Cromwell turned to them and cried: "It is you that have forced me to this, for I have sought the Lord night and day, that He would rather slay me than put me upon the doing this work." Addressing Vane by name, he reproached him with his broken faith, adding that he might have prevented this, but he was a juggler and had no common honesty. Then, taking the bill from the hands of the clerk of the House, he ordered the doors to be locked, and went away.

It remained still to dissolve the Council of State which the Parliament had appointed. In the afternoon, Cromwell came to the Council, and told its members that if they were met as private persons they should not be disturbed; but if as a council, it was no place for them, and they were to take notice that the Parliament was dissolved.

"Sir," replied John Bradshaw, "we have heard what you did at the House this morning, and before many hours all England will hear it; but you are mistaken to think that the Parliament is dissolved; for no power under heaven can dissolve them but themselves: therefore, take you notice of that."

Bradshaw was right: the ideal of constitutional government which the Long Parliament represented would prove stronger in the end than Cromwell's redcoats. That Parliament had all the faults with which Cromwell charged it; but for Englishmen it meant inherited rights, "freedom broadening slowly down," and all that survived of the supremacy of law. With its expulsion, the army flung away the one shred of legality with which it had hitherto covered its actions. Henceforth, military force must put its native semblance on, and appear in its proper shape. Henceforth, Cromwell's life was a vain attempt to clothe that force in constitutional forms, and make it seem something else, so that it might become something else. Yet was there not also something to be hoped from a policy which took its stand on realities instead of legal fictions?

CHAPTER XVI
THE FOUNDATION OF THE PROTECTORATE
1653

The fall of the Long Parliament was received with general satisfaction. "There was not so much as the barking of a dog or any general and visible repining at it," said Cromwell afterwards. His words are justified by the facts. Hyde termed it a most popular and obliging act, and the French Ambassador told his Government that nobility and populace universally rejoiced at General Cromwell's noble deed. Public feeling found vent in ballads. One described the scene of the dissolution, relating what Cromwell had said, and how the members had looked.

"Brave Oliver came to the House like a sprite,

His fiery face struck the Speaker dumb,

'Begone,' said he, 'you have sate long enough;

Do you mean to sit here until Doomsday come?'"

"Cheer up, kind countrymen, be not dismayed," sang another street poet, ending every verse with the exultant chorus: "Twelve parliament men shall be sold for a penny."

For a few weeks, Cromwell was the most popular man in the nation. Royalists whispered that the King would marry Cromwell's daughter, and that Cromwell would content himself with a dukedom and the viceroyalty of Ireland. A more general belief was that he would assume the crown himself. An enthusiastic partisan hung up in the Exchange a picture of Cromwell crowned, with the invitation underneath:

"Ascend three thrones, great captain and divine,

I' th' will of God, old Lion, they are thine."

Cromwell's own view of his position was that, being Commander-in-chief by Act of Parliament, his commission made him the only constituted authority left standing. His desire was to put an end to this dictatorship as soon as he could. The sword must be divested of all power in the civil administration, and the army leaders must prove to the world that they had not turned out the Long Parliament in order to grasp at power themselves. The army itself accepted Cromwell's view, but on the nature of the new civil authority to be set up there were two views amongst the officers. For the present, a temporary Council of State, consisting of thirteen persons, most of whom were officers, carried on the daily business of administration.

As to the future, Major-General Lambert advocated one kind of government, and Major-General Harrison another. Lambert was a gentleman of good family, with some political aptitude and some constitutional knowledge, but less of either than he fancied. A dashing leader and a skilful tactician, he was popular because of his gallant bearing and his genial temper, and believed to be honest because he was good-natured. As a politician he was an intriguer, inscrutable, scheming, and insatiably ambitious. Harrison was a man of no birth and little education, bred on perverted prophecies, full of desperate courage and high-flown enthusiasms,—a man born to lead forlorn hopes and die for lost causes, who did both even to the admiration of his enemies. Unselfish in his own aims, he swayed others by his devotion and his zeal. But he was fitter to command the left wing in the battle of Armageddon than to take any part in the government of earthly states.

Lambert wished to entrust power to a small council of ten or twelve. Harrison wished to give it to a larger council of seventy members like the Jewish Sanhedrin. Lambert's party proposed that the council should be assisted by an elected Parliament, and the authority of both defined by a written constitution. Harrison's followers wished to dispense with a Parliament altogether. The first adhered to the principles laid down in the Agreement of the People, which they had drawn up four years earlier. The second were inspired by the opinions of the Fifth Monarchy men, and believed that the time had come to realise their hopes. Of the four great monarchies of the world's history, the Assyrian and the Persian, the

Macedonian and the Roman, three had fallen, and the fourth was tottering to its fall. At last, as the prophets had foretold, the monarchy of Christ was to begin, and till He came to reign in person, His saints were to rule for Him. A text which Harrison had often in his mouth was—"The saints shall take the kingdom and possess it."

When Cromwell dissolved the Long Parliament, he had no definite plan for the future government of England. He was not a Fifth Monarchy man, but he had no faith in paper constitutions. He was convinced that godly men would make the best governors, but he felt that a government somewhat like a Parliament would be most satisfactory to the nation.

The result was a compromise by which a larger and more representative assembly than Harrison had proposed, was called together. In each county the Congregational Churches were asked to nominate suitable persons, and from this list the council of officers selected those it thought fittest. A hundred and forty persons were thus chosen, of whom five represented Scotland, six Ireland, and the rest England. A writ addressed to each person separately, from Oliver Cromwell, Captain-General, recited that he had been nominated by the General with the advice of his council of officers as one of the men to whom the weighty affairs of the Commonwealth were to be entrusted. All were Puritan notables, combining godliness with fidelity to the cause, and described in the writs as "men fearing God and hating covetousness."

On July 4th, they met at Westminster, and on behalf of the army Cromwell presented them with a deed under his hand and seal, whereby the several persons therein mentioned were constituted the supreme authority. In his opening speech he related the causes which had led to the dissolution of the Long Parliament and their own convocation, adding some advice on the use they were to make of their power. Let them be just and tender to all kinds of Christians, endeavour the promoting of the Gospel, and study to win the support of the nation by their devotion to the public weal. "Convince them that as men fearing God have fought them out of their bondage, so men fearing God do now rule them in the fear of God." In the war, and in the events which had led to the overthrow of the monarchy, there was "an evident print of providence," and now the task of government had come to them "by the way of necessity, by the way of the wise providence of God." "God manifests this to be the day of the power of Christ; having through so much blood, and so much trial as hath been upon these nations, made this to be one of the great issues thereof: to have His people called to the supreme authority." Let them therefore own their call, for never any body of men had come into the supreme authority in such a way of owning God and being owned by Him.

It was not, said Cromwell, by his own design that this had come to pass.

"I never looked to see such a day as this.... Indeed it is marvellous, and it hath been unprojected. It's not long since either you or we came to know of it. And indeed this hath been the way God hath dealt with us all along; to keep things from our eyes all along, so that we have seen nothing in all His dispensations long beforehand—which is also a witness, in some measure, to our integrity."

Since God had brought about so wonderful a thing, why should they not hope for things more wonderful still? "Why should we be afraid to say or think, that this way may be the door to usher in the things that God hath promised and prophesied of, and set the hearts of His people to wait for and expect?" Again and again Cromwell reiterated these hopes. "Indeed I do think somewhat is at the door. We are at the threshold." "You are at the edge of the promises and prophecies." He ended by quoting the 68th Psalm as a prophecy of the glory and the triumph of "the Gospel Churches." "The triumph of that Psalm is exceeding high, and God is accomplishing it."

The assembly to which he spoke was equally confident that its meeting marked the opening of a new era. "They looked," as they declared, "for the long-expected birth of freedom and happiness." "All the world over amongst the people of God" there was "a more than usual expectation of some great and strange changes coming upon the world, which we can hardly believe to be paralleled with any times but those a while before the birth of our Lord and Saviour Jesus Christ." Full of hope, the assembly set to work to fulfil its mission. It voted itself the title of Parliament, invited Cromwell and four other representative officers to take part in its proceedings, elected a new Council of State, and appointed twelve great

Committees for the redress of all kinds of grievances. It took in hand, simultaneously, the reform of the Law and of the Church. The abolition of the Court of Chancery was voted after a single day's debate. Its delays and costliness had long been a scandal, and it was said that twenty-three thousand causes of five to thirty years' standing were lying there undetermined. Next came an Act establishing civil marriage, and providing for the registration of births, marriages, and burials. Acts were passed for the relief of prisoners for debt, for the safe custody of idiots and lunatics, and for the removal of some smaller legal abuses. A committee was appointed to codify the Law, and sanguine reformers talked of reducing its great volumes "into the bigness of a pocket book, as it is proportionable in New England and elsewhere." The Fifth Monarchy preachers at Blackfriars went further, and bade them abolish the law of man, and set up in its place the law of God. They required not a simplification of the laws of England, but a code based on the laws of Moses.

The Church was taken in hand with the same rough vigour as the Law. A proposal to abolish tithes at once was lost by a few votes, but even its opponents were willing to abolish them if lay tithe-owners were compensated, and if some other maintenance were provided for the clergy. So the whole question was referred to a committee. On the other hand, a resolution abolishing patronage was passed by seventeen votes, and a bill ordered to be drawn up to carry it into effect. There were also persistent rumours of an impending attack on the endowments of the universities, and a large party in the House were opposed to any established Church, or any ministry not dependent on voluntary support. Outside Parliament, the Fifth Monarchy preachers denounced the parochial clergy as "hirelings" and "priests of Baal." Their sermons described the Church as an "outwork of Babylon," and a part of the "Kingdom of the Beast." The great design of Christ, they said, was to destroy all anti-Christian forms and churches and clergy all over the world. Their hymns summoned the faithful to follow the Lord to war.

"The Lord begins to honour us,

The Saints are marching on,

The sword is sharp, the arrows swift

To destroy Babylon."

In private, the Fifth Monarchy men were caballing to make Harrison Lord General instead of Cromwell.

Cromwell was dissatisfied and alarmed at the conduct of the Little Parliament and its consequences. Instead of promoting the Gospel, they had threatened to deprive its ministers of the means of subsistence. Instead of allaying sectarian strife their policy had embittered it. His own persistent attempts to reconcile religious animosities met with little success. Vainly he arranged conferences between Presbyterian, Independent, and Baptist ministers to persuade them to live harmoniously together. As he complained to his son-in-law, Fleetwood: "Fain would I have my service accepted of the Saints, if the Lord will, but it is not so. Being of different judgments, and those of each sort seeking most to propagate their own, that spirit of kindness that is to all, is hardly accepted of any." When he tried to mediate between the fighting ecclesiastics, they turned on him as the two Israelites did on Moses, and asked, "Who made thee a prince or a judge over us?" Because he wished to support a national Church the Blackfriars preachers abused him as "The Old Dragon" and "The Man of Sin." Because he had not called a real Parliament, the Levellers accused him of high treason to "his lords the people of England." For what he had done and what he had left undone Cromwell was attacked by fanatics of all parties.

At the same time the position of the Republic had changed for the worse since the Little Parliament began to sit. The Dutch war still continued, and though Monk had gained two decisive victories, on June 3rd and July 31st, over the Dutch fleet, peace was still far off. The chief obstacle to it was the exorbitant terms which the Little Parliament demanded, and on this question also Cromwell was at issue with the men now in power. Peace had become a necessity to England as well as Holland, for in September it was discovered that there would be a deficit of over half a million on the estimates for the navy. A new insurrection, fanned by promises of Dutch aid, had broken out in Scotland. In England there was a marked revival of royalist feeling, and a plot for the surprise of Portsmouth had been discovered. The Levellers were once more raising their heads. Lilburn, defying the penalty imposed by the act of banishment, had returned to England, and in August, 1653, he was tried for his contumacy. Crowds flocked to hear him tried, or to rescue him if condemned, and when he was acquitted their shouting was heard a mile off. Even the soldiers set to guard the Court blew their trumpets and beat their drums for joy, and it seemed as if the agitation suppressed in 1649 was beginning again.

Cromwell was now thoroughly disillusioned and began to repent his part in putting the men of the Little Parliament in power.

In later years, when he referred to his experiment, he called it apologetically "a story of my own weakness and folly."

"And yet," he said, "it was done in my simplicity. It was thought then that men of our own judgment, who had fought in the wars, and were all of a piece upon that account, why surely these men will hit it, and these men will do it to the purpose, whatever can be desired. And such a company of men were chosen and did proceed to action. And this was the naked truth, that the issue was not answerable to the simplicity and honesty of the design."

Besides repenting his own act, Cromwell began to doubt his own motives. Was his eagerness to transfer supreme power to others an honest constitutional scruple, or a cowardly evasion of responsibility? Was it not, perhaps, "a desire, I am afraid sinful enough, to be quit of the power God had most clearly by His providence put into my hands before He called me to lay it down; before those honest ends of our fighting were attained and settled."

Not only the General, but the officers, too, were dissatisfied with their creation. Apart from political or religious considerations, the proceedings of the Little Parliament seriously affected their interests as soldiers. It had touched their honour and threatened their pockets. A point on which the soldiers were justly sensitive was the strict observance of capitulations with royalist commanders, and in one notorious case articles of surrender had been grossly violated, and the Parliament had refused redress. Great opposition had been made to the renewal of the monthly assessment for the maintenance of the army, and a more equitable way of raising the money had been proposed. The soldiers feared that if this new method were adopted their pay would fall behindhand, and they would be obliged to starve or take free quarters. Still further irritation was caused by a motion that, in view of the pressing needs of the State, and the wealth they had obtained in its service, the higher officers should serve without pay for a whole year.

The discontented officers naturally turned to their General for help. Lambert and his party took up once more the idea of a written constitution. In November, a meeting of officers took place at which Lambert's scheme was discussed and adopted. It was a first draft of the Instrument of Government, the main difference being that it placed at the head of the State a King instead of a Protector. At the end of the month, it was submitted to Cromwell. "They told me," he said, "that except I would undertake the government they thought things would hardly come to a settlement, but blood and confusion would break in upon us." But to all their solicitation he replied with refusals. He had two great objections to accepting their offer. One was the aversion to the title of King, which revealed itself again in 1657. The other was that he had empowered the Little Parliament to sit till the end of 1654, and he was not willing to expel a second Parliament by force of arms. Lambert's plot was frustrated by the reluctance of the principal actor, and he retired sulkily to the country.

Cromwell still hoped that the Parliament might be induced to adopt a wiser policy. The strength of the two parties in it was very nearly equal, and a few votes might turn the scale in favour of the moderate section. A final battle on the Church question brought about a new trial of strength. On December 2nd, the Committee on Tithes produced a report containing a regular scheme for the reorganisation of the Church. One clause proposed the appointment of itinerant commissioners to eject unfit ministers and fill up vacant livings. Another provided that the present provision for the maintenance of approved ministers should be guaranteed by Parliament. Others affirmed that tithes were legal property, and suggested a plan for their commutation in case of persons who had conscientious scruples about paying them. Over this report the two parties fought for five whole sittings. The question whether the Church should be reformed or disestablished hung on their decision. At last, on Saturday, December 10th, the extremists triumphed, and the first clause of the report was rejected by fifty-six to fifty-four votes. The supporters of the Church regarded the division as fatal to the whole scheme.

Immediately on this defeat, the moderate party in the Parliament and the malcontents amongst the officers came to an agreement. All Sunday the leaders intrigued and negotiated. The one expedient left was to persuade the Parliament to abdicate, and make way for a more capable government. If the difficulty of getting rid of the Parliament was peaceably solved, those who knew Cromwell felt sure he would accept the accomplished fact, and assume the power offered him. The thing was not impossible, if it was properly worked. Some of the majority had voted on side issues; others might be gained over. Absentees were whipped up; waverers were appealed to through their interests or their fears. An argument which weighed with some was, that the army meant to put a stop to the sitting of the Parliament, and that a decent suicide was the only way to avoid a violent end.

On Monday, December 12th, the Moderates rose early and came to the House betimes. As soon as business began, Colonel Sydenham and other leaders of the party rose up and inveighed against the policy of their opponents. They charged them with seeking to destroy the army by not making sufficient and timely provision for its pay, with endeavouring to overthrow the Law, the Clergy, and the property of the subject. In conclusion they moved, "that the sitting of this Parliament any longer, as it is now constituted, will not be for the good of the Commonwealth, and that therefore it is requisite to deliver up to the Lord General Cromwell the powers which they had received from him."

Everything went off with the precision of a field-day. The debate was very short. One party strove to spin it out till the House grew fuller and their reinforcements came up. The other had resolved to carry the enemy's position by storm. It was no time to debate, said the Moderates, but to do something to prevent the calamities which threatened the State. Old Rouse, the Speaker, who was in the plot himself, ended the discussion by rising from the chair, and left the House without stopping to put the question or to hear the opponents of the motion. In vain they called to him to stop.

Preceded by the mace, and accompanied by the clerk of the House, he marched off with fifty or sixty members to Whitehall. Arrived there, they proceeded to sign their names to a paper returning their powers to Cromwell, and became once more private persons. Eventually about eighty members signed this act of abdication.

About twenty-seven members had stayed behind in the House. They were too few to form a quorum, and could not act as a Parliament. While they were drawing up a protest against the late proceedings, two colonels entered and ordered them to come out. "We are here," said one of the members, "by a call from the General, and will not come out by your desire unless you have a command from him." The colonels had no order from Cromwell to produce, but they fetched in two files of musketeers, and the members took the hint.

Cromwell had taken no part in the plot for procuring the abdication of the Little Parliament. "I can say it," he told the members of the next Parliament, "in the presence of divers persons here who know whether I lie, that I did not know one tittle of that resignation, till they all came and brought it, and delivered it into my hands." As none of the said persons ever contradicted his statement, it may be accepted as true. It sufficed for him to remain passive, and power came back to his hands by a sort of natural necessity. Once more he was in possession of the dictatorship he had sought to lay down. "My power was again by this resignation as boundless and unlimited as before, all things being subject to arbitrariness, and myself a person having power over the three nations without bound or limit set; all government being dissolved, and all civil administration at an end." For the second time Lambert and his allies urged Cromwell to accept the government under the constitution which they had drawn up. The difficulty of getting rid of the Little Parliament no longer stood in the way, and the title of King had been replaced by the title of Protector. They also pointed out to him that the acceptance of the Protectorship in no way increased his power. On the contrary, it put an end to his dictatorship, and reduced his power by imposing constitutional restrictions upon its exercise. It bound him to do nothing without the consent of either a Council or a Parliament. Another argument was still more effective. Once more they warned Cromwell, that, unless he would undertake the government, anarchy was inevitable, and made him responsible for the "blood and confusion" which would be the result. After three or four days' discussion, Cromwell accepted the constitution, to which a general meeting of officers had in the interim given their approval and adhesion. He was solemnly installed as Protector on December 16, 1653, dressed not like a general in scarlet, but like a citizen in a plain black coat, to show all men that military rule was over, and civil government restored.

The new constitution, like the Agreement of the People in 1649, represented the political ideas of the officers of the army. But since 1649 the officers had lost confidence in the people, and they sought now to erect a government based on something firmer than the will of a fickle multitude. A written constitution was asserted to be a better foundation for a government than popular consent, for the express reason that the people would have no power to alter it. There had been enough of commotion, and confusion, and change. "It was high time that some power should pass a decree upon the wavering humours of the people, and say to this nation, as the Almighty Himself said once to the unruly sea: 'Here shall be thy bounds; hitherto shalt thou come, and no farther.'" This was what Lambert and the officers assumed the right to say when they imposed the "Instrument of Government" upon England.

Throughout its provisions their distrust of the English people is evident. Little boroughs were abolished and constituencies made more equal, but the franchise instead of being extended was restricted. In boroughs, the franchise remained unaltered—that is, the right of election was generally in the hands of the corporation; in counties, the forty-shilling freeholders were abolished, and a new franchise was created, which gave the vote to all men possessing property worth two hundred pounds. Henceforth, therefore, Parliament would represent the opinions and interests of the middle classes.

Distrust of the electors was naturally accompanied by distrust of the representatives. For the future, the legislative and executive powers were to be kept permanently separate. The authority and the duration of Parliament were strictly limited. It was to meet once in three years, but to sit for five months only. It had power to legislate as it thought fit, but its laws must not contravene the provisions of the constitution. Its consent to levy money for extraordinary expenses was necessary, but a constant yearly revenue was to be raised to meet the ordinary charge of civil government, army, and navy, which Parliament had no right to diminish.

The Protector possessed the executive power, but his authority was limited also. Except when bills contained something contrary to the constitution, he had no right to veto them. In domestic administration and in foreign affairs, he could not act without the consent of the Council; in taxation and for the employment of the army, he needed the consent of Parliament or Council. The members of the new Council were, in Cromwell's phrase, "the trustees of the Commonwealth in the intervals of Parliament," and possessed far more power than the Council of State erected in 1649. The councillors, most of whom were appointed by the "Instrument" itself, held office for life, and in their hands lay the choice of the Protector's successor.

The object of this complicated system of checks and balances was to prevent either Parliament or Protector from becoming absolute, and to render religious liberty unassailable. None knew better than the leaders of the army how slight a hold upon the nation the principle of toleration had obtained, or how little religious parties were willing to accept it. "This hath been one of the vanities of our contest," said Cromwell. "Every sect saith, 'Oh give me liberty,' but give it him and to his power he will not yield it to anybody else." For the ingenious political devices of the constitution the Protector cared very little, but the religious settlement was a settlement after his own heart. There was to be a national Church, maintained for the present by tithes, in the future, it was hoped, by some better way. Outside the Church, there was to be full liberty of worship for those who did not belong to it, "provided they did not abuse their liberty to the civil injury of others, or to the actual disturbance of the public peace." But this liberty was not to extend to Popery or Prelacy, which were politically dangerous, or "to such as under the profession of Christ hold forth and practise licentiousness."

This was the religious freedom which ever since 1647 the army had demanded, and had at last realised. Yet in spite of all the new constitution promised, there was little prospect that it would obtain the acceptance of the nation. England was the last country in which the attempt to transform a military dictatorship into a sort of constitutional government was likely to succeed.

At the moment, however, the only opposition there was came from the Fifth Monarchy men—hostile to anything which resembled a monarchy or an established Church. Harrison refused to act under the Protector's Government, and was deprived of his commission. Fifth Monarchy preachers raged against the Protector from the pulpit. One called him "the dissemblingest perjured villain in the world." Another identified him with the Little Horn in Daniel's prophecy, which was to make war against the Saints and to be destroyed by them.

Their ravings only strengthened Cromwell's position. What England wanted was a government which would maintain order and preserve property. The interests which the Little Parliament had imperilled welcomed Cromwell's accession to power. His elevation was a bargain, says Ludlow, with the corrupt part of the clergy and the lawyers; he became their Protector and they the humble supporters of his tyranny. So evident was the advantage which Cromwell derived from the events of the last few months that what had happened was freely attributed to his profound statecraft. All was a pageant played by Cromwell, thought Baxter, in order to make his soldiers out of love with democracy and to render his usurpation necessary. He was resolved we should be saved by him or perish.

"He made more use of the wild-headed sectaries than barely to fight for him. They now serve him as much by their heresies, their enmity to learning and ministry, their pernicious demands which tend to confusion, as they had done before by their valour in the field. He can now conjure up at pleasure some terrible apparition of Agitators, Levellers, and such like, who, as they affrighted the King from Hampton Court, shall affright the people to fly to him for refuge: that the hand that wounded may heal them."

Hitherto Cromwell had been the destroyer of old institutions. Now he came forward as the saviour of society. England, therefore, submitted to his government without resistance and without enthusiasm, but with a general feeling of relief. The conversion of the monarchy into a republic had been violent and bloody; the transition from the Republic to the Protectorate was as peaceful as one of the ordinary operations of nature. As such, Waller celebrated it in his poem to Cromwell.

"Still as you rise, the State exalted too

Finds no distemper while 'tis changed by you,

Changed like the world's great scene when without noise

The rising sun night's vulgar lights destroys."

CHAPTER XVII
CROMWELL'S DOMESTIC POLICY
1654–1658

Cromwell came into power as the nominee of the army, and in domestic affairs the programme which he set himself to carry out was that which the army had set forth in its petitions and manifestoes. For the moment he was invested with all the authority of a dictator. According to the "Instrument of Government," the first triennial Parliament was to meet in September, 1654, and in the interval the Protector and his Council were empowered to issue ordinances, which had the force of law "until order shall be taken in Parliament concerning them." Cromwell made a liberal use of this provision, and the period of nine months which followed his accession was the creative period of his government. Between December, 1653, and September, 1654, he issued eighty-two ordinances, nearly all of which were confirmed in 1656 by his second Parliament. Hallam, in a disparaging comparison between Cromwell and Napoleon, concludes by saying that Cromwell, unlike Napoleon, "never showed any signs of a legislative mind, or any desire to fix his renown on that noblest basis, the amelioration of social institutions." In reality, nothing could be farther from the truth, and if Cromwell's reforming zeal has left no trace on the statute book, the reason is that all the laws passed during the Protectorate were annulled at the Restoration.

All the leading principles of Cromwell's domestic policy are contained in the small folio volume of his ordinances. A few are merely prolongations of expiring acts, others are personal or local in their application. There is an ordinance for the relief of poor prisoners, another codifying the law relating to the maintenance of highways, and there are three devoted to the reorganisation of the Treasury. The settlement of Ireland and Scotland, and the completion of the union of the three kingdoms, which the Long Parliament had left unfinished, form the subject of a third series. But none exhibit so plainly the Protector's domestic policy as the three sets of ordinances dealing with the reform of the Law, the reformation of manners, and the reorganisation of the national Church.

Ever since 1647, the army had demanded that the laws of England should be so reformed, "that all suits and questions of right may be made more clear and certain in their issues, and not so tedious nor chargeable in their proceedings." The Long Parliament took the task in hand, made some slight progress, and then stuck fast. The Little Parliament attempted it with so much rude vigour that it seemed likely to end in the subversion of all law. The Protector took up the work where the Long Parliament left off, and persistently pursued it as long as he ruled.

Cromwell realised its difficulty. "If any man," he once said, "should ask me, 'Why, how will you have it done?' I confess I do not know." All he could do was to select the best men for the purpose, and to leave them a free hand. Therefore he applied to the lawyers to co-operate, "being resolved to give the learned of the robe the honour of reforming their profession," and hoping "that God will give them hearts to do it." His chief assistant was Matthew Hale, who was made a judge by the Protector early in 1654. At the opening of Parliament in September, 1654, Cromwell announced that the Government had called together "persons of as great ability and great interest as are in the nation, to consider how the laws might be made plain and short, and less chargeable to the people," and that they had prepared several bills. The most important of these schemes was the ordinance for the regulation of the Court of Chancery, published August 21, 1654, and confirmed by Parliament in 1656. It contained a reduced scale of fees, and embodied, according to modern lawyers, many valuable reforms. Contemporary practitioners, such as Whitelocke, held that there was much in the new procedure which it was impossible or undesirable to carry out, but with some subsequent modifications it was duly put in force.

Cromwell was equally zealous for the reform of the Criminal Law. In April, 1653, as soon as he had turned out the Long Parliament, he gave pardons to all prisoners sentenced to death except those guilty of murder. His object was to make the laws "conformable to the just and righteous laws of God." Some English laws, he told Parliament, were "wicked and abominable laws."

"To hang a man for six and eightpence and I know not what—to hang for a trifle and acquit murder, is in the ministration of the law through ill framing of it.... To see men lose their lives for petty matters is a thing God will reckon, and I wish it may not be laid on this nation a day longer than you have opportunity to give a remedy."

To carry out these schemes required not merely the help of lawyers to devise them, but the co-operation of Parliament to make them law. The Protector's first Parliament spent all its time in constitutional debates, and did nothing to reform the Law. His second, busy most of its existence in the like manner, discussed the bills introduced by the Government for the establishment of county registers and local courts, but allowed them to drop. It completed the abolition of feudal incidents which the Long Parliament had commenced, and which Charles II.'s Parliament finally placed on the statute book, but it left the harshness and cruelty of the criminal code for the nineteenth century to redress.

The "Reformation of Manners" was an object in which the Protector obtained more support from Parliament. All Puritans were eager for it, and the Long Parliament had made a beginning by acts enjoining the stricter observance of Sunday, punishing swearing with greater severity, and making adultery a capital offence. Of the Protector's ordinances, one declared duelling "unpleasing to God, unbecoming Christians, and contrary to all good order and government." A person sending a challenge was to be bound over to keep the peace for six months, and a duellist who killed his opponent was to be tried for murder. A second ordinance supplemented the act against swearing by special provisions for the punishment of carmen, porters, and watermen, "who are very ordinarily drunk and do blaspheme." A third forbade cock-fighting, because it often led to disturbances of the peace and was accompanied by gaming and drunkenness. A fourth suppressed horse-racing for six months, not because of its accompaniments, but because the Cavaliers made use of race-meetings "to carry on their pernicious designs."

When Cromwell's second Parliament met, he appealed to it to further the work.

"I am confident," said he, "our liberty and prosperity depend upon reformation. Make it a shame to see men bold in sin and profaneness and God will bless you. Truly these things do respect the souls of men, and the spirits, which are the men. The mind is the man. If that be kept pure the man signifies somewhat; if not, I would very fain see what difference there is betwixt him and a beast. He hath only some activity to do some more mischief."

Parliament answered by confirming the ordinances against duelling, swearing, and cock-fighting, and passing similar acts of its own. One was directed against the vagrants and "idle, dissolute" persons who abounded in all parts of the country. Amongst them, "the bigots of that iron time" included fiddlers and minstrels taken "playing or making music" in taverns, who were declared punishable as "rogues and vagabonds." A second act was aimed at the professional gamesters about London, who made it their trade "to cheat and debauch the young gentry." A third act enforced the Puritan Sabbath in all its severity. On that day, no shops might be opened and no manufactures carried on. No travelling was to be allowed, except in cases of necessity attested by a certificate from a justice, and persons "vainly and profanely walking on the day aforesaid" were to be punished. Sunday closing was the rule for all inns and alehouses, though the dressing or sale of victuals in a moderate way, "for the use of such as cannot otherwise be provided for," was permitted.

Much of this drastic legislation was ineffective. In some cases it went far beyond the feeling of the times. Juries steadily refused to convict persons charged with adultery under the act of 1650, and it is doubtful whether the capital penalty was ever actually inflicted. In many places, the local authorities were indifferent or timid. "We may have good laws," said the Protector, "against the common country disorders that are everywhere, yet who is to execute them?" Hardly the country justices. "A justice of the peace shall by most be wondered at as an owl, if he go but one step out of the ordinary course of his fellow justices in the reformation of these things." Hence the value in Cromwell's eyes of the Major-Generals established throughout England in the autumn of 1655. They were not simply military officers charged to keep an eye on the political enemies of the government, but police magistrates required to repress crime and immorality in their respective districts. Pride put a stop to bear-baiting in London by killing the bears, and to cock-fighting by wringing the necks of the cocks. Whalley boasted, after he had been a few months in office, that there were no vagrants left in Nottinghamshire, and in every county his colleagues suppressed unnecessary alehouses by the score. Nor was it only humble offenders who were struck at: neither the rich nor the noble escaped the impartial severity of these military reformers. "Let them be who they may that are debauched," said Cromwell, "it is for the glory of God that nothing of outward consideration should save them from a just punishment and reformation." He claimed that the establishment of the Major-Generals had been "more effectual towards the discountenancing of vice and the settling of religion than anything done these fifty years." Their rule ended in the spring of 1657, and Cromwell feared that the work of reformation would come to a stop. But the experiment had infused new vigour into the local administration, which lasted as long as the Protectorate endured.

In spite of these restrictive laws, it must not be imagined that there was any general suppression of public amusements or sports. "Lawful and laudable recreations" even Puritans encouraged. In 1647, when the Long Parliament prohibited the observation of Christmas and of saints' days in general, it passed an act giving servants, apprentices, and scholars a whole holiday once a month, for "recreation and relaxation from their constant and ordinary labours." The Protector himself hunted, hawked, and played bowls, just as if he had been a Royalist country-gentleman. He told Parliament that he suppressed race-meetings not because they were unlawful, but because they were temporarily inexpedient. With all his zeal for Sunday closing, the suppression of unnecessary alehouses, and the punishment of drunkenness, it never occurred to him to stop the sale of drink altogether. He drank wine and small beer himself, and quoted as illogical and absurd "the man who would keep all wine out of the country lest men should be drunk." The idea was contrary to his conception of civil freedom. "It will be found," he said, "an unjust and unwise jealousy to deprive a man of his natural liberty upon a supposition he may abuse it. When he doth abuse it, judge."

In the moral crusade he had undertaken, the Protector relied not so much on restrictive legislation as on the influence of education and religion. It was to their defective education that he attributed much of the misconduct of the "profane nobility and gentry of this nation." "We send our children to France," he said, "before they know God or good manners, and they return with all the licentiousness of that nation. Neither care taken to educate them before they go, or to keep them in good order when they come home." As a party, the Puritans showed a great zeal for education, and the pamphlet literature of the time is full of schemes for its reformation or extension. In these discussions, the modern conception of the duty of the State with regard to education gradually took shape. While the plan of education which Milton published in 1644 was intended only for "a select body of our noble and gentle youth," in 1660, he advocated the foundation of schools in all parts of the nation, in order to spread knowledge, civility, and culture to "all extreme parts which now lie numb and neglected." In his *Oceana*, Harrington asserted that the formation of future citizens by means of a system of free schools was one of the chief duties of a republic.

As usually happens, practical men lagged behind the theorists, but during the Commonwealth a portion of the revenue of confiscated Church lands was systematically devoted to the maintenance of schools and schoolmasters. The Protector pursued the same policy, and publicly declared when appropriating a grant for educational purposes in Scotland, that it was "a duty not only to have the Gospel set up, but schools for children erected and maintenance provided therefor." His government undertook the task of ejecting incapable schoolmasters and of licensing persons fit to teach. It made the proper administration of educational endowments in general a part of its business, and one of Cromwell's earliest ordinances appointed fresh commissioners for the visitation of the universities, and established a permanent board of visitors for the great public schools. Personally, he was far more interested in the reorganisation of the universities than in primary or secondary education. He vigorously defended them against the attacks of the zealots of the Little Parliament who threatened their disendowment or abolition. In 1651, he had been elected Chancellor of Oxford, and held that office till July, 1657, when he was succeeded by his son Richard, signalizing his connection with the university by the foundation of a new readership in Divinity, and the presentation of some Greek manuscripts to the Bodleian. He appointed John Owen his Vice-Chancellor, under whose efficient rule Oxford prospered greatly. Even Clarendon is forced to admit that in spite of visitations and purgings the university "yielded a harvest of extraordinary good and sound knowledge in all parts of learning."

The Protector also endeavoured to found a new university in the north of England. There was a widespread feeling that the two existing universities were not enough for the country. In 1641, petitions were presented praying for the foundation of a university at York or Manchester, and later it was proposed to establish one in London. In 1651, Cromwell strongly recommended the endowment of a school or college for all the sciences and literature, out of the property of the Dean and Chapter of Durham. The scheme, he wrote, was "a matter of great concernment and importance, as that which by the blessing of God may conduce to the promoting of learning and piety in these poor, rude, ignorant parts," and bring forth in time "such happy and glorious fruits as are scarce thought of or foreseen." But Parliament did nothing, and it was reserved for Oliver himself to found a college at Durham in 1657, which throve greatly until the Restoration put an end to its existence.

The Protector encouraged learned men and men of letters. With his relative, the poet Waller, he was on terms of considerable intimacy; he allowed Hobbes and Cowley, both Royalists, to return from exile, and he released Cleveland when he was arrested by one of the Major-Generals, although Cleveland's fame rested mainly on satires against the Puritans. Milton and Marvell were in Cromwell's service as Latin secretaries, and he also employed Marvell as tutor to one of his wards. Brian Walton was assisted in the printing of his Polyglot Bible, and Archbishop Ussher was honoured by a public funeral.

But both learning and education were, in Cromwell's eyes, inseparably connected with religion. When he accepted the Chancellorship he congratulated Oxford on the learning and piety "so marvellously springing up there," adding a hope that it might be "useful to that great and glorious kingdom of our Lord Jesus Christ." Thinking that the chief function of the universities was to provide ministers for the Church, he held piety more important than learning. "I believe," he told his Parliament, five years later, "that God hath for the ministry a very great seed in the youth of the universities, who, instead of studying books, study their own heart." Cromwell's desire to develop higher education, and his defence of the universities against their assailants, were the natural consequences of his resolve to maintain a national Church against those who wished to sever the connection between Church and State. On this question, the army, as a whole, supported Cromwell. In the "Agreement of the People," presented to Parliament in 1649, the army had demanded that "the Christian religion be held forth and recommended as the public profession of this nation," and it included "the instructing of the people thereunto, so it be not compulsive," and "the maintaining able teachers for that end," amongst the legitimate functions of the government. These principles had been embodied in the "Instrument of Government," and the duty of devising means to carry them out fell to the Protector.

The first question to be decided was the question of the maintenance of the clergy. The Little Parliament had proposed to abolish tithes altogether, and in the "Instrument of Government" the substitution of some other provision was suggested. As no satisfactory scheme for the commutation of tithes could be devised, Cromwell felt bound to preserve them. "For my part," said he, "I should think I were very treacherous if I took away tithes till I see the legislative power settle maintenance to ministers another way." To abolish tithes before that was done, would be "to cut the throats of the ministers." Under the Protectorate, as under the rule of the Long Parliament, it was the permanent policy of the government to increase the income of the parochial clergy. The endowments of poor livings were systematically augmented out of the fund supplied by episcopal lands and the fines imposed on royalist delinquents.

The basis of the Protector's plan for the reorganisation of the Church was the scheme which John Owen had presented to the Long Parliament in 1652. On March 20, 1654, Cromwell issued an ordinance "for the approbation of public preachers," which appointed thirty-eight commissioners, lay and clerical, to sit permanently in London and examine into the qualifications of all candidates for livings. Their business was to certify that they found the candidate "to be a person for the grace of God in him, his holy and unblamable conversation, as also for his knowledge and utterance, able and fit to preach the Gospel," and without obtaining this certificate no one was in future to be admitted to a benefice. The commissioners were not empowered to impose any doctrinal tests, and it was expressly declared that approbation by them "is not intended nor shall be construed to be any solemn or sacred setting apart of any person to any particular office in the ministry." All that the "Triers" undertook to do was to see that none but fit and proper persons should receive "the public stipend and maintenance" guaranteed by the State.

After provision for the appointment of the fit, came provision for the elimination of the unfit. A second ordinance, issued in August, 1654, appointed local commissioners in every county to remove scandalous and inefficient ministers and schoolmasters within its limits. Amongst the reasons which justified ejection were included not merely immoral conduct or Popish and blasphemous opinions, but disaffection to the government and the use of the Prayer-book. In September, the work was completed by a third ordinance for the union of small and the division of large and populous parishes.

Cromwell's speeches are full of expressions of satisfaction at the results that these ordinances produced. He was proud of the character of his clergy. "In the times of Episcopacy," said he, "what pitiful certificates served to make a man a minister. If any man understood Latin or Greek, he was sure to be admitted." But now, "neither Mr. parson nor doctor in the university hath been reckoned stamp enough by those that made these approbations, though I can say they have a great esteem for learning." The rule with the Triers was, "that they must not admit a man unless they were able to discern something of the grace of God in him."

He was equally proud of the comprehensiveness of the Church. There were "three sorts of godly men," that is, three sects, to be provided for in it: the Presbyterians, the Independents, and the Baptists. The Triers were drawn impartially from all three bodies, and "though a man be of any of those three judgments, if he have the root of the matter in him he may be admitted." Summing up the work of the Triers and Ejectors, he emphatically declared: "There hath not been such a service to England since the Christian religion was perfect in England."

In the main, Cromwell's satisfaction was justified. Both bodies of commissioners did the work they were charged to do with fidelity. Some good men were expelled merely for royalism or using the liturgy, but the bulk of those who lost their livings deserved their fate, and those admitted were generally fit for their office. The Presbyterian Richard Baxter, an opponent on principle of Cromwell and his works, felt bound to praise the commissioners:

"To give them their due, they did abundance of good to the Church. They saved many a congregation from ignorant, ungodly, drunken teachers. That sort of men that intended no more in the ministry than to say a sermon as readers say their common prayers, and so patch up a few good words together to talk the people asleep with on Sunday, and all the rest of the week go with them to the alehouse and harden them in sin; and that sort of ministers that either preached against a holy life, or preached as men that were never acquainted with it; all those that used the ministry but as a common trade to live by, and were never likely to convert a soul:—all these they usually rejected, and in their stead admitted of any that were able, serious preachers, and lived a godly life, of what tolerable opinion soever they were. So that though they were many of them somewhat partial for Independents, Separatists, Fifth Monarchy-men, and Anabaptists, and against the Prelatists and Arminians, yet so great was the benefit above the hurt to the Church, that many thousands of souls blessed God for the faithful ministers whom they let in."

Outside the bounds of the national Church, the constitution promised liberty of worship to "all such as do profess faith in God by Jesus Christ." Anglicanism and Catholicism, however, labelled Prelacy and Popery, and regarded as idolatrous or politically dangerous, were excepted by name from this promise. In practice, although the use of the liturgy had been prohibited since 1645, many orthodox Anglicans had contrived to retain their livings, sometimes using portions of the Prayer-book from memory, in other cases confining themselves to preaching and to the administration of the sacraments. Many ejected ministers gathered little congregations in private houses, and were not molested by the Government. The royalist insurrection of 1655 led to greater severity, and in October, 1655, Cromwell issued a proclamation prohibiting the employment of the ejected clergy as chaplains or schoolmasters. It was meant as a warning, rather than to be rigidly enforced, and the promise was made that any man whose "godliness and good affection to the present government" were capable of proof should be treated with tenderness. Congregations of Royalists continued to meet in London throughout the Protectorate, and the Government winked at their use of Anglican services and ceremonies. But whenever there was a new plot discovered, their meetings were liable to be interrupted by the soldiery.

The case of the Catholics was harder than that of the Anglicans, although their lot was less hard than it had been. In 1650, the acts imposing fines on recusants for not coming to church were repealed, and there were persistent rumours that the Independents were about to make proposals for their toleration. In June, 1654, a Catholic priest was executed in London for no crime except being a priest. Cromwell, it is said, wished to pardon him, but was prevented by the opposition of his Council. In 1656, Mazarin urged Cromwell to grant toleration to the Catholics.

"I cannot," answered the Protector, "as to a public declaration of my sense on that point; although I believe that under my government your Eminency on behalf of the Catholics has less cause for complaint than under the Parliament. For I have of some and those very many had compassion, making a difference. I have plucked many out of the fire,— the raging fire of persecution, which did tyrannise over their consciences and encroach by arbitrariness of power over their estates. And herein it is my purpose, as soon as I can remove impediments and some weights that press me down, to make a further progress, and discharge my promise to your Eminence."

The Protector's purpose was never fulfilled. Public opinion in England was too hostile to the Catholics to permit of their legal toleration, and the same thing happened when Cromwell wished to readmit the Jews to England. In November, 1655, Manasseh Ben Israel, a learned Portuguese Jew, settled in Amsterdam as a physician, petitioned the Protector to allow the Jews to reside and trade in England, and to grant them the free exercise of their religion. Cromwell, who was personally in favour of their petition, called together a committee of divines, merchants, and lawyers to confer with the Council on the question. The Protector himself took part in the conferences. "I never heard a man speak so well," said one of his hearers, but the divines feared for their religion and the merchants for their trade, so the legal toleration the Jews asked for was not granted. Cromwell, however, granted them leave to meet in private houses for devotion, and showed them such encouragement and favour that their resettlement in England really dates from the Protectorate.

The Protector's tolerant nature showed itself again in his dealings with the Quakers. Under the Commonwealth, the Quakers were persecuted and imprisoned, not simply because their opinions were regarded as blasphemous, but because they were held dangerous to the public peace. Their attacks on the clergy and their misconduct and brawling in churches gave colour to these accusations. Under the Protectorate, this persecution continued, till it was mitigated by the intervention of the Protector and his Council. In 1654, George Fox had a long interview with the Protector. "I spake much to him," writes Fox, "of truth; and a great discourse I had with him about religion, wherein he carried himself very moderately." The earnestness and enthusiasm of Fox impressed Cromwell greatly. "As I spake, he would several times say, it was very good, and it was truth. And as I was turning to go away, he catches me by the hand, and with tears in his eyes, said: 'Come again to my house; for if thou and I were but an hour of a day together we should be nearer one to the other'; adding, that he wished me no more ill than he did to his own soul." Convinced that the Quakers were not inclined to "take up a carnal sword" against his government, the Protector ordered Fox to be set free, and in October, 1656, he released a number of imprisoned Quakers. Again in November, 1657, he issued a general circular to all justices in England and Wales, stating that though he was far from countenancing the mistaken practices or principles of the Quakers, yet as those proceeded "rather from a spirit of error than a malicious opposition to authority," they were "to be pitied, and dealt with as persons under a strong delusion," to be discharged from prison, and to be treated in the future with tenderness rather than severity.

Yet tolerant as Cromwell was, there were limits to his toleration, and certain opinions he regarded as outside the pale. The Instrument refused liberty to "such as under the profession of Christ hold forth and practise licentiousness" and the Petition and Advice added to them those who "published horrible blasphemies."

"As for profane persons," said Cromwell, "blasphemers, such as preach sedition; the contentious railers, evil-speakers, who seek by evil words to corrupt good manners; persons of loose conversation—punishment from the civil magistrate ought to meet with these. Because if they pretend conscience; yet walking disorderly and not according but contrary to the Gospel, and even to natural lights, they are judged by all. And their sins being open make them subjects of the magistrate's sword, who ought not to bear the sword in vain. The discipline of the army was such that a man would not be suffered to remain there, of whom we could take notice that he was guilty of such practices as these."

A well-ordered state, thought Cromwell, should in this respect resemble an army, but, even with regard to opinions which he held blasphemous, he was not willing to suffer the extreme penalties to be inflicted which the law sanctioned and the voice of most Puritans demanded.

In 1656, James Naylor, an old soldier who was one of Fox's early disciples, allowed himself to be hailed by his enthusiastic followers as a new Messiah, and was consequently thrown into prison as a blasphemer. The Parliament then sitting assumed judicial powers, and, after many days' debate, voted that he should be branded, pilloried, whipped, and imprisoned at pleasure. The Protector vainly pointed out to the House that it was going beyond its powers, and all the influence of the Government was required to save Naylor from capital punishment. What the Protector would probably have done if the punishment of Naylor had been left to him was shown by his treatment of John Biddle. Unitarians were by implication excluded from toleration by the Petition and Advice. In 1655, Biddle was prosecuted under the Blasphemy Act of 1648, and would undoubtedly have been sentenced to death. The Protector was petitioned to interfere, and replied by soundly rating the petitioners. "If it be true," said he, "what Mr. Biddle holds, to wit, that our Lord and Saviour Jesus Christ is but a creature, then all those who worship Him with the worship due to God are idolaters." No Christian, was his conclusion, could give any countenance to such a person, but nevertheless he stopped the trial by issuing a warrant for Biddle's confinement at St. Mary's Castle in the Scilly Islands. Biddle's life was undoubtedly saved by this intervention.

In spite of the liberality and comprehensiveness of Cromwell's ecclesiastical policy, there were several sections of Puritans whom it failed to satisfy. Some Independents opposed any established Church, and denied that the State ought in any way to meddle with religious matters. The most distinguished adherents of this view were Vane and Milton. The magistrate, said Milton, had no coercive power at all in matters of religion. It was not his business "to settle religion," as it was popularly termed, "by appointing either what we shall believe in divine things or practise in religious." His duty was simply to defend the Church. "Had he once learned not further to concern himself with Church affairs, half his labour might be spared and the Commonwealth better tended."

Another section, in the name of liberty of conscience, denied the State any right to punish blasphemous or immoral doctrines. "They tell the Magistrate," said the Protector, "that he hath nothing to do with men holding such notions; these are matters of conscience and opinion; they are matters of religion; what hath the Magistrate to do with these things? He is to look to the outward man, not to the inward." Cromwell's own position with regard to dangerous opinions was that, if they were but opinions, they were best left alone. "Notions will hurt none but those that have them." When they developed into actions, it was a different matter, and especially when they led to rebellion and bloodshed. "Our practice hath been," he said in 1656, "to let all this nation see that whatever pretensions to religion would continue quiet and peaceable, they should enjoy conscience and liberty to themselves." But to be quiet and peaceable was the indispensable condition. Fifth Monarchy preachers were frequently arrested for sermons against the government, both before and after the attempted rising of the Fifth Monarchy men in the spring of 1657. On one occasion, some of the congregation of John Rogers, one of their preachers, came to Whitehall to argue with the Protector, complaining that their pastor was suffering for religion's sake. Cromwell answered that Rogers suffered as a railer, a seducer, and a stirrer-up of sedition: that to call suffering for evil-doing suffering for the Gospel was to make Christ the patron of such things. "God is my witness," he concluded, "no man in England doth suffer for the testimony of Jesus. Nay do not lift up your hands and your eyes, for there is no man in England which suffers so. There is such liberty—I wish it be not abused, that no man in England suffereth for Christ."

It was true. Cromwell's was the most tolerant government which had existed in England since the Reformation. In practice, he was more lenient than the laws, and more liberal-minded than most of his advisers. The drawback was, that even the more limited amount of religious freedom which the laws guaranteed seemed too much to the great majority of the nation. Englishmen—even Puritans—had not yet learnt the lesson of toleration. "Is there not yet," said Cromwell in 1655, "a strange itch upon the spirits of men? Nothing will satisfy them unless they can press their finger upon their brethren's consciences to pinch them there." To prevent this, was, he avowed, his task as a ruler.

"If the whole power was in the Presbyterians, they would force all men their way, and the Fifth Monarchy men would do the same, and so the Rebaptised persons; and his work was to keep several judgments in peace, because, like men falling out in the streets, they would run their heads one against another; he was as a constable to part them and keep them in peace."

To induce these jarring sects to co-operate was more difficult, but that also Cromwell attempted to do. In the Puritan Church, which he organised, no agreement about ritual or discipline or doctrine was required, save only the acceptance of the main principles of Christianity. It was not so much a Church as a confederation of Christian sects working together for righteousness, under the control of the State. The absence of agreement in details and of uniformity in externals was no defect in Cromwell's eyes. To him it was rather a merit. "All that believe," he had once written, "have the real unity which is more glorious because inward and spiritual."[8]

The originality of the Protector's ecclesiastical policy lay in this attempt to combine the two principles of toleration and comprehension. It reflected his character. His tolerance was not the result of scepticism or indifference, but arose from respect for the consciences of others. The comprehensiveness of his Church was the outcome of his large-hearted sympathy with every form of Puritanism. To local magistrates in local religious quarrels, he enjoined "a charity as large as the whole flock of Christ"; and the same spirit inspired his exhortation to the Little Parliament.

"Have a care of the whole flock. Love the sheep. Love the lambs. Love all; tend all; cherish and countenance all in all things that are good. And if the poorest Christian, the most mistaken Christian, shall desire to live peaceably and quietly under you: I say if any desire but to live a life of godliness and honesty, let him be protected."

Mr. Greatheart, under whose protection all pilgrims to the Celestial City walked securely—Feeble-Mind and Ready-to-Halt, as well as Valiant-for-Truth,—is but an allegorical representation of what Cromwell was to the Puritans. Cromwell's ecclesiastical system passed away with its author, but no man exerted more influence on the religious development of England. Thanks to him, Nonconformity had time to take root and to grow so strong in England that the storm which followed the Restoration had no power to root it up.

CHAPTER XVIII
CROMWELL'S FOREIGN POLICY
1654–1658

Three aims guided Cromwell's foreign policy: the first was the desire to maintain and to spread the Protestant religion; the second, the desire to preserve and extend English commerce; the third, the desire to prevent the restoration of the Stuarts by foreign aid. The European mission of England, its material greatness, and its political independence were inseparably associated in his mind, and beneath all apparent wavering and hesitation these three aims he consistently pursued.

The Protector had inherited from the Long Parliament a European situation of the greatest complexity. The Dutch war had undone the work of the previous three years. In 1653, England was once more isolated and in danger of a European combination against her. England and France were still carrying on hostilities at sea. Denmark had seized English merchantmen, and closed the Baltic to English trade. Portugal was actually at war with us. There were rumours of the formation of a triple alliance against England, between Holland, France, and Denmark. On the other hand, the war turned more and more against the United Provinces. In the spring of 1654, the English were "perfectly lords and masters of the narrow seas," and no Dutch merchantman could show itself in the Channel.

England had captured over fourteen hundred sail from the Dutch, including 120 men-of-war, and in March, 1654, she had 140 men-of-war at sea, "and better ships," added Cromwell's Secretary of State, "than we have had at any time heretofore." Nevertheless, every motive—solicitude for the Protestant cause, the interest of commerce, the frustration of the designs of the Royalists—all made peace with Holland necessary. Moreover, England was fast sinking under the financial burdens which even successful war imposed. Cromwell, therefore, turned a deaf ear to those who maintained that a little more persistence would force the Dutch to accept the original demands of the Long Parliament, and from the moment he took the negotiations in hand he threw overboard the amalgamation of the two republics. In its place, he at first proposed an offensive and defensive alliance between England and Holland. They were to league themselves together not merely for commercial or national ends, but "for the preservation of freedom and the outspreading of the Kingdom of Christ." "Who could tell," said he, "what God in his own time might intend to accomplish for the deliverance of oppressed nations by means of the two republics?" Other Protestant powers, and even those Catholic powers which allowed their subjects liberty of conscience, might be invited to join the league.

The Dutch envoys, less enthusiastic and more practical, would hear of nothing more than a defensive alliance, and even that proved more than could be realised. The negotiations were slow, for the demands of England were still too high, and France obstructed the progress of the treaty as much as it could. The Protector yielded on some points, but remained inexorable on others, and prepared to renew the war. So the resistance of the Dutch gave way, and by the treaty signed on April 5, 1654, they admitted the supremacy of the British flag in the British seas, abandoned any demand for the modification of the Navigation Act, and promised to pay damages for the losses of English merchants in the East. Each state undertook to expel from its borders the rebels or enemies of the other. Finally, by a private engagement, the province of Holland undertook permanently to exclude the Princes of Orange from command by land or sea. Cromwell had thus attained two of his objects: English commerce was made secure, and the Dutch would no longer help the Royalists to attack the government which England had chosen to set up. At the banquet which he gave the Dutch Ambassadors on the conclusion of the treaty, he dwelt on the advantages of friendship between the two states. They sang the 123d Psalm together: "Behold how good and how pleasant it is for brethren to dwell together in unity." But there was no real restoration of unity, and if the great Protestant alliance of Cromwell's dreams depended on the support of the Dutch, there was little hope of its accomplishment. The commercial jealousy of the two states never slumbered for a moment, and the diplomatists of the Protector found the influence of the Dutch continually obstructing their negotiations.

A few days later than the peace with the United Provinces, Cromwell's Ambassador, Whitelocke, concluded a treaty with Sweden (April 11, 1654). To Cromwell and to Englishmen who had witnessed the exploits of Gustavus Adolphus, Sweden still seemed the champion of Protestantism in northern Europe, and the natural ally of a Puritan England. "The English," wrote Whitelocke in his diary, "are the only people with whom the Swedes may hope for a firm amity and union for the Protestant interest against the common enemy thereof, the Popish party." Apart from this, there were other questions in which the political interests of the two nations coincided, and Cromwell offered to assist the Swedes with a fleet in asserting the freedom of the Sound against Denmark and Holland. Whitelocke was received with the greatest friendliness. "Your General," said Queen Christina to him, "hath done the greatest things of any man in the world: the Prince of Condé is next to him, but short of him." She compared Cromwell to her ancestor, Gustavus Vasa, and predicted that, like him, after being the liberator of his country he would become its king. Nevertheless, the Swedish ministers, fearful of involving their country in a war with Holland, and perhaps with France, declined the proffered alliance. The embassy resulted in a treaty of amity regulating the commercial intercourse of the two states, and providing that Sweden should give no assistance to the cause of Charles II.

Next came a treaty with Denmark, which, as Holland's ally, had been included in the treaty with the Dutch, on condition that the English merchants were compensated for the detention of their ships in the Sound during the war. By the commercial treaty which followed in September, 1654, English vessels were in future to be allowed to pass the Sound on the same terms as the Dutch. Still more important from the commercial point of view was the treaty with Portugal, concluded in July, 1654. English merchants received reparation for their losses, were guaranteed freedom from the interference of the Inquisition, and were given liberty to trade with all Portuguese colonies in the East or West. All these treaties, besides the commercial advantages they brought, gave additional security to the new government against the Royalists, but Cromwell valued those with the Protestant states most, because they also gave increased security to "the Protestant interest abroad." "I wish," said he to his Parliament, "that it may be written upon our hearts to be zealous for that interest. For if ever it were likely to come under a condition of suffering, it is now. And by this conjunction of interests, you will be in a more fit capacity to help them."

In the same speech, the Protector was able to point out the change in the attitude of Europe towards England, which nine months of his rule had produced. "There is not a nation in Europe," he said, "but is willing to ask a good understanding with you." Instead of rumours of coalitions against England, the two greatest powers of the continent were bidding against each other for her alliance. Spain pressed England to land an army in southern France in support of Condé's rebellion, promising help to recover Calais, and large subsidies towards the cost of the English auxiliaries. France offered to abandon the cause of Charles II., and to assist England with men and money to conquer Dunkirk. For some months, Oliver wavered, or seemed to waver. Apparently he was intent only on driving the best possible bargain for England with the two competitors for her support; in reality, he was studying the conditions of the problem and making up his mind how to act. As both were Catholic powers, religious considerations were less decisive than usual. On the one hand, the case of the Huguenots, whose rights under the Edict of Nantes were continually infringed by the French Government, appealed strongly to his Protestant zeal. On the other hand, the Catholicism of France was less bigoted than the Catholicism of Spain, and whatever the wrongs of the Huguenots were, it became clear he could do more to get them redressed by a good understanding with France than by armed intervention. Political considerations also made peace with France desirable. Hitherto, it was true, Spain had been far more friendly to the Republic than its rival, but France was at once the more dangerous enemy and the more valuable ally. Whatever subsidies Spain might promise in return for English aid, it was soon evident that it could pay none. Ere long, Cromwell came to the resolution not to involve England in the European struggle between France and Spain by leaguing himself with either, but to take advantage of the opportunity to settle outstanding disputes, and to maintain, if possible, amicable relations with both. His plan, however, was not so easy of execution as it seemed. When the Protector, as a condition of the renewal of old treaties of commerce and friendship with Spain, demanded that English merchants should have the free exercise of their religion in Spanish ports, and that English colonists and traders in the West Indies should be no longer treated as enemies by the Spaniards, he met with a flat refusal.

"To ask liberty from the Inquisition and free sailing in the West Indies," declared the Spanish Ambassador, "was to ask for his master's two eyes," and no concession could be made on either point. In August, 1654, Cromwell resolved to send an expedition to the West Indies in order to exact reparation for the past and material guarantees for future security. He did not believe that these reprisals would lead to war with Spain in Europe, but if they did he was prepared to take the risk.

Equally unsuccessful were the negotiations with France. The expulsion from that country of Charles II. and his partisans was assented to in principle, and it was agreed that the losses which the traders of the two nations had suffered should be referred to arbitration, but the question of the Huguenots proved an insurmountable obstacle. The Protector demanded that the treaty should expressly recognise his right to intervene on their behalf, if the liberties granted them by the Edict of Nantes were infringed, which France, as was natural, steadfastly refused. Cromwell remained firm. The Protector, wrote Thurloe to an English agent, had espoused the interest of Protestantism, "which is dearer to him than his life and all that he hath," and he could not consent to any clause in a treaty with a foreign power which seemed prejudicial to it. The year 1654 ended without England's coming to an agreement either with France or Spain. Relying upon his army and his fleet of 160 ships, the Protector felt strong enough to maintain a completely independent position, and to assert the interest of England with a high hand in defiance of either. When Penn sailed for the West Indies, in December, 1654, he bore instructions not only to attack the Spanish colonies, but to make prize of any French ships he came across. When Blake in the previous October was despatched to the Mediterranean, he was charged to continue the reprisals against French as well as to protect British trade.

Blake's voyage made the British flag respected and feared throughout the Mediterranean, though the legendary account of the indemnities he exacted from the Grand Duke of Tuscany and the Pope for their unfriendly action during the Dutch war is unsupported by evidence. He made a treaty with the Dey of Algiers, and redeemed the English captives held there. The Dey of Tunis, less amenable to reason, refused reparation, and would not even allow Blake's ships to water in his ports. "We judged it necessary," wrote Blake, "for the honour of our fleet, our nation, and religion, seeing they would not deal with us as friends, to make them feel us as enemies"; so, sailing into the harbour of Porto Farina, he bombarded the Dey's castles, and burnt his ships (April 4, 1655).

Simultaneously with the news of Blake's exploit, England learnt of the massacre of the Vaudois by the troops of the Regent of Savoy. Every Puritan's heart thrilled with sympathy for the sufferings of his fellow Protestants. Milton called on God to avenge the sufferings of the "slaughtered saints" whose bones lay scattered on the Alpine mountains. The armies of the three nations urged Cromwell to action. The Protector needed no prompting. He headed with a gift of two thousand pounds the national subscription raised for the relief of the sufferers. He told the French Ambassador that the sufferings of the poor Piedmontese touched his heart as closely as if they had been his own nearest kin, and refused to sign the treaty with France till their wrongs were righted. By the pen of Milton, he summoned all the Protestant powers to intervene, and he projected employing Blake's fleet to attack Nice or Villa Franca. Diplomatic arguments proved sufficient. Eager to secure the friendship of England, France put pressure on Savoy, the massacres ceased, and the Vaudois were reinstated in their valleys. The Treaty of Pignerol left much unredressed, and Cromwell was far from satisfied with its terms, but by every Puritan in England and every Protestant in Europe he was hailed as the saviour of the Vaudois. Even Englishmen who were no Puritans felt proud to see their country, under his guidance, assert the sovereignty of the seas, punish the pirates of the Mediterranean, and defend the oppressed. Waller's panegyric to the Protector upon "the present greatness of his Highness and this nation," expressed this pride.

"The sea's our own; and now all nations greet,

With bending sails, each vessel of our fleet;

> *Your power resounds as far as winds can blow*
> *Or swelling sails upon the globe may go.*
> *Fame swifter than your winged navy flies*
> *Through every land that near the ocean lies,*
> *Sounding your name, and telling dreadful news*
> *To all that piracy and rapine use.*
> *Whether this portion of the world were rent*
> *By the rude ocean from the continent,*
> *Or thus created, it was sure designed*
> *To be the sacred refuge of mankind.*
> *Hither the oppressed shall henceforth resort*
> *Justice to crave, and succour at your court;*
> *And then your highness, not for ours alone*
> *But for the world's protector shall be known."*

To such a land, with such a leader, asked Waller, what could be thought impossible? Ere long, however, the Protector discovered that even the best-laid schemes did not always prosper. The *Panegyric* was published at the end of May: in August news came to England of the disastrous defeat of the expedition sent to the West Indies at Hispaniola.[2] The Protector fell ill, and everyone attributed his illness to vexation at the evil tidings. Contrary to his expectation also, Spain laid an embargo on English shipping, withdrew its ambassador, and declared war. The breach with Spain was accompanied by the completion of the long-delayed agreement with France, which was signed on the very day that the Spanish Ambassador left England (October 24, 1655). In substance, it was merely a commercial treaty, with a secret clause added for the expulsion of the leading Royalists from France, and the Protector contented himself with a private promise that the rights of the

Huguenots should not be infringed. The conditions under which the agreement took place made a more intimate connection between the two powers inevitable. But for the present Cromwell was busily engaged in negotiations with Sweden, which he hoped to make the basis of a general league of Protestant states. In June, 1655, Charles Gustavus, the successor of Queen Christina, invaded Poland and sent an ambassador to England to ask for aid in men, ships, and money. Cromwell treated the King's envoy with distinguished favour. "They dine, sup, hunt, and play bowls together," and "never was ambassador, or indeed any man, so much caressed and regarded by Cromwell as this man is, nor did he ever seek the friendship of anyone so much as this King of Sweden." From the first he declared his willingness to "enter into a more strict and close alliance" with Sweden both for the sake of the two nations, and for the sake of the Protestant cause. Yet it was impossible to come to an agreement. The Swedish King's conquest of Catholic Poland seemed to the Protector a gain to Protestantism; "Wresting a horn from the head of the Beast," he termed it. But he saw plainly that it was not to the interest of England that the Baltic should fall completely under the dominion of Sweden, and that to support the designs of the King on the Baltic coast-lands would necessarily embroil him with the Danes, the Dutch, and the Brandenburgers. For a time he hoped to turn the arms of Gustavus against the House of Austria, and to convert the offered alliance into the Protestant league he longed for. But it was all in vain, and the sole result of the embassy was a commercial treaty signed in July, 1656.

Meanwhile, at sea, the war with Spain was vigorously prosecuted. During the latter part of 1655 and through 1656, an English fleet cruised on and off the Spanish coast in order to prevent the Spaniards from sending reinforcements to the West Indies and to intercept the silver ships from America. It served also to protect English traders to the Mediterranean, and to force the King of Portugal to carry into effect the treaty of 1654. At one time Cromwell with prophetic foresight proposed the seizure of Gibraltar. "If possessed and made tenable by us," he wrote to Blake, "would it not be an advantage to us and an annoyance to the Spaniards, and enable us, without keeping so great a fleet on that coast, with six nimble frigates lodged there to do the Spaniards more harm than by a fleet and ease our own charge?" But without a force to land, the Admiral judged the design impracticable. Blake's perseverance in the blockade was at last crowned with success. On September 8, 1656, Captain Stayner with a squadron of cruisers detached from his fleet met eight Spanish ships from America off Cadiz, of which he destroyed four bearing treasure worth two millions, and captured a fifth with a cargo of silver valued at six hundred thousand pounds. More glorious, however, was the action at Santa Cruz in Teneriffe on April 20, 1657. Blake sailed into the harbour, where the Spanish treasure-fleet from the West Indies had taken refuge, fought batteries and galleons at close quarters, and sunk or burnt all the sixteen ships without losing one of his own. It was the most brilliant of all his exploits, and the last: he died on his return to England, worn out with the fatigues of the long blockade, just as his ship was entering Plymouth Sound (August 7, 1657).

Meanwhile, events forced Cromwell into closer union with France. The Spaniards had zealously adopted the cause of Charles II., hoping to overthrow Cromwell by means of an insurrection in England. In April, 1656, Philip IV. made a treaty with Charles II. by which he promised him a pension, helped to maintain a little army of English and Irish Royalists in Flanders, and undertook to provide ships for their transport to the English coast. Spanish money, also, was employed to further the plots of the Levellers for the assassination of the Protector. It became evident that, in order to force Spain to peace, it must be attacked on the continent as well as on the seas. On March 23, 1657, Cromwell signed an offensive alliance with France, by which England supplied six thousand soldiers, supported by a fleet, to attack the Spaniards in Flanders, and was to receive Mardyke and Dunkirk as its share of the spoils. He thought that the possession of Dunkirk would give him increased control of the Channel, enable him to exercise a greater pressure upon France, and provide a secure basis for land operations against Spain. "It would be," said Secretary Thurloe, "a bridle to the Dutch, and a door into the continent."

Six weeks later, Sir John Reynolds, with six thousand men, landed at Boulogne and joined the French army under Turenne. Turenne at first employed the English contingent in the interior of Flanders, in sieges and operations which seemed to serve French interests only, and his delay to attack the coast towns made Cromwell suspicious. It seemed, he wrote to

Sir William Lockhart, the English Ambassador, as if the French "would not have us have any footing on that side the water." The French excuses for their delay were but "parcels of words for children." Unless they set about the business at once, he would withdraw his troops and demand the repayment of his expenses. "I desire you to take boldness and freedom to yourself in your dealing with the French on these accounts." Lockhart spoke boldly and freely, and the effect was immediate. The French army drew towards the Flemish coast. Mardyke was besieged, taken, and handed over to an English garrison (October 3, 1657).

When the next campaign opened, Turenne laid siege to Dunkirk, and a Spanish army of fourteen thousand men under Don John and Condé advanced to its relief. Turenne routed them on June 4, 1658, amongst the sandhills on the south of Dunkirk, with the loss of five thousand men. No troops did better service in the battle than the English contingent under Lockhart. The joyful cheer the redcoats gave when they saw their enemy roused the admiration of Turenne, and the Duke of York, who served in the Spanish army, was full of praises of his countrymen's courage. On their hands and knees they stormed the sandhill which was the key of the Spanish left, and at push of pike drove the Spaniards from it. This victory decided the long struggle between France and Spain, and ten days later Dunkirk surrendered. It was all over now with the plans of Charles II.: half his little army had been destroyed in the battle, and the ships provided for their transport had been captured by the English fleet.

Cromwell had at last the foothold on the continent which he desired, and England was safe from attempted invasion, but the Protestant alliance he dreamed of was farther off than ever. A storm had risen in northern Europe which threatened to make any such combination permanently impossible. As soon as Charles Gustavus conquered Poland, his ambition had brought him into collision with his Protestant neighbours. A great coalition was forming against him, and in the spring of 1657 he appealed to Cromwell for help. But before Cromwell would risk either men or money he required as a guarantee the temporary possession of Bremen. It would serve as a basis for military operations, if necessary, and as a means of bringing pressure to bear upon Denmark, if Denmark attempted to break the peace. Gustavus refused, and all Cromwell could do was to endeavour to mediate between

Sweden and Denmark. In May, 1657, the Danes declared war, and forced Gustavus to relax his hold on Poland. Brandenburg, Holland, and Austria joined the coalition, and at the end of 1657, it seemed as if Sweden must succumb. Cromwell had refused to join Gustavus in his designs to partition Denmark, but just as little could he consent to allow Denmark and its allies to complete the overthrow of Sweden. He regarded the coalition as a Catholic plot against a Protestant power—a plot in which misguided Protestant states were furthering the work of the Pope and the House of Hapsburg. In imagination, he saw the Austrian eagle once more stretching her wings towards the Eastern sea and planting herself upon the Baltic, as in the dark days of the Thirty Years' War, before Sweden came to the rescue of the German Protestants.

The speech which the Protector made to Parliament, in January, 1658, was full of these apprehensions. The question, he said, was, "whether the Christian world should be all popery." The Protestant interest abroad was "struck at, nay, quite trodden under foot." The Spanish and Austrian Hapsburgs were leagued together to destroy it. In Poland and in the Empire, Protestants were persecuted and driven out; the Swiss were threatened, and Sweden, the chief champion of the Protestant cause, was in danger. What resistance was there to "this mighty current coming from all parts against all Protestants?" Only that made by Gustavus:

"a poor prince, and yet a man in his person as gallant and as good, as any that these late ages have brought forth."... "A man that hath adventured his all against the Popish interest in Poland, and made his acquisitions still good for the Protestant religion. He is now reduced into a corner, and what adds to the grief of all is that men of our religion forget this, and seek his ruin."

He declared that the success of the coalition threatened the commerce and the maritime power of England. "If they can shut us out of the Baltic Sea, and make themselves masters of that, where is your trade? Where are your materials to preserve your shipping?" Every sailor knew what exclusion from the Baltic meant for England.

The Protector's conclusion was that England must intervene to prevent the King of Sweden from being crushed, and be ready to back him, not only with its fleet, but by landing a force on the continent. "You have accounted yourselves happy," said he, "in being environed with a great ditch from all the world besides. Truly, you will not be able to keep your ditch, nor your shipping, unless you turn your ships and shipping into troops of horse and companies of foot, and fight to defend yourselves on terra firma."

The crisis passed away as rapidly as it had risen, and Gustavus rescued himself without English aid. A winter march over the frozen Belt and the siege of Copenhagen brought Denmark to its knees. In February, 1658, Cromwell's ambassador mediated a peace between the rival powers at Roeschild. But the peace was of short duration. In August, 1658, a month before Cromwell died, the war broke out again, and once more Holland and Brandenburg came to the help of the Danes. The general Protestant league was impossible, because each Protestant power preferred to pursue its private aims and defend its private interests. Ambition and national traditions made Denmark and Sweden irreconcilable foes. Brandenburg was more anxious to secure its own independence than to propagate the faith. The Dutch sought first the interests of their commerce, and preferred, as Oliver complained, "gain to godliness."

In Cromwell's England there were some who, like Morland, held it the greatest glory of the Protector that he had ever identified the interests of England with the interests of European Protestantism. But the merchants of London complained that they were ruined by the cessation of their Spanish trade, and the war with Spain had lost him the hearts of the City. To the commercial classes, and to many republican statesmen, Holland, not Spain, seemed the natural enemy of England, and bitter attacks on the late Protector's policy were heard in the Parliament of 1659. Yet the great position in Europe which Cromwell's energy had gained for England impressed the imagination of contemporaries. "He once more joined us to the continent," sang Marvell, in his lines on Cromwell's death, while Sprat depicted him as waking the British lion from its slumbers, and Dryden as teaching it to roar. Contemporary historians struck the same note. "Cromwell's greatness at home," admitted Clarendon, "was a mere shadow of his greatness abroad." Burnet recorded with approval Cromwell's traditional boast, that he would make the name of Englishman as great as ever that of Roman had been. Still more glorious appeared the policy of the usurper in comparison with that of Charles II. "It is strange," noted Pepys, in 1667, "how everybody do nowadays reflect upon Oliver and commend him, what brave things he did, and made all the neighbour princes fear him."

Then came a change. For a hundred years it was the fashion to say that Cromwell by allying himself with France against Spain destroyed the balance of power in Europe, and produced that preponderance of France against which Europe struggled so long. People forgot that the overgrowth of French power was due to the complicity of Charles II., even more than to Oliver's co-operation, and that, with Oliver as his ally, Louis XIV. would neither have attempted the partition of Holland, nor revoked the Edict of Nantes. With modern historians, it is a commonplace to observe that Cromwell's foreign policy was an anachronism, that the era of religious wars ended with the Treaty of Westphalia, and that material and political motives alone determined thenceforth the relations of European powers. There is much truth in the criticism, but in the years which immediately followed that treaty, religious disputes entered so largely into political quarrels that it was not easy for contemporaries to perceive what is obvious enough to posterity. Least of all was such clearness of vision possible to the Puritan statesman, in whose mind the interest of religion took precedence of all other interests, and to the soldier who regarded war as the instrument with which the God of battles worked out His purpose on earth.

Cromwell's foreign policy was in part a failure, but only in part. He promoted the material welfare of his country, and saved her from foreign interference in her domestic affairs. Where he sought purely national interests he succeeded, but it was impossible for him not to look beyond England. "God's interest in the world," he said, "is more extensive than all the people of these three nations." At another time he told his Council: "God has brought us hither to consider the work we may do in the world as well as at home." Others shared these views, and there were many Puritans who, like Cromwell, held that nations had duties as well as interests. The duty of a free Commonwealth, wrote Harrington, was to relieve oppressed peoples, and to spread liberty and true religion in other lands. "She is not made for herself only," but should be "a minister of God upon the earth, to the intent that the whole world may be governed with righteousness." This was the dream that Cromwell sought to realise through his great Protestant league. Looked at from one point of view, he seemed as practical as a commercial traveller; from another, a Puritan Don Quixote.

CHAPTER XIX
CROMWELL'S COLONIAL POLICY

Cromwell was the first English ruler who systematically employed the power of the government to increase and extend the colonial possessions of England. His colonial policy was not a subordinate part of his foreign policy, but an independent scheme of action, based on definite principles and persistently pursued. As we have seen, it was his extra-European policy which ultimately determined his part in the great European struggle of his days.

All the English colonies had grown up during Cromwell's lifetime. When he was born England had none. He was seven years old when James I. granted a charter to the Virginian Company, and married in the year when the Pilgrim Fathers sailed in the *Mayflower*. It is probable that at one time he thought of emigrating himself, and it is certain that he felt the keenest interest in the Puritan settlers in New England. Ever since 1643, the Protector had been officially connected with the government of the colonies. He was one of the commissioners for the government of the plantations in America and the West Indies whom Parliament appointed in November, 1643, and was reappointed in 1646. But, in spite of their high title, these commissioners had little real power. Their authority might be obeyed in the islands, but on the continent of America it was hardly felt at all. The Civil War tended to loosen the tie which bound the colonies to the mother country. In May, 1643, soon after it began, the four colonies of Massachusetts, Plymouth, Connecticut, and New Haven had formed themselves into a confederation, under the name of "The United Colonies of New England." Strong enough to defend themselves without the aid of the mother country, they were little minded to submit to her control. When malcontents appealed from the courts of Massachusetts to the Parliament, parliamentary orders in their favour were disregarded, and the appellants were punished. At the same time, however, the New England colonies heartily sympathised with the Parliament in its struggle with the King. These outposts of Puritanism across the Atlantic sent many volunteers to the Puritan armies, more than one of whom did distinguished service and rose to high command. Still more important was the influence which the example and the ideas of New England exercised on the development of Democracy and Independency in England. At the time when the Commonwealth was established, the political tie between the English Government and the New England colonies was little more than nominal, but the intellectual sympathy of the two was never stronger.

In the islands, and in the southern colonies, exactly the opposite process took place. There the general feeling was hostile to the Puritans and favourable to the King. When the war ended, fugitive Royalists flocked to Barbadoes and Virginia, just as exiled Puritans had once sought refuge in New England. After the death of Charles I., Virginia, under the government of Sir William Berkeley, proclaimed Charles II., and made it penal to justify his father's execution. Instigated by Lord Willoughby, Barbadoes refused to acknowledge the Republic, suppressed conventicles, banished Roundheads, laid claim to freedom of trade with all nations, and seemed about to declare its independence.

But the statesmen who had made three kingdoms into one Commonwealth by force of arms were not the men to suffer the colonies to shake off their allegiance. In the autumn of 1651, Sir George Ayscue, with a British fleet, was sent to reduce Barbadoes and Virginia to obedience, while at the same time the passing of the Navigation Act proved that the republicans meant to strengthen—not to relax—the hold of the mother land on the colonies. That act bound the colonies to England by ensuring their commercial dependence upon her, and increased the maritime power of England by enriching its shipowners and merchants. But it was not simply the result of the jealousy of English against Dutch merchants, and it was something more than a sign of the rising power of the commercial classes. It was the first attempt on the part of England to legislate for the colonies as a whole, and to treat them as integral parts of one political system. By it the statesmen of the Republic declared that England was to be henceforth regarded not simply as a European power, but as the centre of a world-wide empire.

It is often said that the zeal for maritime and colonial dominion which marked the policy of Cromwell and of the Commonwealth was inspired by Elizabethan traditions, and to a certain extent it is true. But with statesmen and thinkers, this zeal for the expansion of England was also the result of a definite political theory. A stationary state, argued Harrington (and he expressed the views of his contemporaries), was a state doomed to weakness. The policy of the Republic must aim at increase and not merely at preservation. If it was to be lasting, it must lay great bases for eternity. If it was to be strong, it must have room to grow. "You cannot plant an oak in a flower pot," said Harrington; "she must have earth for her roots, and heaven for her branches."

The imperial purpose which had inspired the colonial policy of the Commonwealth found its fullest expression in the actions of the Protector. When Cromwell became Protector, the sovereignty of the English Government was everywhere acknowledged, but it could scarcely be said that it had been cordially accepted. In the southern colonies, there prevailed a strong anti-Puritan feeling; in New England, a growing spirit of independence; while in continent and islands, alike, there was general aversion to the restrictions which the Navigation Act had imposed on colonial trade. Under that act the products of a colony could not be imported to England except in English or colonial ships, and no foreign ships might import to the colonies anything but the products of their own country. From Virginia came loud complaints that the law was "the ruin of the poor planters." In Barbadoes, where the Dutch had carried on a considerable trade, the hostility to the law was still stronger. "It is strange to see how they generally dote upon the Dutch trade," wrote Winslow in 1655. Undeterred, the Protector continued to enforce the act by confiscating Dutch ships caught trading in prohibited commodities to the islands or the southern colonies, though in the New England colonies the non-observance of the act seems to have been tacitly permitted. As a compensation to the colonists, the growing of tobacco in England, where its production was beginning to obtain considerable success, was rigidly suppressed, and some attempt was made to develop a trade in shipping materials with the northern colonies.

In the internal affairs of the colonies, or their relations with each other, Cromwell interfered very little. He protected the Puritan party in the islands, and appointed or removed governors. He endeavoured to arbitrate on the boundary disputes between Maryland and Virginia, and to settle the internal divisions of the Marylanders. In New England, he sought to mediate between Rhode Island and the other colonies, ordering them to give the Rhode Islanders seasonable notice of any wars with the Indians, and to permit them to trade freely. "To maintain a loving and friendly correspondence in all things that may contribute to the common advantage and benefit of the whole," was his advice to the New Englanders about their dealings with Rhode Island, and it aptly defines the aims of the Protector's own policy towards the colonies in general. The corner-stone of his policy was the maintenance of good relations between New England and the Home Government. The New Englanders constituted, as it were, the Puritan garrison in America, and there were weighty political reasons for conciliating them. Apart from this, Cromwell's feeling towards them as brethren in the faith was peculiarly warm, and warmly reciprocated. In 1651, Massachusetts thanked the Lord General for the "tender care and undeserved respect" he had on all occasions manifested towards it, and wished him prosperity in his "great and godly undertakings." When he became Protector, it congratulated him on his being called by the Lord to supreme authority, "Whereat we rejoice, and shall pray for the continuance of your happy government, that under your shadow not only ourselves but all the churches may find rest and peace." Recognising the sensitiveness with which Massachusetts feared any encroachment upon its right of self-government, Cromwell invited rather than commanded it to support his policy, and treated its remonstrances against his proposals with respect. Yet he was not jealous of its growing strength, made no attempt to prevent its coining money, and even favoured its extension over the smaller settlements on its northern border. Citizens of Massachusetts and New Englanders in general were freely employed by him, both in Great Britain and in the colonies themselves. "The great privileges belonging to New England," wrote a Massachusetts agent, were "matter of envy, as of some in other plantations, so of divers in England who trade to those places," but the Protector and many of his Council were "their very cordial friends." When Cromwell died, he was characterised in the diary of a Bostonian as "a man of excellent worth," and one "that sought the good of New England, though he seemed to be wanting in a thorough testimony against the blasphemers of our days."

As characteristic of Cromwell's policy as his love for New England was his zeal for the extension of England's colonial possessions. When he became Protector, the war with the Dutch and the hostile relations existing with France supplied him with an opportunity which he was not slow to seize. At the beginning of the Dutch war, the Long Parliament had called on the New England colonies to attack the Dutch possessions in America, but the New England Confederation was divided, and remained inactive. Massachusetts, partly from conscientious objections to attacking neighbours with whom it had no sufficient ground of quarrel, partly no doubt from political motives, stubbornly opposed the war. Connecticut, New Haven, and Plymouth, whose interests were more directly concerned, were eager to act, but unable to move without the support of their great associate. The confederation seemed threatened with disruption. To some of the colonists, the whole future of New England seemed to depend on the result.

"Our cure is desperate if the Dutch are not removed," wrote William Hooke of New Haven to Cromwell. "They lie close upon our frontiers westward, as the French do on the east, interdicting the enlargement of our borders any farther that way, so that we and our posterity (now almost prepared to swarm forth plenteously) are confined and straitened, the sea lying before us, and a rocky rude desert, unfit for cultivation and destitute of commodity, behind our backs, all convenient places upon the seacoast being already possessed and planted."

Cromwell answered the appeal without a moment's delay. In February, 1654, he despatched three ships and a few soldiers to New England with instructions to capture the Dutch settlements "in the Manhattoes" and on the Hudson. The expedition was commanded by Major Robert Sedgwick of Massachusetts, with whom was associated Captain John Leverett of the same colony—once a captain in the army of the Eastern Association, and to be in future years governor of Massachusetts. Cromwell's letter to the colonial governments told them that he would not enquire why they had not hitherto taken action, but he saw no consideration which should prevent any colony from co-operating with the rest in this work, which concerned their common welfare. When the expedition arrived, even Massachusetts yielded so far as to permit the levy of five hundred volunteers, while the other three colonies were zealous in raising men "to extirpate the Dutch." But before they could march, news came of the conclusion of peace with the Dutch, and the design had to be abandoned (June, 1654).

On this, Sedgwick and his fleet, according to their instructions, made sail for the coast of Acadia to take whatever French ships or settlements they could come across. Old complaints of their aggressions and the state of hostility which existed between France and England in Europe were held to justify the attack. Moreover, this "deluding crew," as Leverett called the French settlers, "had given it out amongst the Indians, that the English were so and so valiant against the Dutch at sea; but that one Frenchman could beat ten Englishmen ashore." "Wherein," he adds, "the Lord hath most obviously befooled them," for Sedgwick with but 130 men took first the Fort of St. John's, next Port Royal (now Annapolis), and finally their strong fort on the Penobscot River. So the whole territory from the Penobscot to the mouth of the St. Lawrence passed under English dominion, and remained in English hands till it was given up by Charles II. in 1668.

After the French and the Dutch, came the turn of the Spaniards. There were grievances more than enough to justify hostilities, and all the diplomatic representations of the Long Parliament had failed to procure their redress. England and Spain had been at peace in Europe ever since 1630, but that peace had never been observed in the western hemisphere. Spain still claimed, by virtue of the Pope's donation, exclusive dominion over islands it left unoccupied, and attacked all foreigners who attempted to colonise them. In 1634, the Spaniards drove out the English settlers from Tortuga; in 1641, a fleet from Cartagena captured and expelled the English colonists of New Providence on the Mosquito coast; in 1651, Santa Cruz was surprised, a hundred English inhabitants killed, and the rest forced to fly from the island. If an English ship sailing to an English colony met a Spanish fleet anywhere in western waters, it was likely to be attacked and plundered. If chance or storm drove an English ship on the coast of Cuba or

Central America, the ship was confiscated, and the crew set to work as convicts.

Mixed with the desire to exact satisfaction for these injuries were other motives. Cromwell was bent on conquest for both religious and economic reasons. The islands Spain held in the West Indies were large and thinly populated, whilst the islands England possessed were small, and filled to overflowing with people. Hispaniola was fertile; "a country beyond compare," people said. Its conquest would provide a vent for the surplus population of the English settlements, for the unruly Highlanders of Scotland, and for the vagrants and criminals of England. Added to this, every piece of territory won from Spain was so much rescued from Catholicism and gained for Protestantism.

In August, 1654, therefore, Cromwell made up his mind to send an expedition to attack the Spanish settlements in the West Indies. General Venables, who was chosen to command it, showed scruples about the justice of attacking the Spaniards. He was told, "that if we had no peace with the Spaniards, then this could be no breach of the peace; if we had peace with them, they had broken it, and then it was but just for the English to seek reparation."

Cromwell did not believe that war with Spain in the West Indies would necessarily lead to war with Spain in Europe. There were many precedents and the practice of the Spaniards themselves to the contrary. The old Elizabethan maxim, "No peace beyond the line," seemed still to hold good. Still more powerful was the recollection of the treasures which the Elizabethan sailors had brought home. What if Spain did declare war? It would be easy to intercept the galleons which brought the silver of Peru from Porto Bello to Havana, and from Havana to Spain. A war with Spain was the most profitable of all wars, and at the worst the profits of the captures would defray the cost of the expedition.

In December, 1654, a fleet of thirty-eight ships, commanded by Admiral Penn, sailed from Portsmouth, bearing General Venables and twenty-five hundred soldiers. With them also went Edward Winslow, once governor of Plymouth Colony, now one of the commissioners appointed to assist Venables in the conduct of the expedition. As the New England colonies had been called on to contribute to the conquest of the Dutch, so the West Indian islands were expected to co-operate in the enterprise against the Spaniards. Nor were Cromwell's expectations disappointed. At Barbadoes and elsewhere, Venables enlisted enough to raise his army to seven thousand men. Some took service in hopes of plunder, expecting to gain "mountains of gold." With others, the desire for new lands was the chief incentive. St. Kitts, "an island almost worn out by reason of the multitudes that live upon it," furnished eight hundred men. But, though the army was large, it was of bad material, badly armed, half drilled, and with very little discipline. The officers knew little of their men, and the old soldiers, drafted from the different regiments in England to form the nucleus of the force, were not enough to leaven the lump. In April, Venables effected a landing on Hispaniola, and marched through the woods to attack its capital, San Domingo. The Spaniards had stopped up the wells, and the soldiers, who had no water-bottles, were worn out by thirst and fatigue before they came in sight of the town. Twice they fell into ambuscades, and were shamefully repulsed by a handful of Spaniards. In the second defeat, they lost eight colours and four hundred men, while Major-General Heane, disdaining to fly, fell pierced by a dozen Spanish lances as he strove to rally his broken regiment. Heavy rains and bad food completed the disorganisation of the troops. "Never did my eyes see men more discouraged," wrote Venables, and when a third attempt was proposed, the officers declined to lead their men, but offered to try to take the town without them.

Hoping for better fortune elsewhere, Venables embarked his forces and sailed to attack Jamaica. Winslow died on the voyage, saying that the disgrace of the defeat had broken his heart. On May 10, 1655, the army landed at Jamaica, occupied its capital, St. Jago de la Vega, without much resistance, and drove the Spaniards to fly to the mountains or to embark for Cuba. But now the troubles of the expedition began again. It was the rainy season, and the army, ill supplied with provisions, tools, and other necessaries, was decimated by sickness. Hundreds died of fevers and dysentery. Venables himself was so ill that his life was despaired of, and he was reported to be dead. In June, Penn with the bulk of the fleet sailed for England, and Venables followed a few days later. Each laid the blame of the failure on the other, and Cromwell, knowing how much their mutual quarrels had contributed to it, sent both to the Tower. They were soon released, but neither was ever employed again.

The Protector was deeply mortified by the result of the expedition. "The Lord," said he, "hath greatly humbled us": but nevertheless he persisted in his projects. Jamaica, he was told by men who knew it, was a better country than Hispaniola, more fertile, more healthful, better situated either for trade or for war, so he resolved to hold it, and to make it the corner-stone of British power in the West Indies. To Major-General Fortescue, whom Venables had left in command, Cromwell promised ample supplies and reinforcements. "We think," he added, "and it is much designed amongst us to strive with the Spaniard for the mastery of all those seas." Writing to Vice-Admiral Goodson, Fortescue's colleague, he reminded him that the war was a war not for dominion only, but for religion.

"Set up your banners in the name of Christ, for undoubtedly it is his cause. And let the reproach and shame that hath been for your sins, and through the misguidance of some, lift up your hearts to confidence in the Lord, and for the redemption of his honour from men who attribute their success to their idols, the work of their own hands.... The Lord himself hath a controversy with your enemies; even with that Roman Babylon of which the Spaniard is the great underpropper. In this respect we fight the Lord's battles."

The battle was long and hard. At the end of 1655, when Robert Sedgwick, the conqueror of Acadia, arrived at Jamaica with the first reinforcements, he found Fortescue dying, and the army

"in as sad and deplorable and distracted a condition as can be thought. The soldiery many dead, their carcases lying unburied in the highways and among bushes; many of them that were alive walked about like ghosts or dead men, who, as I walked through the town, lay groaning and crying out, 'Bread, for the Lord's sake!'"

Much of this suffering was due not to hardships or necessity, but to the mismanagement of the commanders and the misconduct of the men. Though they were dying at the rate of a hundred a week, the survivors would do nothing to secure themselves against the climate, or to provide for their future subsistence. "Dig or plant they neither can nor will, but do rather starve than work," complained Sedgwick. He termed the soldiers a people "so basely unworthy, lazy, and idle, as it cannot enter into the heart of any Englishman that such blood should run in the veins of any born in England."

The Protector looked to New England and the islands to supply him with the planters and farmers whom the new colony needed. Above all, he desired to obtain as its nucleus a body of industrious, God-fearing Puritans, such as New England alone amongst English colonies seemed able to supply. In 1650, he had asked the New Englanders to help in the recolonisation of Ireland, and, undeterred by his failure, he now invited them to remove to Jamaica. "Our desire is," said he, "that this place may be inhabited by people who know the Lord and walk in his fear, that by their light they may enlighten the parts about them, which was a chief end of our undertaking this design." Daniel Gookin of Massachusetts, Cromwell's agent, was commissioned to make large offers to his fellow citizens to induce them to emigrate. Ships were to be furnished for their transportation; they were to be given lands rent free for seven years, and to be free from all taxes for three; they were to be guaranteed as large privileges and rights of self-government as any English city enjoyed. Cromwell felt confident that many would accept the offer, for, remembering the early hardships of the settlers, he regarded New England as barren and unhealthy, and thought his new conquest a much better country. He made his offer, he declared,

"out of love and affection to themselves, and the fellow-feeling we have always had of the difficulties and necessities they have been put to contest with, ever since they were driven from the land of their nativity into that barren wilderness, for their conscience sake; which we could not but make manifest at this time, when, as we think, an opportunity is offered for their enlargement and removing them out of a barren country into a land of plenty."

They had "as clear a call," he told Captain Leverett, to transport themselves from New England to Jamaica, "in order to their bettering their outward condition, as they had had from England to New England."

But the New Englanders were more prosperous than Cromwell imagined, and at the worst their climate was more healthful than that to which he invited them to remove. New Haven—threatened just then by an Indian war—was the only colony which seriously considered the proposal, and in the end it answered in the negative. In the reply of Massachusetts, "intelligence from Jamaica of the mortality of the English race there," was the only definite objection mentioned. Its people thanked the Protector for his good intentions with humble and effusive piety, promised him their prayers, and made it quite clear that they meant to stay where they were. Two or three hundred New Englanders accepted the invitation, but that was all.

As little feasible was it to people Jamaica from Scotland or Ireland. Cromwell thought of transporting Lowland vagrants and turbulent Highlanders on a large scale, but was told that any plan for compulsory emigration would set all Scotland in a blaze. There was a scheme discussed for transporting one thousand Irish boys and as many Irish girls to Jamaica, but it came to nothing. Jamaica was colonised by the surplus population of the other West Indian islands. St. Kitts, Barbadoes, and the Bermudas sent numerous settlers, while the island of Nevis furnished seventeen hundred with its governor at their head. By degrees the mortality amongst soldiers and colonists diminished; cultivation spread, and a little trade in colonial products sprang up. Under Sedgwick's rule, the work of plantation really began. He died in May, 1656, and was succeeded as governor by Major-General William Brayne, an officer who had been serving in Scotland under Monk, and to whose wisdom the pacification of the Western Highlands was chiefly due. Brayne died in September, 1657, "infinitely lamented," wrote a colonist, "being a wise man, and perfectly qualified for the command and design." To him succeeded Colonel Edward Doyley, who governed Jamaica till after the restoration of Charles II.

All this time the infant colony was engaged in an active war with the Spaniards, both by sea and land. The fleet lay in wait for the Spanish treasure-ships, or attacked the towns on the Spanish main. In 1655, Goodson took Santa Martha; in 1656, Rio de la Hacha. Sedgwick was much opposed to these buccaneering raids, thinking them not only unprofitable but harmful. "We are not able," he wrote, "to possess any place we attack, and so in no hope thereby to effect our intention in dispensing anything of the true knowledge of God to the inhabitants." To the Indians and blacks he added, "we shall make ourselves appear a cruel, bloody, and ruinating people," which "will cause them, I fear, to think us worse than the Spaniard." Few shared these conscientious scruples. In 1657, Captain Christopher Mings took Coro and Cumana, in Venezuela, bringing home "more plunder than ever was brought to Jamaica," and enriching the whole island. The buccaneering spirit, which produced such demoralising results in later years, tainted the colony from its birth.

On their part, the Spaniards made repeated attempts to reconquer Jamaica. Some still lurked in the forests and mountains, and, aided by the mulattoes and negroes, cut off small parties of settlers. Spain sent fresh soldiers to Cuba, and expeditions from Santiago or Havana landed more than once on the northern coast of Jamaica. In 1657, Doyley killed or took a party of three hundred. In 1658, he defeated thirty companies of Spanish foot, who had established themselves near Rio Nova, killing three hundred, taking one hundred prisoners, and storming the fort they had built. He sent ten flags as trophies to Cromwell, but the Protector was dead ere the news of the victory reached him. "So," writes a colonial historian, "he never had one syllable of anything that was grateful from the vastest expense and the greatest design that was ever made by the English."

Yet, though to Cromwell himself the history of his West Indian expedition must have seemed a dreary record of failure, it was in reality the most fruitful part of his external policy, and produced the most abiding results. Through it, the Spaniards were forced to refrain from molesting the English colonies in the West Indies, and England obtained, as he desired, "the mastery of those seas." Unlike other parts of his policy, it was not reversed but maintained at the Restoration. Charles II. kept Jamaica, and forced Spain with a high hand to submit to its retention by England. He succeeded in effecting the conquest of Dutch America, which Cromwell had been so eager to undertake. He ceded Acadia to France, but his successors won it back, and won all Canada too. Under him and under them the power of the Home Government was systematically directed to the defence of existing colonies and the foundation of new ones. Thus the colonial policy which Cromwell and the statesmen of the Republic had initiated became the permanent policy of succeeding rulers, and it became so because it represented not the views of a particular party, but the aspirations and the interests of Englishmen in general.

CHAPTER XX
CROMWELL AND HIS PARLIAMENTS

From 1654 to 1658, the fundamental question of English politics was, whether Cromwell would succeed in securing the assent of the nation to the authority which the army had conferred upon him. Foreigners saw the situation clearly. After the famous Swedish chancellor, Oxenstiern, had heard Whitelocke's account of the foundation of the Protectorate, he told him there was but one thing remaining for the Protector to do and that was "to get him a back and breast of steel." "What do you mean?" asked Whitelocke. "I mean," replied the Chancellor, "the confirmation of his being Protector by your Parliament, which will be his best and greatest strength." Cromwell himself was not content to remain the nominee of the soldiers, and wished to govern by consent and not by force. But two great obstacles stood always in his way. One was the rooted aversion of Englishmen to the rule of the sword, which was the origin of his power. The other was the traditions of the House of Commons. In January, 1649, it had claimed to be the supreme power in the state in the right of the sovereign people it represented, and that claim, once made, could never be forgotten. To one section of the Republicans, the only legitimate Government was the expelled Long Parliament, granted by statute the right never to be dissolved but by its own consent. To another section, any elected Parliament was as all-powerful as the people from which its rights were derived. To admit the right of any external power to limit the authority of Parliament, seemed to both a betrayal of the liberty of the nation.

The first Parliament elected under the provisions of the Instrument of Government met in September, 1654. The majority of its members were Presbyterians or moderate Independents, for the extreme men of the Little Parliament had been rejected at the polls. It soon became evident that while the House was prepared to accept Cromwell as head of the state, it was not willing to accept the constitution which the officers had devised. Instead of contenting itself with the functions of a legislature, it claimed to be a constituent assembly. The Protector might exercise the executive power, provided the representatives of the people settled the terms upon which he held it. "The government," ran the formula adopted, "should be in the Parliament and a single person limited or restrained as the Parliament should think fit." The co-ordinate and independent power which the Instrument of Government gave the Protector was thus called in question, and Parliament once more laid claim to sovereignty.

Cromwell thought it necessary to intervene to maintain his own authority and that of the constitution. He offered a compromise. Parliament might revise the constitution if its essentials were left untouched. "Circumstantials" they might alter; "fundamentals" they must accept. Those fundamentals he summed up in four principles: government by a single person and Parliament; the division of the control of the military forces between Parliament and the Protector; limitation of the length of time which a Parliament might sit; and, finally, liberty of conscience. As for himself, Cromwell asserted that his title to rule had been ratified by the nation. The army, the City, most of the boroughs and counties of England had by their addresses signified their approval. The judges by taking out new commissions had accepted his authority. The sheriffs by proceeding to elections in accordance with his writs, and the members themselves chosen in those elections, had thereby owned it too. Either directly or indirectly therefore his power was founded on the acceptance and consent of the people. For the good of these nations and their posterity he would maintain the present settlement against all opposition. "The wilful throwing away of this Government, so owned by God, so approved by men,—I can sooner be willing to be rolled into my grave and buried with infamy, than I can give my consent unto."

About a hundred members were excluded from the House for refusing to sign an engagement to be faithful to the Commonwealth and the Protector, and not to alter the government as settled in a single person and Parliament. The rest, accepting the Protector's invitation, proceeded to revise the constitution. Many days they spent in these debates, wasting much time in futile disputes about words, but making some judicious amendments. They made the office of Protector elective, and the Council more dependent upon Parliament. On the other hand, they restricted the Protector's veto over legislation, and sought to limit the toleration granted by the constitution. A list of damnable heresies was to be drawn up, and twenty articles of faith were to be enumerated, which no man was to be permitted to controvert. At this both the army and the Protector took alarm, and Cromwell was petitioned by the officers to intervene. In the end, it was agreed that the question of heresy should be left to the joint decision of Protector and Parliament, but another question remained behind, on which no compromise was possible. By the "Instrument," the Protector was empowered to maintain a standing army of thirty thousand men, but at the close of 1654, the forces actually on foot in the three nations amounted to fifty-seven thousand. The annual expenditure of the state had risen to £2,670,000, while the revenue amounted only to two millions and a quarter. Parliament was eager to reduce taxation, and above all to reduce the cost of the army, which amounted to £1,560,000 per annum. It demanded the reduction of the army to the legal maximum, voted after much discussion a revenue of one million three hundred thousand pounds, which it held to be sufficient to maintain an army of thirty thousand, and promised to provide money to pay off the twenty-seven thousand men to be disbanded. At the same time, it insisted that the control of the military forces of the nation should belong to Parliament, not to the Protector. On this question Oliver could not yield. In his opinion and in the opinion of his Council, thirty thousand men were not sufficient to keep the three nations in peace.

The royalist rising in Scotland was only just put down, and Ireland, though subdued, was seething with discontent. In England, preparations for an insurrection were in progress, encouraged by the disputes between Parliament and the Protector. "Dissettlement and division, discontent and dissatisfaction," he said, "together with real dangers to the whole, have been more multiplied within these five months of your sitting than in some years before. Foundations have been laid for the future renewing of the troubles of these nations by all the enemies of them abroad and at home."

The Cavaliers, said Cromwell, had been for some time furnishing themselves with arms; "nothing doubting but that they should have a day for it, and verily believing that whatsoever their former disappointments were, they should have more done for them by and from our divisions than they were able to do for themselves." The Levellers were working in concert with the Cavaliers, "endeavouring to put us into blood and confusion, more desperate and dangerous confusion than England ever yet saw." Republicans of position were joining with the Levellers to create discontent and mutiny amongst the soldiers, and the delay to vote money for the payment of the army and the insufficiency of the sum yet voted had furthered these designs. The army in Scotland was thirty weeks behindhand with its pay, and in danger of being reduced to take free quarters. A plot had been discovered to seize Monk, make someone else general, and march the army into England to overthrow the Government. Under such conditions, it was impossible for the Protector to consent to so great a reduction of the army, or to give up the control of it. "If," said he, "the power of the militia should be yielded up at such a time as this, when there is as much need of it to keep this cause, as there was to get it, what would become of us all?" Nor was it possible for him at any time to surrender the control of the army if the balance of the constitution was to be preserved. Unless that control were equally shared between the Protector and Parliament, said Cromwell, it would put an end to the Protector's power "for doing the good he ought, or hindering Parliament from perpetuating themselves, from imposing what religion they please on the consciences of men, or what government they please upon the nation." If this fundamental principle were abandoned, all the others would be endangered. "Therefore," he concluded, "I think it my duty to tell you that it is not for the profit of these nations, nor for common and public good, for you to continue here any longer."

The plots of which Cromwell had spoken were widespread and dangerous, but the vigilance of the Government nipped them in the bud. Major-General Overton, whom the Scottish mutineers had pitched upon as their leader, was imprisoned first in the Tower and then in Jersey. Major-General Harrison, whom the Fifth Monarchy men in England relied upon to head them, was sent to Carisbrooke Castle. Major Wildman, the chief of the Levellers, was arrested in the act of dictating a "Declaration of the free and well affected people of England now in arms against the tyrant, Oliver

Cromwell." The seizure of many royalist agents paralysed the plots of the Cavaliers. Their rising had been fixed to take place on February 13th, but it was adjourned for three weeks, and when March came, though there were gatherings in half a dozen places, so few obeyed the signal that the conspirators generally dispersed, and went home again. The only actual outbreak took place at Salisbury, where Colonel Penruddock and Sir Joseph Wagstaff got together three or four hundred men, and proclaimed Charles II. Then they made for Cornwall, where royalist feeling was still strong, but they were overtaken and routed by Cromwell's soldiers at South Molton in Devonshire. Penruddock and a few others were executed, and some scores of their followers were transported to the West Indies to work in the sugar plantations.

As soon as the insurrection was over, Cromwell, to show his desire to diminish the burdens of the nation, and his wish to meet as far as possible the reasonable demands of the late Parliament, took in hand the reduction of the army. During the summer and autumn of 1655, ten or twelve thousand men were disbanded, and the pay of those maintained in the service was diminished. Then followed an extension of military rule which brought more odium upon the Protector than any other act of his Government. England was divided into twelve districts, and over each was set an officer with the local rank of major-general, and the special duty of maintaining the order of his district. He was charged to put in force an elaborate system of police regulations meant to prevent conspiracies against the Government, and to see to the execution of all laws relating to public morals. He had command of the local militia, and of a troop of horse raised in every county to supplement it.

This "standing militia of horse" as it was termed, consisted of about six thousand men, paid a small sum as a retaining fee, and liable to be called out at a day's notice. The eighty thousand pounds a year required to maintain them was to be procured by a tax of ten per cent. on the income of the royalist gentry, the assessment and collection of which were entrusted to the major-generals assisted by local commissioners.

As a measure of police the institution was a great success, but politically it was a great mistake. It was a reversal of the policy which Cromwell had hitherto followed. By the amnesty he had carried in 1652, and by the repeal of the compulsory engagement to be faithful to the Commonwealth, Cromwell had sought to induce the Royalists to forget their defeat and to become good citizens. In the declaration now published, to justify his proceedings for securing the peace of the nation, he adopted the view that the Royalists were irreconcilable. They had laboured, he complained, to keep themselves distinct and separate from the well-affected, "as if they would avoid the very beginning of union." They bred their children under the ejected clergy, and confined their marriages within their own party, "as if they meant to entail their quarrel and prevent the means to reconcile posterity." People might say it was unjust to punish all the Royalists for the fault of a few, but "the whole party generally were involved in this business," either directly or indirectly. Therefore, "if there were need of greater forces to carry on the work, it was a most righteous thing to put the charge on that party which was the cause of it."

The defence convinced only the supporters of the Government. To the rest of England, the arbitrary and inquisitorial proceedings of the major-generals were sufficient to condemn the institution. It was evident that the military party amongst the Protector's advisers had obtained the upper hand of the lawyers and civilians. The Protectorate, which had hitherto striven to seem a moderate and constitutional government, stood revealed as a military despotism.

Meanwhile a legal opposition more dangerous than royalist plots threatened the Protector's authority. The lawyers began to call in question the validity of his ordinances, and the judges to manifest scruples about enforcing them. Whitelocke and Widdrington, two of the Commissioners of the Great Seal, resigned their posts because of scruples about executing the ordinance for the reform of Chancery. Judges Newdigate and Thorpe declined to act on the commission appointed for the trial of the insurgents in the north. A merchant named Cony refused to pay customs duties not imposed by act of Parliament, and his counsel, Serjeant Twysden, asserted that their levy by Cromwell's ordinance was contrary to Magna Carta, Chief-Justice Rolle, before whom the case came, resigned his place to avoid determining the question.

Cromwell met this opposition by arresting those who refused to pay taxes, sending Cony's lawyers to the Tower, and replacing the doubters by more compliant judges. Cony, intimidated or cajoled, withdrew his plea, and the lawyers apologised and submitted. Necessity was the Protector's only excuse for these despotic acts. "The people," he had asserted when he dissolved Parliament, "will prefer their safety to their passions, and their real security to forms, when necessity calls for supplies." Convinced that the maintenance of his Government was for the good of the people, he was resolved to maintain it by force, and did not shrink from the avowal. "'Tis against the will of the nation: there will be nine in ten against you," Calamy is reported to have told Cromwell, when he assumed his protectorship. "Very well," said Cromwell, "but what if I should disarm the nine, and put a sword in the tenth man's hands. Would not that do the business?"

Nevertheless, neither the argument from necessity nor the appeal to force could persuade the Republican leaders to recognise the authority of the Government. Men like Vane and Ludlow steadily refused even an engagement not to act against it.

"Why will you not own this Government to be a legal government?" said Lambert to Ludlow. "Because," replied Ludlow, "it seems to me to be in substance a re-establishment of that which we all engaged against, and had with a great expense of blood and treasure abolished." "What is it you would have?" asked the Protector himself. "That which we fought for," said Ludlow, "that the nation might be governed by its own consent." "I am as much for government by consent as any man," answered Cromwell, "but where shall we find that consent?"

That was the difficulty. Ludlow said that the consent required was that of "those of all sorts who had acted with fidelity and affection to the public." Vane in his *Healing Question* said that a convention representing "the whole body of adherents to this cause" was the only body that had a right to determine the government of the nation. Both were blind to the fact that the divisions of the Puritan party had made agreement impossible, and that government by consent would necessarily bring about the restoration of the Stuarts.

In the summer of 1656, the Protector summoned a second Parliament, although according to the terms of the "Instrument" he need not have done so till 1657. He needed money to carry on the war with Spain, and the major-generals told him that they could secure the election of members favourable to the Government. When the elections came, the major-generals had an unpleasant surprise. Everywhere the arbitrary measures of the last eighteen months had aroused general discontent. "No courtiers, nor swordsmen," was the popular cry, and in the counties, where the electorate was too large to be overawed, a large number of opposition candidates were returned. When Parliament met, the Protector's Council assumed the right to decide on the qualifications of the persons elected, and excluded a hundred members as disaffected to the Government.

Those excluded protested, but their protest was unheeded; those allowed to sit submitted with hardly a murmur. They were in general moderate Presbyterians or Independents, willing to support any Government which promised tranquillity to a nation weary of political strife. Their willingness to accept Cromwell as Protector was shown by an act annulling the title of the Stuarts to the throne, and by another making it high treason to plot for the overthrow of his Government. The capture of the Spanish treasure ships by Stayner, which happened just about the opening of the session, gave Cromwell's foreign policy the prestige of success, and the House responded to his appeal for supplies by approving the Spanish war and voting £400,000 for its expenses.

On other questions, it soon appeared how little even adherents of the Protectorate sympathised with the Protector's hostility to religious persecution, and how much they resented the arbitrary proceedings of the major-generals. In the case of James Naylor the House assumed judicial power, and many members were eager to punish his blasphemies with death. Cromwell's intervention was repulsed and Naylor was sentenced to be branded, scourged, and imprisoned at pleasure. Still more bitter was the struggle over the bill for continuing the "decimation" tax imposed on the Cavaliers for the support of the new militia. The major-generals were attacked from all quarters of the House, and the tax was denounced as unjust, and as a breach of the public faith. Cromwell's son-in-law, Claypole, spoke against the bill, and so did his trusted councillor, Lord

Broghill. Excepting the soldiers themselves, few defended it, and it was finally negatived by an overwhelming majority.

While these debates were still in progress, a new plot against the Protector's life was discovered. Miles Sindercombe, a discharged soldier of Levelling principles, after the failure of several schemes for shooting Cromwell from a window on his way to Hampton Court, or assassinating him in his coach as he took the air in Hyde Park, attempted to set Whitehall Chapel on fire, hoping to find a better opportunity in the confusion. When an account of the plot was laid before Parliament, Mr. Ashe, a Presbyterian member of little note, moved a startling addition to the address of congratulation. "It would tend very much to the preservation of himself and us," he declared, "that his Highness would be pleased to take upon him the government according to the ancient constitution. Both our liberties and peace and the preservation and privilege of his Highness would then be founded upon an old and sure foundation."

The same suggestion had often been made outside the walls of the House. In the first draft of the "Instrument of Government," the officers had offered Cromwell the title of King instead of Protector, and he had refused it. In August, 1655, a petition had been circulated in London pressing Cromwell to assume the title of King or Emperor, but its author had been reprimanded by the Council, and the petition suppressed. At the close of 1656, the victories over the Spaniards had roused a widespread feeling that Cromwell was worthy to be enrolled amongst English kings. It found expression in Waller's verses on the capture of the Spanish treasure ships.

> "Let it be as the glad nation prays," sang the poet.
>
> "Let the rich ore forthwith be melted down,
>
> And the state fixed, by making him a crown;
>
> With ermine clad and purple, let him hold
>
> A royal sceptre made of Spanish gold."

But neither foreign glories nor domestic dangers were so strong a motive for the revival of monarchy as the desire to return to constitutional government. The reaction against the rule of the Fifth Monarchy men had made Cromwell Protector, the reaction against the rule of the swordsmen produced the attempt to make him King. "They are so highly incensed against the arbitrary actings of the major-generals," wrote an observing member of Parliament, "that they are greedy of any power that will be ruled and limited by law." Ashe's suggestion was denounced as a crime by a few staunch Republicans, but it fell upon fruitful ground. Five weeks later, Alderman Pack, one of the members for London, brought in a bill proposing a revision of the constitution and a revival of monarchy. Republicans regarded the scheme as prompted by Cromwell himself, but in reality it was the work of the merchants and the lawyers of the middle party. Again the military element in the House took one side and the civil the other. The major-generals, backed by the soldiers and the Republicans, stubbornly contested the Bill, article by article, but at last, on March 25th, the House resolved, by 123 to 62 votes, that the Protector should be asked to assume the name and office of King. On the 31st of March, the scheme was presented to the Protector for acceptance, under the title of "The Humble Petition and Advice" of Parliament.

Cromwell's answer was hesitating and ambiguous. He expressed his thanks for the honour done him, and his approval of the new constitution, but ended with a refusal. He said that as he could not accept a part of the scheme without accepting the whole, he could not "find it his duty to God and the Parliament to undertake this charge under that title." For the next five weeks committees of Parliament argued with the Protector to remove his scruples and to prove the necessity of his accepting the crown. The title meant everything to them.

"Parliament," wrote Thurloe, "will not be persuaded that there can be a settlement any other way. The title is not the question, but it's the office, which is known to the laws and to the people. They know their duty to a king and his to them. Whatever else there is will be wholly new, and upon the next occasion will be changed again. Besides they say the name Protector came in with the sword, and will never be the ground of any settlement, nor will there be a free Parliament so long as that continues, and as it savours of the sword now, so it will at last bring all things to be military."

But the same reasons which made the revival of monarchy seem so desirable to Parliament and the lawyers, made it obnoxious to the army. A month before the offer of the crown to Cromwell, Major-General Lambert and a hundred officers petitioned him to refuse it. Cromwell answered with firmness; to him their objections to the title seemed overstrained and unreasonable. "Time was," he reminded them, "when they boggled not at the word king." "For his own part," he added, "he loved the title as little as they did." It was only "a feather in a hat." But the policy of the officers had failed. The constitution they had drawn up needed mending. The experiment of the major-generals had ended in failure. "It is time," he concluded, "to come to a settlement, and to lay aside arbitrary proceedings so unacceptable to the nation."

Cromwell was desirous to accept the constitution drawn up by Parliament, because it seemed to secure that settlement by consent of the nation, so long and so vainly sought. "I am hugely taken with the thing, settlement, with the word, and with the notion of it," declared Cromwell to the parliamentary committee. "I think he is not worthy to live in England that is not."

In itself the constitutional scheme contained in the Petition and Advice seemed a good scheme. There was the monarchical element which Cromwell had pronounced desirable in 1657. There were the checks on the arbitrary power of the House of Commons which he always thought necessary, not only in the existence of a written constitution, such as the officers had devised in 1653, but in the revival of a Second Chamber as a balance to the Commons. Civil liberty seemed fully provided for, and "that great natural and civil liberty, liberty of conscience," securely guaranteed. "The things provided in the Petition," asserted Cromwell, "do secure the liberties of the people of God so as they never before had them."

For five weeks these conferences continued. "I do judge of myself," said the Protector soon after they began, "that there is no necessity of this name of king, for the other name may do as well." He was even disposed to think that God had blasted the title as well as the family which had borne it. Moreover, he told Parliament, many good men could not swallow the title, and they should not run the risk of losing one friend or one servant for the sake of a thing that was of so little importance. If left to himself the Protector would probably have waived his scruples, and accepted, but this last consideration decided his answer. From many a staunch Cromwellian outside the army, letters and pamphlets against kingship reached Cromwell. He was plainly told that for him "to re-edify that old structure of government" which God by his instrumentality had overthrown, and to set up again that monarchy which Parliament had declared burdensome and destructive to the nation, would be "a fearful apostacy." In the army, it was clear that his acceptance of the crown would create an irreconcilable schism. When the day for his final answer came, Fleetwood, Desborough, and Lambert threatened to lay down their commissions if he accepted, and that morning about thirty officers presented a petition to Parliament, begging it to press the Protector no more, and protesting against the revival of kingship. On May 8, 1657, Cromwell answered Parliament with another refusal, saying: "Though I think the act of government doth consist of very excellent parts in all but that one thing of the title as to me, I cannot undertake this government with the title of King."

Parliament, though much disappointed, took the hint these words contained. Had Cromwell definitely refused when the Petition and Advice was first offered to him, Parliament would have thrown up the whole scheme in disgust. As it was, in its anxiety to obtain his acceptance, it had adopted all the amendments which he suggested during the conferences, and had gone too far to abandon the constitution so carefully elaborated. On May 25th, the Petition and Advice was presented to Cromwell again, with the title of Protector substituted for that of King, and this time he gave his assent to it. In Westminster Hall, on Friday, the 26th of June, he was for the second time installed as Protector, with great pomp and ceremony. The Speaker, as representative of Parliament, invested him with a robe of purple velvet, lined with ermine, "being the habit anciently used at the investiture of princes," presented him with a Bible, girt a sword to his side, and put a golden sceptre into his hands. He took the oath to maintain the Protestant religion and to preserve the peace and the rights of the three nations, and sat down in the chair of state. The trumpets sounded, the people shouted "God save the Lord Protector," and the heralds made proclamation after the ancient fashion when kings were crowned.

Cromwell had gained what he desired. At last his authority rested upon a constitutional basis. Henceforth he was not merely the nominee of the army, but the elect of the representatives of the people. Moreover, under the Petition and Advice his powers were more extensive than they had been under the Instrument of Government. He had acquired the right to nominate his own successor and to appoint, subject to the approval of Parliament, the seventy members of the new Second Chamber. He had obtained a permanent revenue of one million three hundred thousand pounds, which Parliament held sufficient to cover the ordinary expenditure of Government in time of peace, while for the next three years he had been granted an additional revenue of six hundred thousand pounds to meet the cost of the war. On the other hand, the authority of Parliament had been enlarged, and that of the Protector's Council diminished. Parliament had gained control over its own elections, and the arbitrary exclusion of its members was made henceforth impossible. But it remained to be seen whether a Parliament, representing all sections of the Puritan party, would accept a settlement made by a packed Parliament, or whether the newly devised Second Chamber would be a more effectual check to the Lower House than the paper limitations of the Instrument of Government.

In January, 1658, when Parliament met again after a six months' vacation, the situation was altered. About forty of the Protector's chief supporters in the Lower House had been called to the new Second Chamber, and their places had not been filled up by fresh elections. At the same time all the leading Republicans, excluded at the opening of the first session,—old parliamentary hands, skilful in debate, and bitterly hostile to the Protectorate,—swelled the ranks of the Opposition. Instead of there being a strong Government majority, the two parties in the House of Commons were pretty equally balanced. Nevertheless, the Protector's opening speech was full of hope and confidence. Looking back on the past work of this Parliament and the settlement achieved by it, his heart overflowed with gratitude and gladness. "How God hath redeemed us as we stand this day! Not from trouble and sorrow and anger only, but into a blessed and happy estate and condition, comprehensive of all interests." We have "peace and rest out of ten years' war," religious freedom after years of persecution. "Who could have forethought, when we were plunged into the midst of our troubles, that ever the people of God should have had liberty to worship God without fear of enemies?" Let them own what God had done, and build on this foundation of civil and spiritual liberties which he had given them.

"If God shall bless you in this work," continued Cromwell, "and make the meeting happy on that account, you shall be called the blessed of the Lord. The generations to come shall bless us. You shall be 'the repairers of breaches, and the restorers of paths to dwell in.' And if there be any higher work which mortals can attain unto in the world beyond this, I acknowledge my ignorance of it."

Cromwell was speedily undeceived. As soon as the proceedings began, it was evident that a breach between the two Houses was imminent. In Cromwell's second speech to them, four days after the session began, he spoke of his fears rather than his hopes. Abroad, he said, the Protestant cause was in danger through the complications in Northern Europe, and Charles II. had got together an army and was projecting a landing in England. At home, the Cavaliers were planning another insurrection, but the greatest danger lay in their own divisions. "Take us in that temper we are in: it is the greatest miracle that ever befell the sons of men that we are got again to peace." Consider how many different sects and parties there were in the nation, each striving to be uppermost. "If God did not hinder, it would all make up one confusion. We should find there would be but one Cain in England, if God did not restrain; we should have another more bloody civil war than ever we had in England." What stood between England and anarchy except the army, and except the Government established by the Petition and Advice? "Have you any frame or model of things which would satisfy the minds of men if this be not the frame?"

The Republican leaders, who had now obtained the guidance of the Lower House, were deaf to these arguments. They were pledged by oath to be true and faithful to the Lord Protector, and not to contrive anything against his lawful authority, and they were careful to keep the word of promise to the ear. But they insisted on discussing the Petition and Advice over again, taking nothing for granted which had been done during their absence. "Unless you make foundations sure, it will not do your work," said Haslerig. "We who were not privy to your debates upon which you made your resolutions should have liberty to debate it over again," added another. With great acuteness they fixed upon the authority of the new Second Chamber as the point of attack, denied it to be a House of Lords as Cromwell styled it, and insisted that its proper title, according to the Petition and Advice, was "the other House."

If it were suffered to call itself a House of Lords, it would claim all the legislative and judicial powers the old Lords had possessed: and then what would become of the rights of the people? The people, said Scot, had been by the providence of God set free from any authority which could exercise a veto on their resolutions. "Will they thank you, if you bring such a negative upon them? What was fought for, but to arrive at a capacity to make your own laws?" "The Commons of England," chimed in Haslerig, "will quake to hear that they are returning to Egypt." For seven whole sittings these debates continued, and the Lower House refused to have any dealings with the Upper House till this question was decided. To the republicans the title meant everything. "Admit Lords and you admit all," argued Ashley Cooper. "I can suffer to be torn in pieces," cried Haslerig, "I could endure that; but to betray the liberties of the people of England, that I cannot."

The Republican leaders did not confine their opposition to words. Some of them entered into communication with the malcontents in the city and the army. It was arranged that a petition should be presented, signed by ten thousand persons in London, demanding the limitation of the Protector's power over the army, and the recognition of the House of Commons as the supreme authority in the nation. In reply, the House was to vote an address asserting both these principles, and if need be to appoint Fairfax commander-in-chief instead of Cromwell. The Republicans expected to be backed by part of the army, for there were rumours of disaffection in the ranks. Soldiers had been heard to say that under pretence of liberty of conscience they had been fooled into betraying the civil liberties of their country, and all to make one family great. And nowhere was the hostility to the new House of Lords stronger than amongst the officers of the Protector's own regiment of horse.

The scheme came to Cromwell's ears, and the next morning he sent a sudden summons to both Houses to meet him (February 4, 1658). He was Protector, he told them, by virtue of the Petition and Advice. "There is not a man living can say I sought it, no, not a man nor woman treading upon English ground." They had petitioned and advised him to undertake his office, and he looked to them to make their engagements good. Then, addressing himself to the members of the Commons, he complained that, instead of owning the settlement made by their consent, they were attempting to upset it. "The nation is in likelihood of running into more confusion in these fifteen or sixteen days that you have sat, than it hath been from the rising of the last session to this day. Through the intention of devising a Commonwealth again, that some people might be the men that might rule all." Some were "endeavouring to engage the army to carry that thing," others "to stir up the people of this town into a tumulting." These things tended "to nothing else but the playing of the King of Scots' game," and could end in nothing but blood and confusion. "I think it high time," he concluded, "that an end be put to your sitting, and I do dissolve this Parliament. And let God be judge between you and me."

"Amen," responded the defiant Republicans.

CHAPTER XXI
THE DEATH OF CROMWELL
1658–1660

To contemporaries, the Protectorate had never seemed stronger than it did in the summer of 1658. "From the dissolution of Cromwell's last Parliament," writes Clarendon, "all things at home and abroad seemed to succeed to his wish, and his power and greatness to be better established than ever it had been." Military mutiny, royalist insurrection, projected invasion—the three dangers which threatened his rule in the spring—had all been successfully overcome. The conspiracies were frustrated by the timely arrest of their leaders. Some disaffected officers lost their commissions, a few of the Fifth Monarchy men were imprisoned, while about a dozen Royalists were tried by a High Court of Justice, of whom five suffered on the scaffold or the gallows. Abroad, the victory of the Dunes and the capture of Dunkirk shed new lustre on English arms, and raised Cromwell's fame still higher in Europe, while the splendid reception of Lord Fauconberg at the French Court, and the complimentary mission sent by Louis XIV. to the Protector, attested the value which the most powerful sovereign in Europe set on Cromwell's friendship.

Modern historians have taken a less favourable view of the situation than contemporaries did. Some have assumed that Cromwell's power was tottering to its fall, and that he must have succumbed to the difficulties which surrounded him. He was faced, it has been said, by the certainty of bankruptcy without a supply from Parliament, and the certainty of overthrow if he summoned Parliament. Both statements are exaggerated, for neither difficulty was insuperable. Cromwell had been faced by both ever since he began to rule, and his Government had contrived to live through them.

In 1658, the financial difficulty was more serious than the parliamentary difficulty. When the Long Parliament was expelled, the national finances were in a state of chaos. The monthly property tax had risen to £120,000 per mensem, there was a debt of about £700,000, and the Crown lands, Church lands, and confiscated estates—which were the great resource of the treasury in emergencies—had almost all been sold. During the Protectorate the financial administration was improved, public money thriftily husbanded, and taxation reduced. The monthly assessment was lowered first to £90,000, then to £60,000, and finally to £50,000. But as the reduction of the expenditure of the state did not proceed at the same pace, the receipts did not balance the outgoings. The income of Cromwell's Government for 1657–1658 may be estimated at about £1,900,000, while its expenses were about £400,000 more. The army cost about £1,100,000, the navy about £900,000, and the civil government about £300,000. The causes of this large deficit were two. One was the cost of holding down Ireland and Scotland, the revenues of which were insufficient to defray the cost of their garrisons, so that the English treasury had to supply about a quarter of a million a year for that purpose. The second cause was the Protector's foreign policy. It was calculated by financiers that less than half a million was enough to maintain a fleet sufficient for defensive purposes. But a navy strong enough to fight Spain for the mastery of the Western seas, blockade the Spanish coasts, and interfere in the disputes of the Baltic powers, cost twice that sum. The consequence of this was that the Protector's Government was always embarrassed for money, and that a considerable debt accumulated. By the spring of 1659, that debt amounted to about a million and three quarters. Had the financiers of the Protectorate, like the financiers of the time of William III., adopted the device of funding the debt, and raising loans to cover the deficits caused by war, the difficulty would have been temporarily solved. But as the conditions of the time and the want of skill amongst Cromwell's financial advisers prevented the adoption of that plan, the only course was to reduce expenditure, or to obtain larger supplies from Parliament, neither of which things was easy, but neither impossible. After the successful campaign of 1658, it became evident that Spain would be forced to make peace, and a reduction both in naval and military expenditure became feasible. In the opinion of the French Ambassador (a shrewd observer, and deeply concerned in forming a right estimate of the question), there was nothing in the financial embarrassments of the Government to endanger its stability. As little danger, according to his view, was there of its overthrow by Parliament. The temporary success of the Republicans in the second session of the last Parliament was due to a cause which would not recur, that is, the weakening of the Government majority by the withdrawal of forty of its supporters to form the new Second Chamber. The Protectorate had gained, rather than lost, parliamentary strength. While the result of the Parliament of 1654 had been to weaken the authority of the Protector, the result of that of 1656 had greatly increased it. In the summer of 1658, therefore, the Protector resolved to summon another Parliament towards the close of the year, and but for his death the intention would have been fulfilled. It was confidently expected on all hands that the offer of the Crown would have been renewed by that body, and, as the elections of December 1658 proved, the Government would have had a majority of at least three to two. The support which Richard Cromwell obtained from Parliament negatives the theory that the opposition would have succeeded in the attempt to overthrow his father.

Events proved clearly that the maintenance of the Protectorate depended on the fidelity of the army. At the commencement of the Protectorate, it numbered not less than sixty thousand men. In December, 1654, there were still fifty-three thousand men in arms in the three nations, in spite of recent reductions. By the end of the Protectorate it numbered, including the troops employed in Flanders and Jamaica, about forty-eight thousand men. During this period a considerable change had taken place in its character and composition. Officers opposed to the Government had been, one after another, deprived of their commands: Harrison in December, 1653, Overton and four other colonels in 1654, Lambert in 1657, Packer and five captains of Cromwell's own regiment in the spring of 1658. By 1658 the superior officers were generally either personal adherents of the Protector or professional soldiers who took little interest in political questions. Men of the type of Monk had taken the place of men of the type of Harrison. Amongst the subordinate officers and non-commissioned officers there were many Republicans, but they were without sufficient influence to be dangerous. All Anabaptists and Fifth Monarchy men had been purged out of the ranks; private soldiers in general looked to military service as a livelihood, and might become mutinous if their pay was too much in arrears, but hardly for the sake of maintaining political principles.

The history of the Protectorate is the history of the gradual emancipation of the Protector from the political control of the army. Twice he had successfully frustrated attempted alliances between the parliamentary opposition and the malcontents in the army, and each attempt had strengthened his authority over the army.

It was this sense of the hopelessness of insurrectionary movements, so long as Cromwell lived, which caused the repeated conspiracies of Royalists and Levellers for Cromwell's assassination. In 1654, some of the people round Charles II. issued a proclamation in the King's name offering five hundred pounds, knighthood, and a colonel's commission, to any one who succeeded in killing "a certain mechanic fellow" called Oliver Cromwell, "by pistol, sword, or poison." Charles was cognisant of these plots, and stipulated only that the Protector's assassination should be connected with a general royalist rising, not an isolated act. There were many subsequent designs of the same nature, especially after the alliance between the Levellers and the Royalists. Lieutenant-Colonel Sexby, once a soldier in Cromwell's own regiment, undertook to arrange the assassination of the Protector, and was supplied with money by the Spanish Government for that purpose. Sindercombe, whose plot was detected in January, 1657, was his agent. In the following May, Sexby published a tract entitled *Killing No Murder*, the object of which was to prove that it would be both a lawful and a glorious act to kill the Protector. "Let every man," said he, "to whom God hath given the spirit of wisdom and courage be persuaded by his honour, his safety, his own good, and his country's, to endeavour by all rational means to free the world from this pest. Either I or Cromwell must perish," announced Sexby. But, visiting England in disguise to make further arrangements for this purpose, Sexby was arrested, and died a prisoner in the Tower.

Cromwell was kept well informed of these designs by his police, and spoke of them with great contempt. "Little fiddling things" he termed them in one of his speeches. "It was intended first for the assassination of my person," he told Parliament of the plot of 1654, "which I would not remember as anything at all considerable to myself or to you, for they would have had to cut throats beyond human calculation before they could have been able to effect their design."

As a precaution against such designs, the Protector's life-guard, which had originally consisted simply of the forty-five gentlemen forming the life-guard of the Commander-in-chief, was raised in 1656 to 160 men. Royalist accounts say that during the last months of his life Cromwell was "much more apprehensive of danger to his person than he had used to be," and that in consequence he surrounded himself with guards, never returned from Hampton Court by the road by which he went thither, and rarely slept twice in the same bed. These are legends for which there is no solid foundation. The Protector took reasonable, but not exaggerated precautions. He was not a man whose nerves could be shaken by threats, but he knew as well as his enemies did how much depended on his life, and how little the permanence of his work was assured.

The real danger to the Protectorate was that Cromwell was growing old. He was now in his fifty-ninth year. The fatigues of campaigning had injured his health before he began to rule. He had one dangerous illness in the spring of 1648, and another in the spring of 1651. "I thought I should have died of this sickness," he said of the latter. Under the fatigues of government, his health was still more impaired. The despatches of foreign ambassadors have frequent references to the ill health of the Protector as one of the causes which retarded their negotiations. The difference between his signatures in 1651 and in 1657 is very remarkable. The bold firm hand of the first date becomes shaky and feeble six years later. His speeches prove that he felt the weight which rested upon his shoulders. "It has been heretofore," he said in 1657, "a matter of, I think, but philosophical discourse, that a great place, a great authority, is a great burden. I know it is." Danton, disillusioned by failure, cried that it was better to be a poor fisherman than a ruler of men. Cromwell sometimes regretted the quiet country life he had exchanged for the cares and vicissitudes of supreme power. "I can say in the presence of God, in comparison of whom we are but like poor creeping ants upon the earth, I would have lived under my woodside, to have kept a flock of sheep, rather than undertook such a government as this is."

He met each new difficulty with his old resourcefulness and courage, but when one was overcome another rose before him, and the incessant struggle made increasing demands upon his vital forces. In the opinion of his steward, Maidston, "being compelled to wrestle with the difficulties of his place as well as he could without parliamentary assistance," after the dissolution of his second Parliament, was a fatal addition to his burdens. "I doubt not to say it drank up his spirits, of which his natural constitution afforded a vast stock, and brought him to his grave."

Private griefs also contributed their share to his load. In February, 1658, Robert Rich died, the husband of Cromwell's youngest daughter Frances, married only four months earlier. On the 6th of August following, died Elizabeth Claypole, his favourite daughter, after a long and painful illness. The Protector was much with her in her last days, and his "sense of her outward misery in the pains she endured took deep impression upon him."

A little time after his daughter's funeral, Cromwell fell ill of an ague, or intermittent fever, but in a few days he seemed to shake it off and to regain strength. On August 20th, George Fox, going to Hampton Court to plead with the Protector "about the sufferings of Friends," met him riding in the Park at the head of his guards. "Before I came to him," says Fox, "I saw and felt a waft of death go forth against him, and when I came to him he looked like a dead man." The next day Cromwell fell sick again, but he felt certain that the prayers put up for him would be answered, and was assured that he would recover. "Banish all sadness from your looks, and deal with me as you would with a serving man," he said to a doubting physician. "You may have skill in the nature of things, yet nature can do more than all physicians put together; and God is far above nature." When the fit was past, his physicians ordered him to remove to Whitehall, thinking that he would be benefited by the change of air.

At Whitehall, his condition became worse instead of better: he was racked by alternate heats and chills; all recognised that the danger was great; "our fears are more than our hopes," wrote Thurloe to Henry Cromwell. On Tuesday, the last day of August, the French Ambassador told his Government that the Protector was at death's door, but the same evening he rallied, and hope gained the upper hand again. That night, one who watched in Cromwell's bedchamber heard him praying, and remarked that "a public spirit to God's cause did breathe in him to the very last." For he prayed, not for himself or for his family, but for Puritanism and for all Puritans—for "God's cause" and "God's people." "Thou hast made me," he said, "though very unworthy, a mean instrument to do them some good, and Thee service. And many of them have set too high a value upon me, though others wish and would be glad of my death. But, Lord, however Thou dost dispose of me, continue and go on to do good for them. Give them consistency of judgment, one heart, and mutual love, and go on to deliver them.... Teach those who look too much upon Thy instruments to depend more upon Thyself. Pardon such as desire to trample upon the dust of a poor worm, for they are Thy people too. And pardon the folly of this short prayer, even for Jesus Christ's sake, and give us a good night, if it be Thy pleasure."

Cromwell hourly grew weaker. Through the night of Thursday, the 2nd of September, he was very restless, speaking often to himself in broken sentences difficult to hear. "I would be willing," he said once, "to live to be further serviceable to God and His people, but my work is done." "God will be with His people." He resigned himself to die.

A physician offered him something to drink, bidding him to take it, and to endeavour to sleep, but he answered: "It is not my design to drink or to sleep, but my design is to make what haste I can to be gone." Towards morning he spoke again "using divers holy expressions, implying much inward consolation and peace," and with them he mingled "some exceeding self-debasing words, annihilating and judging himself." After that he was silent, and at four o'clock on the afternoon of Friday he died.

It was the 3rd of September, his fortunate day, the anniversary of Dunbar and Worcester.

As Marvell sang:

"No part of time but bare his mark away

Of honour—all the year was Cromwell's day,

> *But this, of all the most auspicious found,*
>
> *Thrice had in open field him victor crowned,*
>
> *When up the armèd mountains of Dunbar*
>
> *He marched, and through deep Severn, ending war:*
>
> *What day should him eternise, but the same,*
>
> *That had before immortalised his name?"*

Sometime during his illness Cromwell had verbally nominated his eldest son as his successor, so, about three hours after Oliver's death, Richard was proclaimed Protector. Addresses from counties, cities, and regiments poured in to the new ruler, and foreign powers hastened to congratulate and to recognise him. There was no more opposition than if he had been the descendant of a long line of hereditary sovereigns. "There is not a dog that wags his tongue, so great a calm are we in," wrote Thurloe to Henry Cromwell.

Richard's first care was his father's funeral. The body of the late Protector was embalmed and removed from Whitehall to Somerset House, there to lie in state, as that of James I. had done. His waxen effigy, clad in royal robes of purple and ermine, with a golden sceptre in the hand and a crown on the head, was for many weeks exhibited. The corpse was privately buried in the chapel of Henry VII., in Westminster Abbey, on September 26th, but the public funeral took place with extraordinary pomp on November 23rd. All the great officers of state and public officials, with officers from every regiment in the army, walked in solemn procession from Somerset House to the Abbey, through streets lined with soldiers in new red coats with black buttons.

The funeral ceremonies cost sixty thousand pounds, and this profusion, which the Government could ill afford, excited angry criticism amongst the Republicans. Their dissatisfaction would have mattered little, but there were already signs of coming trouble in a more dangerous quarter. A quarrel began between the civil and the military faction in the Protector's council. Oliver had been Commander-in-chief, as well as Protector, but now the superior officers demanded a commander-in-chief of their own choosing, and put forward Fleetwood as their candidate. Their aim was to shake off the control of Richard's civilian advisers, and make the army independent of the civil power. Richard firmly refused their demand, and the storm seemed to blow over, but the officers only waited for a more convenient opportunity.

In January, 1659, the necessity of providing money for the public service obliged Richard to call a Parliament. All the Republican leaders obtained seats, but more than two-thirds of the members elected were supporters of the Government. There was a long struggle over the recognition of Richard as Protector, followed by excited debates about the right of the members for Scotland and Ireland to sit in Parliament, and over the old question of the House of Lords. On all these points, the Government carried the day, but in the meantime the agitation in the army had begun again, and a council of officers repeated the demands made in the previous autumn. The Protector, backed by his Parliament, which was indignant at military dictation, ordered the council to cease meeting. The military leaders, allying themselves with the Republican minority in the House, refused obedience. A few colonels adhered to the Protector, and obeyed his orders, but they were deserted by their men, and all the regiments in London gathered round Fleetwood at St. James's. On behalf of the council of officers, Fleetwood and Desborough demanded the immediate dissolution of Parliament. "If he would dissolve Parliament," said Desborough, "the officers would take care of him; if he refused, they would do it without him and leave him to shift for himself." Richard might have resisted with some chance of success, for Monk and the army in Scotland remained faithful, and Henry Cromwell, with the Irish army, would have supported him. But he trusted the promises of his uncles, and, whatever the result to himself, he shrank from beginning a civil war. "I will not have one drop of blood spilt for the preservation of my greatness," he is reported to have said. Yielding to the pressure put upon him, he dissolved Parliament (April 21, 1659), and a fortnight later he had ceased to reign.

Thus the Protectorate fell before that alliance between the Republicans and the malcontents in the army which Cromwell had always been strong enough to prevent. Fleetwood had no wish to overthrow his brother-in-law,

Desborough no animosity to his nephew; they meant to make him their tool, and to govern under his name. But the inferior officers declared for the restoration of the Republic, and threw over the House of Cromwell. On May 7th, the Long Parliament was restored to power by the men who had expelled it in April, 1653, and the Revolution was completed.

There was no real union between these temporary allies. The fifty or sixty members of the Long Parliament who governed England in the name of the Republic had learnt nothing and forgotten nothing. The soldiers, conscious that the Government could not live for a day without their support, grew restive and indignant when their claims were ignored and their requests slighted. After the suppression by Major-General Lambert of a royalist insurrection in August, 1659, Parliament and army came to an open breach. Parliament cashiered Lambert and eight other officers for promoting a petition which it had declared seditious, and Lambert retaliated (October 13, 1659), by putting a stop to its sittings.

Lambert—the real leader of the army, though Fleetwood was its nominal head—stood now in the position which Cromwell had occupied in April, 1653; but this time the army was divided. In Scotland, Monk declared for the restitution of the Parliament, and by dilatory negotiations kept Lambert and Fleetwood from acting until the desertion of their soldiers, the defection of the fleet, and the opposition of London obliged them to give way. At the end of December, 1659, the Long Parliament was a second time restored, and Monk, with six thousand men, entered England unopposed. It was not zeal for that assembly which caused its restoration, but hostility to military government. Under the opprobrious nickname of "The Rump," Parliament was the laughing stock of every ballad-maker, but for the moment it represented all that was left of the constitution. Weary of experiments, and most weary of the rule of the sword, the English people wished to return to the known laws and the old government. As Monk marched to London, petitions poured in urging him to declare for a free Parliament, and every petitioner knew that a really representative Parliament meant the restoration of Charles II. Monk answered by protesting unalterable fidelity to the Republic, but made up his mind to use his power to let the nation determine freely its own future. When he reached London he availed himself of the disaffection of the City to oblige

Parliament to readmit the Presbyterian members whom Pride had expelled in 1648 (Feb. 21, 1660). Having thus secured a majority ready to do his bidding, he obliged the House to vote its own dissolution, and issue writs for the calling of a free Parliament (March 16, 1660). As commander-in-chief, he maintained the freedom of the elections, kept the army under control, and watched over the peace of the nation.

Monk's greatest service to England was not the restoration of Charles II. After the breach between army and Parliament that was inevitable. "The current," said Cowley, "was so irresistible, that the strongest strove against it in vain, and the weakest could sail with it to success." Monk's merit was that he brought about the Restoration without a civil war. His dexterous and unscrupulous policy blinded the Republicans to his intentions till it was too late for them to resist, and made the army instrumental in effecting what the bulk of it would have fought to prevent. But for him, England would have been, in Cromwell's phrase, "one Cain." Thanks to him, the transition from the government of an armed minority to the government which an overwhelming majority of the nation desired was a peaceable and constitutional revolution. So the rule of Puritanism, founded with blood and iron, fell without a blow. The alliance between the Presbyterians and the Royalists, begun thirteen years ago, was now at last completed. The once triumphant Independents were divided and powerless. Maidston, the steward of Cromwell's household, in a letter to John Winthrop, wrote the epitaph of militant Independency.

"The interest of religion lies dreadfully in the dust, for the eminent professors of it, having achieved formerly great victories in the war, and thereby great power in the army, made use of it to make variety of changes in the government, and every one of those changes hazardous and pernicious.... They were all charged upon the principles of the authors, who, being Congregational men, have not only made men of that persuasion cheap, but rendered them odious to the generality of the nation."

At the end of April, 1660, a free Parliament met, the first for twenty years. On May 29th, Charles II. re-entered London "with a triumph of above twenty thousand horse and foot, brandishing their swords and shouting with inexpressible joy; the ways strewed with flowers, the bells ringing, the streets hung with tapestry, the fountains running with wine."

"I stood in the Strand and beheld it, and blessed God," wrote John Evelyn. "And all this was done without one drop of blood shed, and by that very army which rebelled against him; but it was the Lord's doing, for such a restoration was never mentioned in any history, ancient or modern, since the return of the Jews from the Babylonish captivity; nor so joyful a day, and so bright, ever seen in this nation, this happening when to expect or to effect it was past all human policy."

In the constitutional settlement which followed the King's return, England reverted to the state of things which had existed before the Civil War began. Cromwell's legislation and all the laws made by the Long Parliament were regarded as null and void. There was a general amnesty for all political offenders excepting the Regicides and a few persons regarded as specially dangerous. Twelve Regicides suffered the penalties of high treason, and Hugh Peters and Sir Henry Vane shared their fate. About twenty escaped into foreign parts, and about five and twenty were imprisoned for life. After the punishment of the living, came vengeance against the dead. In November, 1660, a bill for the attainder of Cromwell and other dead Regicides was introduced into the House of Commons. During its progress, Captain Titus stood up and observed,

"that execution did not leave traitors at their graves, but followed them beyond it, and that since the heads of some were already put upon the gates, he hoped that the House would order that the carcases of those devils who were buried at Westminster—Cromwell, Bradshaw, and Ireton—might be torn out of their graves, dragged to Tyburn, there to hang some time, and afterwards be buried under the gallows."

It was voted without any opposition, though many present must have agreed with Pepys, whom it "troubled, that a man of so great courage as Cromwell should have that dishonour done him, though otherwise he might deserve it well enough."

Accordingly, on Saturday, January 26, 1661, the bodies of Cromwell and Ireton were disinterred from their graves in Westminster Abbey, and on the Monday conveyed from Westminster to the Red Lion Inn, in Holborn. Finally, on the morning of January 30th, the twelfth anniversary of the execution of Charles I., their bodies, and that of Bradshaw, were drawn upon sledges from Holborn to Tyburn. "All the way, as before from Westminster, the universal outcry and curses of the people went along with them." "When these three carcases were at Tyburn," continues the newspaper, "they were pulled out of their coffins, and hanged at the several angles of that triple tree, where they hung till the sun was set; after which they were taken down, their heads cut off, and their loathsome trunks thrown into a deep pit under the gallows." The common hangman took the heads, placed them on poles, and set them on the top of Westminster Hall, Bradshaw's head in the centre, Ireton's and Cromwell's on either side.

Yet, though all this was done in the face of day, as many places claim to be Cromwell's sepulchre as once contended for the honour of being Homer's birthplace. Strange rumours spread abroad that the body subjected to all these indignities was not Cromwell's. Two years later, a French traveller in England was told that Cromwell had caused the royal tombs in Westminster Abbey to be opened and the bodies transposed, so that none might know where his own body was laid. Pepys repeated the story to one of the late Protector's chaplains, who answered, "That he believed Cromwell never had so poor a low thought in him as to trouble himself about it." Another rumour was that Cromwell's body was secretly conveyed away, and buried at dead of night on Naseby Field. According to a third, Cromwell's daughter, Lady Fauconberg, foreseeing changed times, had ere this removed her father's body from Westminster, and reinterred it in a vault at Newburgh Abbey, in Yorkshire. All these stories found, and find, believers, but there is no reasonable ground for doubting that it was Cromwell's body which hung on the gallows at Tyburn, or that it was duly buried in the pit beneath them. Where Connaught Square now stands, a yard or two beneath the street, trodden under foot and beaten by horsehoofs, lies the dust of the great Protector.

CHAPTER XXII
CROMWELL AND HIS FAMILY

"Mr. Lely," said Cromwell to the painter, "I desire you would use all your skill to paint my picture truly like me, and not flatter me at all; but remark all these roughnesses, pimples, warts, and everything, otherwise I never will pay a farthing for it." Doubtless the Protector would have given a similar charge to his biographers, but their task is more difficult; much contemporary evidence is merely worthless gossip, much is vitiated by party spirit, and on many points the authorities are silent.

John Maidston, the steward of Cromwell's household, supplies us with what he terms "a character of his person:"

"His body was well compact and strong, his stature under six foot (I believe about two inches), his head so shaped as you might see it a storehouse and a shop both of a vast treasury of natural parts. His temper exceeding fiery, as I have known, but the flame of it kept down for the most part, or soon allayed with those moral endowments he had. He was naturally compassionate towards objects in distress, even to an effeminate measure; though God had made him a heart, wherein was left little room for fear but what was due to himself, of which there was a large proportion, yet did he exceed in tenderness towards sufferers. A larger soul I think hath seldom dwelt in house of clay than his was. I believe if his story were impartially transmitted, and the unprejudiced world well possessed with it, she would add him to her nine worthies."

The numerous portraits of Cromwell help to complete Maidston's description. Like most Puritan gentlemen he wore his hair long; the thick light brown locks which began to grow grey before he became Protector covered his collar and almost reached his shoulders. His eyes, according to Cooper's and Walker's portraits, were blue or grey, and his eyebrows strongly marked. His nose was long, thick, and slightly arched, with full nostrils—the beak of a vulture, said royalist pamphleteers, and even political friends jested about its size. "If you prove false," said the downright Haslerig to Cromwell, "I will never trust a fellow with a big nose again." The mouth was large, firm, and full-lipped. Strength, not grace, marked both face and figure. But the rough-hewn features have an air of kindness and sagacity mingled with the resolution and energy which are their most marked characteristics. In some portraits there is an air of melancholy.

The dignity of the Protector's outward bearing was admitted even by opponents:

"When he appeared first in Parliament," writes Clarendon, "he seemed to have a person in no degree gracious, no ornament of discourse, none of those talents which use to reconcile the affections of the standers by; yet as he grew into place and authority his parts seemed to be renewed, as if he had concealed faculties till he had occasion to use them; and when he was to act the part of a great man, he did it without any indecency through the want of custom."

To another Royalist, Sir Philip Warwick, he appeared "of a great and majestic deportment and comely presence," and he made a similar impression on foreign observers.

When the Protector gave audience to ambassadors or received official deputations an elaborate ceremonial of a quasi-regal character was strictly observed. Sir Oliver Fleming, who had been one of the continental agents of Charles I., and was skilled in all the niceties of diplomatic etiquette, acted as Cromwell's master of the ceremonies. But the Protector transacted much important business in less formal interviews with the representatives of foreign states. He was easily accessible to his subjects in general, and petitioners found no great difficulty in putting their grievances before him. Opponents of his policy were allowed opportunity to set forth their objections, and he argued with them freely in reply. Even religious enthusiasts contrived to deliver their messages from the Lord or, like Fox, to explain what their religious views really were. About three times a month the Protector took part in the proceedings of the Council of State, but most of his political or administrative work was transacted with small committees or with Secretary Thurloe alone. With these trusted councillors he freely unbent.

"He would sometimes be very cheerful with us," says Whitelocke, "and laying aside his greatness he would be exceeding familiar with us, and by way of diversion would make verses with us, and everyone must try his fancy. He commonly called for tobacco, pipes, and a candle, and would now and then take tobacco himself; then he would fall again to his serious and great business."

Whitelocke also gives some account of the Protector's recreations. Cromwell retained throughout his life the tastes of a country gentleman. At Hampton Court he often amused himself with bowls, but his favourite sports were hunting and hawking. As he rode from Worcester to London after his victory in 1651, he diverted himself, on the way, with hawking, and he sometimes practised the same sport on Hounslow Heath after he was Protector. When he entertained the Swedish Ambassador at Hampton Court in 1654, after dinner was over the Protector, the ambassador, and the rest of the company "coursed and killed a fat buck" in the park. Cromwell was a bold jumper, and it was noticed that the ambassador "would not adventure to leap ditches after the Protector, but was more wary."

Good horses of every kind were always Cromwell's delight. English diplomatic agents in the Levant were employed to procure Arabs and Barbs for his riding or for breeding purposes. "Six gallant Flanders mares, reddish grey," had drawn the General's coach when he set out for the reconquest of Ireland, and six white horses drew the Protector's coach when it conveyed the Spanish Ambassador to his place of embarkation. Of these white horses it was said that they were a finer team than any king of England had ever possessed. Another team of six horses—presented by the Count of Oldenburg in 1654—ran away in Hyde Park when the Protector himself was driving them. Cromwell, who was flung off the box upon the pole, got entangled in the harness, and was dragged for some distance by one foot, but he escaped in the end with nothing more than a few bruises. Andrew

Marvell and George Wither both published poems celebrating the Protector's deliverance, and the incident furnished several royalist wits with a theme for satires and epigrams.

Another recreation which found great favour with Cromwell was music. When he gave a banquet to foreign ambassadors or members of the House of Commons, "rare music, both of instruments and voices," was always an important part of the entertainment. The same thing took place in hours of relaxation or domestic festivities, for the Protector, according to a contemporary biographer, was "a great lover of music, and entertained the most skilful in that science in his pay and family." In the great hall at Hampton Court he had two organs, and his organist, John Hingston, was a pupil of Orlando Gibbons. James Quin, a student of Christ Church, Oxford, who had been deprived of his place by the Puritan visitors of that university, obtained his restoration to it through the Protector's love of music. Quin was not a very skilful singer, but he had a bass voice "very strong and exceeding trolling." Some of his friends brought him into the company of the Protector, "who loved a good voice, and instrumental music well." Cromwell "heard him sing with very great delight, liquored him with sack, and in conclusion said, 'Mr. Quin, you have done well; what shall I do for you?' To which Quin made answer, with great compliments, that his Highness would be pleased to restore him to his student's place, which he did accordingly."

A few other notices of the Protector's personal habits may be gleaned from contemporary sources. In his diet his tastes were very simple; according to a contemporary pamphleteer, it was "spare and not curious"; no "French quelquechoses" were to be found on his table, but plain, substantial dishes. His ordinary drink, according to the same authority, consisted of "a very small ale" known by the name of "Morning Dew." He also drank freely a light wine which his physicians had recommended to him as good for his health.

In dress Cromwell's tastes were marked by the same simplicity. When he expelled the Long Parliament in 1653, he was wearing "plain black clothes with grey worsted stockings." At his installation in the following December he had on "a plain black suit and cloak," though a few weeks later when he was entertained by the Lord Mayor he wore "a musk colour suit and coat richly embroidered with gold." When Protector, his dress was naturally more sumptuous than it had been before, and Sir Philip Warwick, who had so contemptuously criticised the cut of his clothes in 1640, attributed the improvement in his appearance to a better tailor as well as to converse with better company. But even then a young Royalist fresh from the French Court described the Protector as "plain in his apparell," and "rather affecting a negligence than a genteel garb."

The Protector's household was naturally organised on a more magnificent scale than that which had sufficed him as General. The sum allowed for its maintenance was sixty thousand pounds during the first Protectorate, and a hundred thousand pounds during the second. But many other expenses were defrayed from this fund, and Cromwell spent a large amount in charity; according to one biographer as much as forty thousand pounds a year. Speaking of the Protector's second installation, and the increased state which was its consequence, Sir Philip Warwick says: "Now he models his household so that it might have some resemblance to a Court, and his liveries, lackies, and yeomen of the guard are known whom they belong to by their habit." The forty or fifty gentlemen employed in the internal service of Whitehall and Hampton Court, or in attendance upon the Protector's person, wore coats of grey cloth with black velvet collars, and black velvet or silver lace trimming. And besides these "yeomen of the guard" he had the life-guard of horse which has been mentioned before. All this show and state offended many rigid Puritans, to whom even the semblance of a Court was hateful. Others held that it was "necessary for the honour of the English nation" that its head should be surrounded by a certain amount of pomp, and this opinion was generally accepted.

Both newspapers and private letters make frequent mention of the Protector's family. When Cromwell took up his residence at Whitehall in April, 1654, his aged mother removed with him. But she took no pleasure in her son's grandeur, and it was said that she "very much mistrusted the issue of affairs, and would be often afraid when she heard a musket that her son was shot, being exceedingly dissatisfied unless she might see him once a day at least." She died in November, 1654, in her ninety-fourth year, and a little before her death, gave her blessing to her son, in words which show

how fully she sympathised with the aims of his life. "The Lord cause His face to shine upon you, and comfort you in all your adversities, and enable you to do great things for the glory of the most High God, and to be a relief unto His people. My dear son, I leave my heart with thee: good night."

Of the Protector's wife, "her Highness the Protectress" as she was officially styled, little mention is ever made. There is no doubt some foundation for the account of her methodical and economical management of the Protector's household, which is contained in a contemporary pamphlet, but the main object of the pamphleteer was to sneer at her "sordid frugality" and unfitness for the station in which fortune had placed her. Mrs. Hutchinson, while owning that Cromwell "had much natural greatness and well became the place he had usurped," describes his wife and children "as setting up for principality," which suited them no better than fine clothes do an ape. The Protector's daughters according to her were "insolent fools," with one exception. The exception was Bridget, the eldest, who after the death of her first husband, Ireton, became the wife of Lieutenant-General Fleetwood. She alone "was humbled and not exalted with these things."

Elizabeth Claypole, the Protector's second and favourite daughter, was in her father's opinion in danger "of being cozened with worldly vanities and worldly company," while some of the sharp sayings attributed to her account for Mrs. Hutchinson's severe judgment. On the other hand we have the evidence of James Harrington, the author of *Oceana*, that "she acted the part of a princess very naturally, obliging all persons with her civility, and frequently interceding for the unhappy." Harrington owed to her the restoration of the confiscated manuscript of *Oceana*, and she often interceded with her father on behalf of imprisoned Royalists. Perhaps it was owing to this that, when the bodies of the Protector and Admiral Blake and many other great Parliamentarians were exhumed from their graves in Westminster Abbey, hers was left undisturbed, and lies there still.

Mary, the third daughter, who was born in 1637, married Thomas Belasyse, Lord Fauconberg, in November, 1657, while Frances, the youngest, became in the same month the wife of Robert Rich, grandson of the Earl of Warwick.

Both weddings were celebrated by festivities which scandalised some Puritans. The wedding feast of Frances was kept at Whitehall, "when," says a news-letter, "they had forty-eight violins and much mirth with frolics, besides mixt dancing, (a thing heretofore accounted profane) till five of the clock yesterday morning." That of Mary Cromwell was at Hampton Court, and songs for the occasion were composed by Andrew Marvell, in which the bride was introduced as Cynthia, Fauconberg as Endymion, and the Protector himself as Jove.

Both these two ladies lived to see the Revolution, Mary dying in 1712, and Frances in 1721. Lady Fauconberg was childless, and Mrs. Claypole's children died unmarried. But after the death of Robert Rich, Frances Cromwell married Sir John Russell of Chippenham, and from her or her sister Bridget many existing families can trace their descent.

The Protector's sons fare little better at Mrs. Hutchinson's hands than his daughters. According to her, Henry Cromwell and his brother-in-law Claypole were "two debauched, ungodly cavaliers," while Richard though "gentle and virtuous" was yet a "peasant in his nature" and "became not greatness." Richard's education had not fitted him for greatness. Cromwell, until his second Protectorate at least, never contemplated being succeeded in power by one of his sons. He objected on principle to hereditary governments, and declared, in 1655, that if Parliament had offered to make the Government hereditary in his family he would have rejected it. Rulers should be chosen for their love to God, to truth, and to justice, not for their birth. "For as it is in the *Ecclesiastes*, who knoweth whether he may beget a fool or a wise man?" Cromwell therefore made at first no attempt to advance either of his sons. For six or seven years after his marriage, Richard lived on his property in Hampshire, devoting himself to hunting and other amusements. His father's complaints show that he was idle, ran into debt, neglected the management of his estate, and made "pleasure the business of his life." In November, 1655, however, the Protector appointed him one of the Council of Trade, in order, no doubt, to give him some training in public business. In 1657, after the Protector's second installation, a further change took place. Richard was suddenly brought to the front; he succeeded his father as Chancellor of the University of Oxford, was made a member of the Protector's council, and was given the command of a regiment of horse. When he travelled about the country, he was received by the local authorities as if he were the destined heir of his father's authority. It was a poor training for a future ruler, and, after he became Protector, Richard was heard to complain that "he had thought to have lived as a country gentleman, and that his father had not employed him in such a way as to prepare him for such employment; which he thought he did designedly." Yet though Richard showed no political ability during his brief reign, he was far from being the country clown which royalist satires represented him. In his public appearances he displayed a dignity of bearing which surprised even his friends, and an oratorical power which they had never suspected. After the Restoration, the debts which he had contracted as Protector, and the jealous suspicion with which the Government of Charles II. always regarded him, obliged him to live many years in exile. "I have been alone thirty years," he wrote to his daughter in 1690, "banished and under silence, and my strength and safety is to be retired, quiet, and silent." After his return to England, which took place about 1680, he thought it safer to adopt a feigned name, and lived in complete retirement. He died in 1712, leaving three daughters, and his eldest son, who died in 1705, left no issue.

Henry Cromwell, though a man of much greater natural capacity than his brother, was also for a time kept back by his father. From 1650 to about 1653, he was colonel of a regiment of horse in Ireland, and was reputed to be a good officer. In August, 1654, the Protector's council nominated him to command the forces in Ireland, but the Protector was reluctant to allow his son to take the post, and kept him a year longer in England. "The Lord knows," wrote Cromwell to Fleetwood, "my desire was for him and his brother to have lived private lives in the country; and Harry knows this well, and how difficultly I was persuaded to give him his commission." As Commander-in-chief and a member of the Irish council Henry proved his ability, and in November, 1657, he succeeded his brother-in-law, Fleetwood, as Lord Deputy of Ireland.

His task, like his father's task in England, was to establish civil government in place of military rule, and to unite all Protestant sects in support of the Protectorate. He had many difficulties to contend with, both political and financial; the Anabaptists and a faction amongst the officers gave continual trouble. The land settlement was but half completed, prosperity was slow to return, and order hard to re-establish. Yet he was more successful than could have been expected, and with the majority of the Protestant colony in Ireland he gained great popularity. Rigid Puritans held that his way of living and his ostentation in dress savoured too much of the world, but in other respects his conduct was blameless. His chief defect was an infirmity of temper. He was very sensitive to criticism and very impatient of opposition; insomuch that his father warned him against making it a business to be too hard for his opponents.

It is sometimes said that if the Protector had made Henry his successor instead of Richard, the Protectorate might have lasted. But the choice of Cromwell was dictated by the circumstances in which he was placed. Among his councillors and generals there was no man whom the rest would willingly have accepted as their ruler, and of his sons Richard was far more acceptable to the chief supporters of the Protectorate than his abler and more masterful brother would have been. The military cabal which overthrew Richard would have proved too strong for Henry, to whom, moreover, some of its leaders were personally hostile.

A month after the fall of his brother, Henry Cromwell resigned the government of Ireland, and rejecting all the overtures of the Royalists, acquiesced in the re-establishment of the Republic. He declared that he had formerly had an honourable opinion of the Republic, but was satisfied also of the lawfulness of the "late government under a single person."

"And whereas my father (whom I hope you yet look upon as no inconsiderable instrument of these nations' freedom and happiness), and since him my brother, were constituted chief in those administrations, and the returning to another form hath been looked upon as an indignity to these my nearest relations, I cannot but acknowledge my own weakness to the sudden digesting thereof, and my own unfitness to serve you.... And as I cannot promote anything which infers the diminution of my late father's honour and merit, so I thank the Lord, for that He hath kept me safe in the great temptation, wherewith I have been assaulted to withdraw my affection from that cause wherein he lived and died."

At the Restoration, Henry, thanks to his friends amongst the Royalists, and to the moderation with which he had used his power, was not molested, though he lost a portion of his estates by the change. He lived in retirement on his property in Cambridgeshire, dying there in 1674. Henry's great-grandson, Oliver Cromwell of Cheshunt, who died in 1821, was the last descendant of the Protector in the male line.

CHAPTER XXIII
EPILOGUE

Either as a soldier or as a statesman Cromwell was far greater than any Englishman of his time, and he was both soldier and statesman in one. We must look to Cæsar or Napoleon to find a parallel for this union of high political and military ability in one man. Cromwell was not as great a man as Cæsar or Napoleon, and he played his part on a smaller stage, but he "bestrode the narrow world" of Puritan England "like a colossus."

As a soldier he not only won great victories, but created the instrument with which he won them. Out of the military chaos which existed when the war began he organised the force which made Puritanism victorious. The New Model and the armies of the Republic and the Protectorate were but his regiment of Ironsides on a larger scale. As in that regiment, the officers were carefully chosen. If possible, they were gentlemen; if gentlemen could not be had, plain yeomen or citizens; in any case, "men patient of wants, faithful and conscientious in their employment." Character as well as military skill was requisite. A colonel once complained that a captain whom Cromwell had appointed to his regiment was a better preacher than fighter. "Truly," answered Cromwell, "I think that he that prays and preaches best will fight best. I know nothing that will give the like courage and confidence as the knowledge of God in Christ will. I assure you he is a good man and a good officer." Inefficiency, on the other hand, certain heresies which were regarded as particularly blasphemous, and moral backslidings in general, led at once to the cashiering of any officer found guilty of them.

Officers, it has been well said, are the soul of an army; and the efficiency and good conduct which Cromwell required of his, they exacted from the rank and file. Most of the private soldiers were volunteers, though there were many pressed men amongst them, and it cannot be said that all those who fought for Puritanism were saints in any sense of the word. But regular pay and severe discipline made them in peace the best conducted soldiers in

Europe, and in war an army "who could go anywhere and do anything." A common spirit bound men and officers together. It was their pride that they were not a mere mercenary army, but men who fought for principles as well as for pay. Cromwell succeeded in inspiring them not only with implicit confidence in his leadership, but with something of his own high enthusiasm. He had the power of influencing masses of men which Napoleon possessed. So he made an army on which, as Clarendon said, "victory seemed entailed"—"an army whose order and discipline, whose sobriety and manners, whose courage and success, made it famous and terrible over the world."

Cromwell's victories, however, were due to his own military genius even more than to the quality of his troops. The most remarkable thing in his military career is that it began so late. Most successful generals have been trained to arms from their youth, but Cromwell was forty-three years old before he heard a shot fired or set a squadron in the field. How was it, people often ask, that an untrained country gentleman beat soldiers who had learnt their trade under the most famous captains in Europe? The answer is that Cromwell had a natural aptitude for war, and that circumstances were singularly favourable to its rapid and full development. At the outset of the war he showed an energy, a resolution, and a judgment which proved his possession of those qualities of intellect and character which war demands of leaders. The peculiar nature of the war, the absence of any general direction, and the disorganisation of the parliamentary forces gave him free scope for the exercise of these qualities. In the early part of the war each local leader fought for his own hand, and conducted a little campaign of his own. Subordinate officers possessed a freedom of action which subordinates rarely get, and with independence and responsibility good men ripened fast. At first, Cromwell was matched against opponents as untrained as himself, till by constant fighting he learnt how to fight. In a happy phrase Marvell speaks of Cromwell's "industrious valour." If he learnt the lessons of war quicker than other men it was because he concentrated all his faculties on the task, let no opportunity slip, and made every experience fruitful.

It was as a leader of cavalry that Cromwell earned his first laurels. In attack he was sudden and irresistibly vigorous. Like Rupert he loved to head his charging troopers himself, but in the heat of battle he controlled them with a firmer hand. When the enemy immediately opposed to him was broken he turned a vigilant eye on the battle, ready to throw his victorious squadrons into the scale, either to redress the balance or to complete the victory. At Marston Moor, as on many another field, he proved that he possessed that faculty of coming to a prompt and sure conclusion in sudden emergencies which Napier terms "the sure mark of a master spirit in war." When the fate of the battle was once decided he launched forth his swordsmen in swift and unsparing pursuit. "We had the execution of them two or three miles" is the grim phrase in which he describes the conclusion of his fight at Grantham, and after Naseby Cromwell's cavalry pursued for twelve miles.

When he rose to command an army, Cromwell's management of it in battle was marked by the same characteristics as his handling of his division of cavalry. In the early battles of the Civil War there was a strong family likeness: there was an absence of any generalship on either side. The general-in-chief exhibited his skill by his method of drawing up his army and his choice of a position; but when the battle began the army seemed to slip from his control. Each commander of a division acted independently; there was little co-operation between the different parts of the army; there was no sign of a directing brain. Cromwell, on the other hand, directed the movements of his army with the same purposeful energy with which he controlled his troopers. Its different divisions had each their definite task assigned to them, and their movements were so combined that each played its part in carrying out the general plan. The best example of Cromwell's tactical skill is the battle of Dunbar. There, though far inferior in numbers, Cromwell held in check half the enemy's army with his artillery and a fraction of his forces, while he attacked with all his strength the key of the enemy's position, and decided the fate of the day by bringing a strong reserve into action at the crisis of the battle. Whenever the victory was gained it was utilised to the utmost. At Dunbar the Scots lost thirteen thousand men out of twenty-two thousand; after Preston less than a third of Hamilton's army succeeded in effecting their return to Scotland: after Worcester, not one troop or one company made good its retreat.

Cromwell's strategy, compared with that of contemporary generals, was remarkable for boldness and vigour. It reflected the energy of his character, but it was originally dictated by political as well as military considerations. "Without the speedy, vigorous, and effectual prosecution of the war," he declared in 1644, the nation would force Parliament to make peace on any terms. "Lingering proceedings, like those of soldiers beyond seas to spin out a war," must be abandoned, or the cause of Puritanism would be lost. Therefore, instead of imitating the cautious defensive system popular with professional soldiers, he adopted a system which promised more decisive results. "Cromwell," says a military critic,. "was the first great exponent of the modern method of war. His was the strategy of Napoleon and Von Moltke, the strategy which, neglecting fortresses and the means of artificial defence as of secondary importance, strikes first at the army in the field."

In his Preston campaign Cromwell had to deal with an invading army more than twice the strength of his own, which ventured because of that superiority to advance without sufficient scouting and without sufficient concentration. He might have thrown himself across Hamilton's path and sought to drive him back; he chose instead to fall upon the flank of the Scots, and thrust his compact little force between them and Scotland. Thus he separated the different divisions of Hamilton's army, drove Hamilton with each blow farther from his supports, and inflicted on him a crushing defeat instead of a mere repulse. In 1650 and 1651, Cromwell had a much harder task given him. He had to invade a country which presented many natural difficulties, and which was defended by an army larger than his own under the command of a man who was a master of defensive strategy. All his efforts to make Leslie fight a pitched battle in the open field completely failed until one mistake gave him the opportunity which he seized with such promptitude at Dunbar. In the campaign of 1651, Cromwell found himself brought to a standstill once more by Leslie's Fabian tactics. As Leslie gave him no opportunity he had to make one, and with wise audacity left the way to England open in order to tempt the Scots into the invasion which proved their destruction.

In his Irish campaigns Cromwell had an entirely different problem to solve. The opposing armies were too weak to face him in the field and too nimble to be brought to bay. The strength of the enemy consisted in the natural and artificial obstacles with which the country abounded: fortified cities commanding points of strategic value; mountains and bogs facilitating guerrilla warfare; an unhealthy climate, a hostile people, a country so wasted that the invader must draw most of his supplies from England. Under these conditions the war was a war of sieges, forays, and laborious marches, but there were no great battles. Cromwell combined the operations of his army and his fleet so as to utilise to the full England's command of the seas. He attacked the seaports first, and after mastering them secured the strong places which would give him the control of the rivers, thus gradually tightening his grasp on the country till its complete subjugation became only a matter of time.

Opinions may differ as to the comparative merits of these different campaigns. What remains clear is that Cromwell could adapt his strategy with unfailing success to the conditions of the theatre in which he waged war and to the character of the antagonists he had to meet. His military genius was equal to every duty which fate imposed upon him.

Experts alone can determine Cromwell's precise place amongst great generals. Cromwell himself would have held it the highest honour to be classed with Gustavus Adolphus either as soldier or statesman. Each was the organiser of the army he led to victory, each an innovator in war— Gustavus in tactics, Cromwell in strategy. Gustavus was the champion of European Protestantism as Oliver wished to be, and each while fighting for his creed contrived to further also the material interests of his country. But whatever similarity existed between their aims the position of an hereditary monarch and an usurper are too different for the parallel to be a complete one. On the other hand, the familiar comparison of Cromwell with Napoleon is justified rather by the resemblance between their careers than by any likeness between their characters. Each was the child of a revolution, brought by military success to the front rank, and raised by his own act to the highest. Each, after domestic convulsions, laboured to rebuild the fabric of civil government, and to found the State on a new basis. But the revolutions which raised them to power were of a different nature and demanded different qualities in the two rulers.

Cromwell's character has been the subject of controversies which have hardly yet died away. Most contemporaries judged him with great severity. To Royalists he seemed simply, as Clarendon said, "a brave, bad man." Yet while Clarendon condemned he could not refrain from admiration, for though the usurper "had all the wickedness against which damnation is pronounced, and for which hell fire is prepared, so he had some virtues which have caused the memory of some men in all ages to be celebrated." Though he was a tyrant he was "not a man of blood," and he possessed not only "a wonderful understanding in the natures and humours of men," but also "a great spirit, an admirable circumspection and sagacity, and a most magnanimous resolution."

The Republicans regarded the Protector as a self-seeking apostate. "In all his changes," said Ludlow, "he designed nothing but to advance himself." He sacrificed the public cause "to the idol of his own ambition." All was going well with the State, a political millennium was at hand, "and the nation likely to attain in a short time that measure of happiness which human things are capable of, when by the ambition of one man the hopes and expectations of all good men were disappointed."

Baxter, a Presbyterian, though as convinced an opponent of the Protector as Ludlow, was a more generous critic. According to him, Cromwell was a good man who fell before a great temptation. He

"meant honestly in the main, and was pious and conscionable in the main course of his life, till prosperity and success corrupted him. Then his general religious zeal gave way to ambition, which increased as successes increased. When his successes had broken down all considerable opposition then was he in face of his strongest temptations, which conquered him as he had conquered others."

But like Milton's Satan, even after his fall "all his original virtue was not lost." As ruler of England "it was his design to do good in the main, and to promote the interest of God more than any had done before him."

Eighteenth-century writers judged Cromwell with the same severity as his contemporaries. "Cromwell, damned to everlasting fame," served Pope to point a moral against the desire of making a name in the world. Voltaire summed up Cromwell as half knave, half fanatic, and Hume termed him a hypocritical fanatic. Even as late as 1839, John Forster quoted as "indisputably true" Landor's verdict that Cromwell lived a hypocrite and died a traitor.

Six years later, Carlyle published his collection of *Cromwell's Letters and Speeches*, which for every unprejudiced reader effectually dispelled the theory of Cromwell's hypocrisy. "Not a man of falsehoods, but a man of truths," was Carlyle's conclusion, and subsequent historians and biographers have accepted it as sound. It is less easy to answer the question whether Cromwell was a fanatic or not. Fanaticism, like orthodoxy, is a word which means one thing to one man and something else to the next, and to many besides Hume enthusiast and fanatic are synonymous terms. It is plain, however, that Cromwell was a statesman of a different order from most. Religious rather than political principles guided his action, and his political ideals were the direct outcome of his creed. Not that purely political considerations exercised no influence on his policy, but that their influence instead of being paramount was in his case of only secondary importance.

In one of his speeches Cromwell states in very explicit language the rule which he followed in his public life. "I have been called to several employments in this nation, and I did endeavour to discharge the duty of an honest man to God and His people's interest, and to this Commonwealth."

What did these phrases mean? If anyone had asked Cromwell what his duty to God was in public affairs, he would have answered that it was to do God's will. "We all desire," he said to his brother officers in 1647, "to lay this as the foundation of all our actions, to do that which is the will of God." He urged them to deliberate well before acting, "that we may see that the things we do have the will of God in them." For to act inconsiderately was to incur the risk of acting counter to God's design, and so "to be found fighting against God."

But, in the maze of English politics, how were men to ascertain what that will was? Some Puritans claimed to have had it directly revealed to them, and put forward their personal convictions as the dictates of Heaven.

Cromwell never did so. "I cannot say," he declared in a prayer-meeting where such revelations had been alleged, "that I have received anything that I can speak as in the name of the Lord." He believed that men might still "be spoken unto by the Spirit of God," but when these "divine impressions and divine discoveries" were made arguments for political action, they must be received with the greatest caution. For the danger of self-deception was very real. "We are very apt, all of us," said he, "to call that Faith, that perhaps may be but carnal imagination." Once he warned the Scottish clergy that there was "a carnal confidence upon misunderstood and misapplied precepts" which might be termed "spiritual drunkenness."

For his own part, Cromwell believed in "dispensations" rather than "revelations." Since all things which happened in the world were determined by God's will, the statesman's problem was to discover the hidden purpose which underlay events. When he announced his victory at Preston he bade Parliament enquire "what the mind of God is in all that and what our duty is." "Seek to know what the mind of God is in all that chain of Providence," was his counsel to his doubting friend, Colonel Hammond. With Cromwell, in every political crisis this attempt to interpret the meaning of events was part of the mental process which preceded action. As it was difficult to be sure what that meaning was, he was often slow to make up his mind, preferring to watch events a little longer and to allow them to develop in order to get more light. This slowness was not the result of indecision, but a deliberate suspension of judgment. When his mind was made up there was no hesitation, no looking back; he struck with the same energy in politics as in war.

This system of being guided by events had its dangers. Political inconsistency is generally attributed to dishonesty, and Cromwell's inconsistency was open and palpable. One year he was foremost in pressing for an agreement with the King, another foremost in bringing him to the block; now all for a republic, now all for a government with some element of monarchy in it. His changes of policy were so sudden that even friends found it difficult to excuse them. A pamphleteer, who believed in the honesty of Cromwell's motives, lamented his "sudden engaging for and sudden turning from things," as arguing inconstancy and want of foresight. Moreover the effect of this inconsistency was aggravated by the violent zeal with which Cromwell threw himself into the execution of each new policy. It was part of his nature, like "the exceeding fiery temper" mentioned by his steward. "I am often taken," said Cromwell in 1647, "for one that goes too fast," adding that men of such a kind were disposed to think the dangers in their way rather imaginary than real, and sometimes to make more haste than good speed. This piece of self-criticism was just, and it explains some of his mistakes. The forcible dissolution of the Long Parliament in 1653 would never have taken place if Cromwell had fully appreciated the dangers which it would bring upon the Puritan cause.

On the other hand, this failure to look far enough ahead, while it detracts from Cromwell's statesmanship, helps to vindicate his integrity. He was too much taken up with the necessities of the present to devise a deep-laid scheme for making himself great. He told the French Ambassador in 1647, with a sort of surprise, that a man never rose so high as when he did not know where he was going. To his Parliaments he spoke of himself as having seen nothing in God's dispensations long beforehand. "These issues and events," he said in 1656, "have not been forecast, but were sudden providences in things." By this series of unforeseen events, necessitating first one step on his part and then the next, he had been raised to the post of Protector. "I did out of necessity undertake that business," said he, "which place I undertook, not so much out of a hope of doing any good, as out of a desire to prevent mischief and evil which I did see was imminent in the nation."

Conscious, therefore, that he had not plotted to bring about his own elevation, Cromwell resented nothing so much as the charge that he had "made the necessities" to which it was due. For it was not merely an imputation on his own honesty, but a kind of atheism, as if the world was governed by the craft of men, not by the wisdom of God. People said, "It was the cunning of my Lord Protector that hath brought it about," when in reality these great revolutions were "God's revolutions." "Whatsoever you may judge men for, however you may say this is cunning, and politic, and subtle, take heed how you judge His revolutions as the product of men's invention."

Cromwell said this with perfect sincerity. He felt that he was but a blind instrument in the hands of a higher power. Yet he had shaped the issue of events with such power and had imposed his interpretation of their meaning upon them with such decision, that neither contemporaries nor historians could limit to so little the sphere of his free will.

It was possible to "make too much of outward dispensations," and Cromwell owned that perhaps he did so. His system of being guided by events instead of revelations did not put an end to the possibility of self-deception, though it made it less likely. "Men," as Shakespeare says, "may construe things after their fashion clean from the purpose of the things themselves." But if Cromwell sometimes mistook the meaning of facts he never failed to realise their importance. "If the fact be so," he once said, "why should we sport with it?" and the saying is a characteristic one. He was therefore more practical and less visionary than other statesmen of his party; more open-minded and better able to adapt his policy to the changing circumstances and changing needs of the times. To many contemporary politicians, the exact carrying out of some cut-and-dried political programme seemed the height of political wisdom. The Levellers with their Agreement of the People and the Scottish Presbyterians with their Covenant are typical examples. The persistent adhesion of the Covenanters to their old formulas, in spite of defeats and altered conditions, Cromwell regarded as blindness to the teaching of events. They were blind to God's great dispensations, he told the Scottish ministers, out of mere wilfulness, "because the things did not work forth their platform, and the great God did not come down to their minds and thoughts." He would have felt himself guilty of the same fault if he had obstinately adhered either to a republic or a monarchy under all circumstances. Forms of government were neither good nor bad in themselves. Either form might be good: it depended on the condition of England at the moment, on the temper of the people, on the question which was more compatible with the welfare of the Cause, which more answerable to God's purpose as revealed in events. It was reported that Cromwell had said that it was lawful to pass through all forms to accomplish his ends, and if "forms" be taken to mean forms of government, and "ends" political aims, there can be no doubt that he thought so. However much he varied his means, his ends remained the same.

To understand what Cromwell's political aims were, it is necessary to enquire what he meant when he spoke of his discharging his duty to "the interest of the people of God and this Commonwealth." The order in which he places them is in itself significant. First, he put the duty to a section of the English people; last, the duty to the English people in general. Cromwell was full of patriotic pride. Once, when he was enumerating to Parliament the dangers which threatened the State, he wound up by saying that the enumeration should cause no despondency, "as truly I think it will not; for we are Englishmen: that is one good fact." "The English," he said on another occasion, "are a people that have been like other nations, sometimes up and sometimes down in our honour in the world, but never yet so low but we might measure with other nations." Several times in his speeches he termed the English "the best people in the world." Best, because "having the highest and clearest profession amongst them of the greatest glory—namely, religion." Best, because in the midst of the English people there was as it were another people, "a people that are to God as the apple of His eye," "His peculiar interest," "the people of God." "When I say the people of God," he explained, "I mean the large comprehension of them under the several forms of godliness in this nation"; or, in other words, all sects of Puritans.

To Cromwell the interest of the people of God and the interest of the nation were two distinct things, but he did not think them irreconcilable. "He sings sweetly," said Cromwell, "that sings a song of reconciliation between these two interests, and it is a pitiful fancy to think they are inconsistent." At the same time the liberty of the people of God was more important than the civil liberty and interest of the nation, "which is and ought to be subordinate to the more peculiar interest of God, yet is the next best God hath given men in this world." Religious freedom was more important than political freedom. Cromwell emphatically condemned the politicians who said, "If we could but exercise wisdom to gain civil liberty, religion would follow." Such men were "men of a hesitating spirit," and "under the bondage of scruples." They were little better than the carnal men who cared for none of these things. They could never "rise to such a spiritual heat" as the Cause demanded. Yet the truth was that half the

Republican party and an overwhelming majority of the English people held the view which he condemned.

Cromwell wished to govern constitutionally. No theory of the divine right of an able man to govern the incapable multitude blinded his eyes to the fact that self-government was the inheritance and right of the English people. He accepted in the main the first principle of democracy, the doctrine of the sovereignty of the people, or, as he phrased it, "that the foundation of supremacy is in the people and to be by them set down in their representatives." More than once he declared that the good of the governed was the supreme end of all governments, and he claimed that his own government acted "for the good of the people, and for their interest, and without respect had to any other interest." But government for the people did not necessarily mean government by the people. "That's the question," said Cromwell, "what's for their good, not what pleases them," and the history of the Protectorate was a commentary on this text. Some stable government was necessary to prevent either a return to anarchy or the restoration of the Stuarts. Therefore he was determined to maintain his own government, with the assistance of Parliament if possible, without it if he must. If it became necessary to suspend for a time the liberties of the subject or to levy taxes without parliamentary sanction, he was prepared to do it. In the end the English people would recognise that he had acted for their good. "Ask them," said he, "whether they would prefer the having of their will, though it be their destruction, rather than comply with things of necessity?" He felt confident the answer would be in his favour.

England might have acquiesced in this temporary dictatorship in the hope of a gradual return to constitutional government. What it could not accept was the permanent limitation of the sovereignty of the people in the interest of the Puritan minority whom Cromwell termed the people of God. Yet it was at this object that all the constitutional settlements of the Protectorate aimed. It was in the interest of this minority that the Instrument of Government restricted the power of Parliament and made the Protector the guardian of the constitution. It was in their interest that the Petition and Advice re-established a House of Lords. That House, as Thurloe said, was intended "to preserve the good interest against the uncertainty of the

Commons House," for, as another Cromwellian confessed "the spirit of the Commons had little affinity with or respect to the Cause of God."

Cromwell trusted that the real benefits his government conferred would reconcile the majority of the nation to the rule of the minority and "win the people to the interest of Jesus Christ." Thus the long hostility between the people and "the people of God" would end at last in reconciliation.

It was a fallacious hope. Puritanism was spending its strength in the vain endeavour to make England Puritan by force. The enthusiasm which had undertaken to transform the world was being conformed to it. A change was coming over the party which supported the Protector; it had lost many of the "men of conscience"; it had attracted many of the time-servers and camp-followers of politics; it was ceasing to be a party held together by religious interests, and becoming a coalition held together by material interests and political necessities. Cromwell once rebuked the Scottish clergy for "meddling with worldly policies and mixtures of worldly power" to set up that which they called "the kingdom of Christ," and warned them that "the Sion promised" would not be built "with such untempered mortar." He had fallen into the same error himself, and the rule of Puritanism was founded on shifting sands. So the Protector's institutions perished with him and his work ended in apparent failure. Yet he had achieved great things. Thanks to his sword absolute monarchy failed to take root in English soil. Thanks to his sword Great Britain emerged from the chaos of the civil wars one strong state instead of three separate and hostile communities. Nor were the results of his action entirely negative. The ideas which inspired his policy exerted a lasting influence on the development of the English state. Thirty years after his death the religious liberty for which he fought was established by law. The union with Scotland and Ireland, which the statesmen of the Restoration undid, the statesmen of the eighteenth century effected. The mastery of the seas he had desired to gain, and the Greater Britain he had sought to build up became sober realities. Thus others perfected the work which he had designed and attempted.

Cromwell remained throughout his life too much the champion of a party to be accepted as a national hero by later generations, but in serving his Cause he served his country too. No English ruler did more to shape the future of the land he governed, none showed more clearly in his acts the "plain heroic magnitude of mind."

www.ingramcontent.com/pod-product-compliance
Lightning Source LLC
Chambersburg PA
CBHW051856160426
43209CB00006B/1319